SEARCHING FOR THE
MESSIAH

SEARCHING FOR THE
MESSIAH

Unlocking the Psalms of Solomon and
Humanity's Quest for a Savior

BARRIE A. WILSON

PEGASUS BOOKS
NEW YORK LONDON

SEARCHING FOR THE MESSIAH

Pegasus Books Ltd.
148 W 37th Street, 13th Floor
New York, NY 10018

Copyright © 2020 by Barrie A. Wilson

First Pegasus Books edition August 2020

Interior design by Maria Fernandez

Library of Congress Cataloging-in-Publication Data is available.

ISBN: 978-1-64313-450-5

10 9 8 7 6 5 4 3 2 1

Printed in the United States of America
Distributed by Simon & Schuster
www.pegasusbooks.com

for
Jacob, Noah, Eden,
Bari, Dylan,
Ryder, Beau,
Cooper, Mackenzie,
Thalia, and Jackson

∽

The future is bright.
Enjoy!

CONTENTS

Preface   ix

I: JESUS AS A MESSIAH—SOME QUESTIONS   1
      1: A Breakthrough Insight   3
      2: Curious Silences   14
      3: About the Gospels   24
      4: Strange Inconsistencies   36
      5: Going Incognito   51

II: HOW DID THE IDEA OF THE MESSIAH COME ABOUT?   67
      6: Messiah as Anointed Leader   69
      7: Biblical Superhero Saviors—Male and Female   84
      8: A Savior, a Messiah, and a Redemption   98
      9: World Transformation   113

III: WHAT'S A MESSIAH?   127
      10: A Mysterious, Neglected, Ancient Manuscript   129
      11: Messiah—Job Description   141

IV: HOW DID THE CONCEPT OF THE MESSIAH EXPLODE
      ONTO THE WORLD STAGE?   151
      12: Jesus—the Kingdom of God   153
      13: The Problem—No Kingdom   166
      14: Paul and the Messiah as Christ   172
      15: Unfinished Business   190
      16: Modern Political Saviors   202
      17: Superhero Saviors: Superman, Batman, Wonder Woman   221

V: WHERE IS TOMORROW'S MESSIAH TO BE FOUND?   237
      18: "Someone Else"   239
      19: The Real Messiah   250

Selected References   263
Acknowledgments   267
Index   269

PREFACE

———⚬⚬⚬———

Lois, you say the world doesn't need a savior,
but every day, I hear people crying for one.

(Superman in *Superman Returns*)

For millennia, people around the world have embraced the search for a rescuer or messiah. Christians, Jews, and Muslims in particular have been caught up in this pursuit, either looking for a returning messiah or one yet to come. Religious scholars, megachurch pastors, and television evangelists pour over ancient manuscripts and prophecies looking for signs when the messiah will arrive to set things right.

Even Hollywood has become caught up in messianic fervor. People around the globe flock to blockbuster films whose superhero saviors rescue humanity and pack theaters, generating huge fortunes for their studios.

The search for a messiah has never been timelier, or more important, than right now. Currently many people dread the state of the world. Things are clearly a mess.

A deadly pandemic has swept the world, creating in its wake fear, anxiety, and economic uncertainty. Hit by medical and financial threats simultaneously, people are overwhelmed with major concerns: personal and family health, job security, income, investments, and social contact with others.

Politically, citizens in many countries are at loggerheads with each other. Holding little respect for different views, opposing camps viciously lambast each other with personal attacks. Angry people confront one another over politics, religion, lifestyles, and moral choices. Adding to the fray, traditional and social media have become increasingly polarized. Retreating to comfortable ideological niches, they create confusion and uncertainty concerning authentic *versus* fake information.

The past century has witnessed massive world wars, unimaginable horrors and atrocities, a Holocaust, famines, and genocides in many parts of the globe. The Middle East is constantly on fire and powerful new entities—Russia, China, and Iran among them—have emerged to challenge American and Western might and leadership. Climate and economic refugees fleeing unsustainable environments face huge barriers, nations that have slammed the door shut with the attitude that "none is too many." Countless millions live each day in fear for their lives and those of their children.

All-seeing drones, job-threatening artificial intelligence devices, and invasive cyber capabilities—all these add to modern-day anxiety about the future.

What's next?

Since people and governments have made such a mess of things, people search for a way out. Where's messiah when we need him the most?

If the messiah were to appear, how would we recognize him? Do we even know what are we searching for?

Put simply, what's a messiah? Without the answer to that question, how can we identify a genuine one from a mere charlatan?

These seem like simple questions, but they aren't.

A natural place to start our search is with the Bible. Surprisingly, it doesn't tell us what a messiah *is*. The Hebrew Bible, or the Old Testament,* says very

---

* Jewish scholars prefer the terms "Hebrew Bible" and "Christian Scriptures," whereas Christians use "Old Testament" and "New Testament." When the latter phrases are used in this book, no theological significance is attached to "New" and "Old" as if one replaced the other.

little about the criteria for being a real messiah. There's not one book, not even one chapter, devoted to the idea of a messiah. There's more in these scriptures on diagnosing and curing skin diseases than on the topic of the messiah.

And yet, Christians claim that Jesus is not just a messiah, but *the* messiah. How can we evaluate this claim without an idea of what being a messiah means? What did Jews of Jesus's time understand by the term "messiah"? Why did some say Jesus was the messiah and others say that he was not? The Christian Scriptures, or the New Testament, also caution us about being misled by "false messiahs." How can we identify such unreliable individuals without a job description?

The search for a messiah is not just rooted in religious contexts. Some modern political leaders cultivate savior imagery, promising people better times ahead. Barack Obama, for instance, touted his "Audacity of Hope" promise, while Donald Trump pledged to "Make America Great Again." Younger, more radical rivals have surfaced who challenge conventional ways of thinking about the climate, economy, healthcare, immigration reform, and international relations.

Add to these the many political leaders of the past century who have sung the messianic siren song. These include not only dictators such as Adolf Hitler, Joseph Stalin, Mao Zedong, and Fidel Castro who held out hope for their people, but also visionaries such as Woodrow Wilson who was hailed as the "Savior of Humanity" for his work helping to end World War I. International bodies—the League of Nations, the United Nations—were created with high expectations to save us from war, only to disappoint time and time again. Why do people so eagerly respond to these would-be saviors?

Increasingly, saviors are to be found in popular new cosmologies, fictitious though they may be. Superman, Batman, Wonder Woman, Aquaman, Captain Marvel, Spider-Man, and many others saturate our popular culture as superheroic individuals with amazing powers. They fight evil forces to make the world a safer and better place. In so doing these rescuers have created new rival alternate universes, different conceptual frameworks for understanding the world in which we live.

Why has the superhero genre become so popular recently as the DC Extended Universe and the Marvel Cinematic Universe vie for cultural supremacy? What does this preoccupation with superhero saviors tell us about the world in which we live today?

Why is the search always for "someone else" to clean up the mess? Why is it always "someone else's" job?

Why do we look to religion, politics, and pop culture for a messiah, savior, or rescuer? Have we perhaps been looking in all the wrong places?

∞

In this book, I aim to tackle these key questions by providing the most current historical scholarship and groundbreaking research on issues which have never been more timely—or more important. Along the way we'll discuss an important neglected ancient manuscript penned just a few decades before the birth of Jesus. It tells us definitively what Jews meant by "messiah."

The book explores the hopes and dreams generated by messiahs, superheroes, and other saviors who promise better times, coming soon. It is meant for those who like to "wrestle" with complex issues.

Written from a historical perspective, not a faith one, it should appeal to those who enjoy searching for understanding important ideas based on textual evidence. The results of the investigation should yield new insights and provide an excellent catalyst for discussion.

Barrie Wilson, PhD
Professor Emeritus & Senior Scholar
Humanities and Religious Studies
York University, Toronto

I

JESUS AS A MESSIAH—
SOME QUESTIONS

1

A BREAKTHROUGH
INSIGHT

⚬⚬⚬

A Long Trek

J esus, it's hot!"

So might Peter have exclaimed as he and the rest of Jesus's students trudged over the rocky barren hills north of Capernaum.

As is usual with summers in northern Israel, it's hot . . . very hot. Temperatures in the midafternoon soar into the upper 90s. The year is 30 BCE. Jesus and his band of weary followers are on the move northward, having left the village of Bethsaida and their home base, the tiny fishing town of Capernaum. As the Gospel of Mark puts it, "Jesus went on with his disciples to the villages of Caesarea Philippi" (Mark 8:27).*

---

*   The New Revised Standard Version (NRSV) is the translation used throughout for passages from the Christian Scriptures/New Testament. See *The New Oxford Annotated Bible with the Apocrypha*, College Edition. Edited by Bruce M. Metzger, Roland E. Murphy. New York: Oxford University Press, 1991. This Christian translation is widely used throughout North American colleges and universities.

We can imagine them looking back from the top of the long sloping hills above Capernaum. From there they could see the mud-brick homes of their lakefront village nestled along the northern edge of the Sea of Galilee. The Sea of Galilee wasn't, of course, a real "sea," but it deserved this name being the largest freshwater lake in the Middle East. From their vantage point high above the village, both the eastern and western sides of the lake stood out. In the sweltering haze, they could dimly make out the southern edge, only 13 miles distant.

The lake looked very small indeed. But it represented life. The Sea of Galilee provided abundant fish for Jesus and his followers to eat to supplement their staples. It offered refreshing breezes in the hot summer evenings, and, above all, it gave fresh water. Some talked eventually of building fish farms like those in the wealthier village of Magdala just a few miles west, along the coast. Most fished daily to feed their families, taking their boats out onto the usually calm lake. Capernaum, they all thought, was beautiful. It was, after all, home.

Not far inland from the shore in Capernaum rose an impressive synagogue, built out of black basalt. They could clearly see that edifice—the largest in the village—rising above the houses and marketplace. Jesus had taught there and in villages around the lake, especially on the east side of the Sea of Galilee.

Today, however, Jesus and his band of students were on the move. Why were they headed towards Caesarea Philippi far in the north? They were venturing away from home and their familiar daily routines. These included fishing, fetching water, looking after their growing families, and studying Torah. The latter was the Jewish Law or Teaching as expressed in the first five books of the Bible, Genesis through Deuteronomy.

Jesus's ragtag group of some 12 individuals had gradually made its way northwards, mile after arduous mile, perhaps with Peter upfront and Judas bringing up the rear. Who else joined in the excursion, we might well ask? The disciples' wives, for instance? Some older children in for the adventure? A few admirers—groupies, perhaps?

Very likely, Mary the Magdalene was in the entourage. She was, after all, a wealthy woman, the closest associate of Jesus, perhaps even his life partner. She helped fund his mission, along with several other wealthy women such as

Joanna, the wife of Herod Antipas's chief of staff, and Susanna (Luke 8:1–3). A two-week sojourn to northern Israel and back for 13 or more individuals was an expensive undertaking. Jesus was fortunate to have such well-heeled, and, in the case of Joanna, politically well-placed patrons.

What about Jesus's brothers—Jacob (whom we call James); Joseph, or José for short; Judas or Jude, and Simon (Mark 6:3)? Had they tagged along as well, perhaps with their families?

The trek was challenging—about 40 miles. They would have thought of it as a three or four-day walk. All in the steamy heat. To undertake such a journey required a serious purpose. What was the reason for this trip? As students of Jesus, these disciples were used to travel. This tiny group was, after all, on an urgent and vital mission, alerting people to the coming Kingdom of God, the coming of a time when the whole world would be transformed. A far better world, they thought, and likely they sensed they'd have a prominent place in it, along with their teacher. Prepare, Jesus preached, for this new social and political order. In this connection, he emphasized performing acts of kindness, compassion, and mercy, as well as forgiving others.

A few miles north of Capernaum and Bethsaida, they would join the well-trodden ancient highway that had connected Egypt with Asia and Europe for centuries. Along the way they would encounter caravans, merchants, and missionaries promoting strange religions from the East, as well as Egyptian sages, Greek philosophers, religious leaders, and brave travelers like themselves. They'd pass by soldiers, too, and foreigners, not only from lands north and east, but also local settlers from Greece and Rome who had built ten non-Jewish cities in Galilee. They would have brought water with them, flat bread, and some lentils. From time to time they'd purchased figs and dates from passing merchants. They walked over barren, rocky hills with few trees, their skin parched by the hot sun. They crossed a marsh with myriads of mosquitoes infected with malaria.

Caesarea Philippi

Finally, the group reached what appeared to be their destination. They were approaching a mountainous area, with abundant shade trees. Off in the distance, snow-capped peaks beckoned the weary sojourner. It was a welcome sight, the promise of a cooler climate . . . and rest. Is this why they had ventured so far? Was this a holiday or did Jesus have some other purpose in traveling so far away from their usual haunts?

Jesus had traveled with his disciples into the area known as Caesarea Philippi. Situated on a terrace overlooking a valley, the city was flanked to the north by Mount Hermon, an impressive mountain range towering in some places 9000 feet above sea level. The area was lush, with groves of trees providing shade from the scorching summer sun. Through dense forests, water gushed up from the earth—a multitude of cascading springs that combined eventually to form the Jordan River.

The religious significance of the terrain was not lost on ancient peoples. The area around Caesarea Philippi was devoted to the worship of the god Pan. Pan was an amusing deity, a playful Greek god of nature and wildlife. He was the custodian, or shepherd, of the untamed outdoors, an energetic and sexually active god. Not as stern as Zeus, nor as wise or as nurturing as Artemis, Pan appealed to those who sought a bit of joy in the midst of a harsh existence. The religious rites associated with Pan provided people with a much-needed break from the ordinary, a time out for exuberant celebrations—a far cry from the daily grind of providing shelter, safety, and food for their families.

At the time of Jesus, there were shrines and grottos all around Caesarea Philippi dedicated to this much-beloved deity, Pan. So popular was this accommodating god that most townspeople simply called their city Caesarea Paneas. It was a sacred site to which Jesus had led his small group.

But why? Why were they here? Why so far afield? And why had they come to a center of pagan worship?

Caesarea Philippi was doubly sacred. Devoted not only to Pan, this town was also dedicated to none other than Caesar, the supreme ruler of the Mediterranean world, sometimes thought of as human, sometimes as divine, and most of the time, probably as a bit of both.

Caesar's influence and presence exerted itself in far-flung places, remote from Rome. Troops, traders, settlers, and visitors all played a role in proclaiming the power of Roman rule. Rome was never far away. Roman laws, language, literature, religion, and troops—all these manifestations of imperial might lay right on their doorsteps in the Gentile cities that dotted the Galilean landscape. Locals could never forget that fact of life. Rome was almost as close as next door. Nazareth, for instance, the small village of Jesus's youth, lay just a few miles southeast of a much larger non-Jewish city, Sepphoris, a bastion of Roman power and prestige.

Caesarea Philippi was Caesar's city just as much as it was Pan's.

Jesus's Identity

It is in this magnificent setting of Caesarea Philippi, with two gods before him—the divine-human Roman ruler and the maverick god Pan—that Jesus poses the famous question to his disciples: "Who do people say that I am?" (Mark 8:27)

Note, here in Mark, the earliest gospel, Jesus is not asking his disciples for *their* impressions. He is asking a different question: how do the *people* to whom he had been speaking about the Kingdom of God understand him? It isn't a test question: it's a research poll. Jesus is simply probing for information, some feedback on what they had heard.

In modern terms, we might think of Jesus's trek with his closest followers to the region of Caesarea Philippi as an off-site meeting, a chance to reflect, to measure results to date and plan for the future. Jesus had been speaking to crowds around the Sea of Galilee for some time. Here was a chance, away from his familiar scene, to find out from his students what they had heard. What was the reaction? How did ordinary people size him up?

Jesus's students oblige. They report that people consider him to be either like John the Baptist, Elijah, or one of the prophets (Mark 8:28). It's also interesting what the disciples do not report: the crowds do not think of him as a king or as a priest.

John the Baptist? Elijah? A prophet? Jesus does not reject any of these three responses and they are all worthy of serious consideration. They are, after all, impact statements, perceptions of Jesus by fellow Galileans. Each response tells us something about how this itinerant Jewish preacher was understood by the people in the Galilee in the late 20s.

Jesus as John the Baptist

Those who perceive Jesus to be like John the Baptist would have understood him as a charismatic leader. John was a contemporary, and a cousin of Jesus. He was a strange character, an ascetic. He dressed oddly. Wearing a garment made out of camel's hair, he sported a leather belt and lived out in the harsh Judean wilderness, amongst wild animals, insects, and snakes, eating honey and locusts (Mark 1:6). He attracted followers, notably Andrew (Simon Peter's brother), and his group of followers survived alongside Jesus's disciples well into the Common Era.[*]

John the Baptist and his disciples lived by the shores of the Jordan River, only a few miles north of the strict Torah-observant community at Qumran. This was the Dead Sea Scroll Community. They were likely a reclusive group called Essenes although not all scholars agree with this identification. Was this community in touch with John the Baptist and his entourage? Did the two groups share similar views? The evidence is unclear.

Whereas the people at Qumran were turned inward, building up their own community of righteousness, John's focus was outgoing and he responded well to the throngs of people who sought him out. He immersed Jewish individuals in the flowing water of the Jordan River. This act symbolized personal repentance (Mark 1:4), a serious commitment to turn one's life around, to become less secular and more religious.

The Jewish historian Josephus noted that John the Baptist's actions were popular. People poured out of Jerusalem to meet this enigmatic religious figure. According to Josephus, John urged "the Jews to exercise virtue, both as to righteousness towards one another, and piety towards God." (*Jewish Antiquities*, Book 18, Chapter 5, Section 2)

Piety to God and righteousness towards others—these two pillars form the foundation laws of the Torah (or Jewish Law): the Ten Commandments (Deuteronomy 5:6–21; Exodus 20:1–17). The first commandments express piety towards God—having one and only one God, for instance,

---

[*] For a critical introduction to what we can now reliably know about John the Baptist, see Rivka Nir, *The First Christian Believer: In Search of John the Baptist*. Sheffield, UK: Sheffield Phoenix Press, 2019.

not making idols, and observing the Sabbath. The remaining commandments express righteousness towards others—not committing murder, for instance, honoring parents and not envying a neighbor's possessions or spouses. According to Josephus, John the Baptist's mission was simply to encourage people to become more Torah-observant, to return to the roots of their religion.

That was one way in which Jesus was perceived. Like John the Baptist, Jesus was regarded by some as advocating strict adherence to the commandments of Torah, the need for repentance and a corresponding change of lifestyle.

Jesus as Elijah

Others, the disciples report, think of Jesus as the Elijah-figure.

Elijah was the great 9th century BCE* prophet who vigorously defended monotheism against the polytheistic Canaanites (1 Kings 17:1–2 Kings 2:11). This powerful figure also performed many miracles including a resurrection; weather control including stopping and starting storms; and zapping enemies by causing fire from heaven to descend upon them. Since Elijah was presumed not to have died—he was simply taken up into heaven in a whirlwind—it was popular belief that he would return from heaven at the dawning of the messianic era.

We find this view expressed in the book of the Hebrew prophet Malachi:

> Lo, I [God] will send the prophet Elijah to you before the coming of the awesome, fearful day of the Lord. (JPS, Malachi 3:22, 23; NRSV, Malachi 4:4, 5)†

---

* BCE = Before the Common Era. Same as BC, Before Christ. Dates not marked BCE are dates from the Common Era (CE), same AS AD (*Anno Domini*).

† Two translations are used for the Hebrew Bible/Old Testament. "JPS" is *JPS Hebrew–English Tanakh*, a standard Jewish translation (*Tanakh* being a Hebrew acronym for the books of the Law, Prophets, and Writings that make up the Hebrew Bible). "NRSV" is *New Revised Standard Version*, a standard Christian translation widely used in North American colleges and universities.

A returning Elijah would be a messenger. In modern terms, he'd function as an emergency alert, putting the world on notice of impending momentous events.

For Malachi, the return of Elijah at some future point in history heralds the time when God will identify and separate the righteous from the wicked. During these bleak times, the wicked will be burned like straw, while the righteous will be encouraged to remain faithful to the teachings of Torah (JPS, Malachi 3:22; NRSV, Malachi 4:4). Then, just before "the awesome, fearful day of the Lord," Elijah will reappear precipitating a time of tremendous turmoil and bloodshed.

An earlier prophet, Amos, had depicted this terrifying "day of the Lord" graphically:

Ah, you who wish
For the day of the Lord!
Why should you want
The day of the Lord?
It shall be darkness, not light!—
As if a man should run from a lion
And be attacked by a bear;
Or if he got indoors,
Should lean his hand on the wall
And be bitten by a snake! (Amos 5:18–19)*

So those who thought of Jesus as Elijah might have viewed him as the messenger sent to wake up the world to terrifying and catastrophic events.

There is another possibility, however. Elijah was the celebrated defender of faith in one God *versus* the polytheistic prophets of Ba'al. It is intriguing, then, that this report of Jesus as Elijah takes place before the sanctuaries of the pagan deity Pan and the divine-human Roman emperor. Perhaps Jesus is the new Elijah, a teacher who advocates strict monotheism against all competing theologies. That would recall one of the most important of

---

* Unless otherwise stated, the JPS translation is used throughout for passages from the Hebrew Bible/Old Testament.

the Ten Commandments—have no other gods (Deuteronomy 5:7)—or the *Shema*—"Hear, O Israel! The Lord is our God, the Lord alone" (Deuteronomy 6:4). Perhaps that is what some people meant when they thought of Jesus as Elijah, a new monotheistic preacher.

Or, since Elijah was known for having performed amazing miracles, perhaps some simply understood Jesus to be a miracle worker.

We do not know how they thought of Jesus when they linked him to Elijah. All these associations are possibilities and maybe all were entertained.

Jesus as a Prophet

Those weren't the only popular perceptions of Jesus's identity. Some, the disciples report, view Jesus as a prophet. This makes sense, because the Gospel of Mark positions him as a prophet, coming on the scene in Galilee announcing the coming Kingdom of God (Mark 1:15). Jesus promises that a new world will take shape before the eyes of those currently alive (Mark 9:1). That soon! With life expectancies at the time being in the mid-30s for most people, that means the Kingdom would materialize within a decade or two. Like the oracles of the ancient prophets, Jesus's message is urgent: people have to prepare, now. *They* have to prepare, not their grandkids nor their great-grandchildren. There is no time to lose.

The ancient Hebrew prophets had emphasized a number of important themes: for example, repentance, warnings of impending disaster, new beginnings, rededication to the demands of the Torah, faithfulness to the worship of the one true God, integrity in worship, apocalyptic scenarios, and so on. Some prophets were largely negative. Amos, for instance, focused on the sins of the people in his era and outlined the likely consequences—invasion, destruction, and death.

Other prophets, however, were encouraging. A prophet like Malachi looked positively towards the future, to an era when God will reward the righteous and punish the wicked. Living at the end of the Babylonian Exile, Isaiah in Chapters 40 to 55 was also an enthusiastic prophet. He encouraged people to return to Israel and to live out the type of life that

God mandated. He wrote: "A voice rings out: 'Clear in the desert a road for the Lord!'" (Isaiah 40:3). Isaiah's passage refers to Jews in exile in the Babylonian Empire. The voice is God's: he is announcing that the way of the Lord is being prepared in the desert. The exiles can return and, metaphorically speaking, desert valleys will be raised, and hills lowered to make their sojourn home easier.

Like Malachi, the Isaiah of Chapters 40 to 55 is positive and uplifting. For Isaiah, a brand-new future now awaits the exiles. Take comfort in this historic development. Pack up and get moving. That's his upbeat message.

So, some people perceive Jesus to be a prophet, someone who perhaps, like Isaiah, could motivate others to take seriously the idea of a better world coming soon, and to prepare for it.

This feedback—Jesus as John the Baptist, or as Elijah returned, or as a prophet—should not be glossed over. They are, after all, testimonials from Jesus's closest associates concerning what they had heard from the people to whom Jesus had been speaking. They are reports of the various impressions Jesus had created in the minds of his audience. People of the late 20s associated Jesus with the message of a rapidly changing world and with the need to prepare for it through repentance and rededication to the obligations of the Torah.

Jesus, all his disciples, and the people to whom he was speaking around the Sea of Galilee were, of course, Jews and the Torah forms the backbone of the Jewish lifestyle. The Torah refers to the teachings or laws found in the first five books of the Hebrew Bible, that is, in the Old Testament of the Christian Bible.* According to the disciples' reports, in light of coming social changes on a massive scale, Jesus was regarded as a teacher. Return to your religious roots, repent, and change your ways. Why? Because the Kingdom of God was imminent. That's the message Jesus seems to have been conveying to the crowds around the Sea of Galilee in the late 20s.

---

* "Torah" can mean either the Books of the Torah, that is, the first five books of the Bible, or the actual commandments themselves expressed in those five books. Jewish scholars have identified 613 commandments—some applicable to all Jews, some only to men, others only to women and some only to priests. The Hebrew Bible or Old Testament as a whole contains three major sections: Torah, the Prophets, and the Writings.

Jesus as Messiah (*Christos*)

Jesus does not comment on any of these perceptions. Instead, he proceeds to ask his disciples a follow-up question: "But who do *you* say I am?" (Mark 8:29, italics added). That shifts the ground significantly.

Peter immediately blurts out: "You are the Messiah (*Christos* in Greek)."

Of course, Peter, like Jesus, did not speak Greek: he spoke Aramaic. He would have said *Mashiach*. All the writings of the New Testament are in Greek, however, and so we have *Christos*, or 'Christ' as the translation.

Here's the breakthrough insight: Peter says that Jesus is the messiah. That claim represents a huge imaginative leap, catapulting Jesus into superhero savior status. Note that it is not Jesus who self-identifies as messiah: it's Peter's impression and his alone. None of the other disciples back up Peter's assessment.

Moreover, the disciples' reports have not prepared us for this stunning announcement. Jesus as the messiah was not one of the reported impressions. Clearly, the people Jesus had been speaking to around the Sea of Galilee did not think of him in these terms.

So why did Peter think of him as "the messiah?" What did he mean by this description? What are we to make of Jesus's immediate response: "And he [Jesus] sternly ordered them not to tell anyone about him" (Mark 8:30)?

What a spectacular setting for Peter's dramatic utterance! That momentous declaration is set against the magnificent backdrop of Caesar's city and home to the Greek god Pan. Is this staging symbolic? Is there a hint of some looming power struggle between the forces of destiny—government, gods, and Jesus?

2
CURIOUS SILENCES

～≈≈≈～

B ut is our original question really answered? We now know that, some four decades after the event in question, around the year 70, the author of the Gospel of Mark says that Peter declared Jesus to be the Messiah. Presumably the writer of Mark intends his late 1st century readers to agree as well. Perhaps the search for messiah has ended.

Immediately, however, more difficult questions arise.

For one thing, we do not know what Peter, or the disciples or, for that matter, what Jesus meant by this claim. What did they understand by "messiah"? Did Jesus qualify as one? If so, on what basis? How can we tell? Why should we believe Peter, especially since his impression of Jesus is so much at odds with the perceptions of ordinary people around the Galilee to whom Jesus had spoken? Why this disconnect?

For another, how does the claim that Jesus is the messiah relate to Jesus's primary concern; that is, spreading the word to his contemporaries that the Kingdom of God is imminent? How are the ideas of messiah and Kingdom connected? Peter's claim looks "off message," taking the focus off a new social and political reality—the Kingdom—and placing it instead on the person of Jesus. That represents a major shift in emphasis.

Mark points out:

> . . . Jesus came to Galilee, proclaiming the good news of God, and saying, "The time is fulfilled, and the kingdom of God has come near; repent, and believe the good news." (Mark 1:14, 15)

What is the gospel* or "good news"? As this passage makes clear, the good news is that the Kingdom of God is about to appear. People are to "believe," that is, take seriously Jesus's claim that it's going to happen by preparing for this world-shattering event. They must be *doers*—they must repent. In so doing they will change themselves.

Repentance isn't a cozy mental state, a momentary one-time confession of sins. Rather repentance represents an ongoing activity involving the whole person. It's an entire makeover, a change in lifestyle. In the Jewish context of Jesus and his audiences, repentance means becoming more Torah-observant with all the attitudes, choices, decisions, and behaviors this requires . . . keeping the Sabbath and major festivals, observing the dietary laws, trusting the one God, being just in dealings with other people, forgiving others, being kind and compassionate, and so on. In other words, personal transformation is required before world transformation can possibly occur.

This emphasis by Jesus and John the Baptist on repentance and a corresponding change in lifestyle is consistent with what Malachi had said centuries before. When God sends Elijah before the coming of the "awesome, fearful day of the Lord (*YHVH*†)," people are to be faithful to the teachings of the Torah (Malachi 3:22–24 JPS; Malachi 4:4, 5 NRSV). So, people must "shape up" and prepare themselves and their families for the coming Kingdom.

The coming Kingdom of God, the need to prepare for it, and taking the practices of Judaism seriously—that's how Jesus is introduced in the

---

* The word "gospel" is old English for "good news" (*godspel*).

† *YHVH* is the sacred name of God. It is not uttered in Jewish circles being read instead as either *"Adonai"* (the Lord) or *HaShem* (the Name). Christian scholars might insert two vowels, vocalizing it as "Yahveh" or "Yahweh." Older English Bibles insert three vowels and express the name as "Jehovah" as do many older Christian hymns as in "Guide me, O Thou great Jehovah."

Gospel of Mark. It's a call to action. Why, in the midst of this, do we suddenly get messiah talk instead of some sustained discussion of the nature of the Kingdom? Jesus's audiences around the Galilee, the first readers of the Gospel of Mark, as well as us here today—we'd all expect that Jesus will provide more details about his central message. A new world order, a Kingdom of God—that was the really exciting news. When would it appear? What impact would this new society have on peoples' lives and families? Would the arduous daily grind and drudgery cease? Would life become easier? Would the world be somehow better? If so, how?

Moreover, why should we believe Jesus? What evidence does he have that the Kingdom is about to be made manifest? Why should we turn our lives around simply because he asked us to?

These are the kinds of considerations we would demand today. Very likely those in antiquity would have been at least as inquisitive.

There's another problem. If Jesus were the messiah, why did nobody other than Peter think he was one? According to the disciples' report, nobody—absolutely nobody—had placed him in this category. They just didn't think of him in those terms. Peter's idea that he might be messiah crops up "out of the blue." There is no groundwork for understanding his mission in those terms and no indication that any of Jesus's other disciples shared Peter's opinion. No groundswell of approval is mentioned—no round of applause, no instant great acclamation. Peter's statement is just left out there, hanging.

Moreover, if Jesus *were* to promote himself publicly as a messiah, what would the crowds have associated with that claim? What would they have understood by the term "messiah"? In other words, what did Jews in the 1st century Galilee think a messiah would be?

Surely the Gospel of Mark will go on to probe all these issues, in detail.

But, surprisingly, that is not the case.

Everyone Goes Silent: Jesus, Peter, Disciples

Jesus does not comment on Peter's dramatic insight. The Gospel of Mark simply informs us that Jesus "sternly ordered them not to tell anyone about him" (Mark 8:30). So, the injunction is to keep quiet about this grandiose claim.

Why silence? Why did Jesus press the mute button, at least with respect to this role?

Silence is curious. Surely if this insight were so important, presumably Jesus—and especially the author of the Gospel of Mark—would be eager to explain the significance of this conceptual breakthrough. What does this claim mean? What's the job description? Does Jesus measure up?

These are the questions that should drive the narrative. But this is not what happens. The author of the Gospel of Mark immediately drops the topic of Jesus as a messiah. Jesus remains silent. The disciples do not discuss the insight. Peter offers no explanation of what he meant by his sudden declaration. There is no discussion, no elaboration, and no explanation why Peter's view is so at odds with those of the crowds Jesus had spoken to. If being a messiah is what Jesus wanted his audience to understand about him, why no analysis of this serious miscommunication? It does not bode well for his political and religious mission to be so far off the mark when it comes to establishing an identity, a brand. No one identifies him as messiah . . . except Peter. And Jesus does not reinforce this perception.

So what might this silence mean?

There are various explanations.

At this point in the Gospel of Mark's narrative—halfway through, the eighth out of 16 chapters—silence may represent a secret understanding between Jesus and his students. They now know—and he knows they now know—his true identity. Silence may therefore represent a tacit endorsement, a secret pact shared by Jesus and his closest associates. A century ago, William Wrede dubbed this Mark's "messianic secret."* He put forward this view to help explain why there is no unambiguous claim in the gospel that Jesus is the messiah: Jesus colludes with his closest associates to keep it a secret.

That's one interpretation. However, there is no evidence for this view other than silence. That's reading a lot into the absence of discussion.

---

* William Wrede, *The Messianic Secret.* Trans. J. C. G. Greig. London: James Clarke & Co., 1971. First published in German in 1901.

There are other ways of construing silence. Perhaps Jesus entertained reservations about the possible consequences of announcing his messiahship prematurely. Maybe he judged the time was not ripe for this disclosure. He would have known that to put himself forward as a messiah would be a radical and, possibly, a life-threatening step.

Jesus as the messiah represents a much more powerful claim than being an Elijah, a monotheistic miracle worker, and forerunner of God's Kingdom. It's a more important title than that of prophet. It's also a much stronger claim than saying he was like the charismatic John the Baptist, however much he and John were alike in their missions to transform people's commitments.

So, messiah? Proclaiming him as such would bring powerful and challenging forces into play. Entrenched political and religious interests would immediately raise the threat level to "severe" or "critical." Jesus would become a marked man, singled out for special attention from both Jewish and Roman officials concerned with protecting their power base from any upstart political operative. Maybe Jesus was just not ready for such a momentous step. Perhaps the foundations for such a bold move had not yet been sufficiently laid. Maybe it was just too risky for him to declare his candidacy.

After all, in his day, there were no messiahship primaries. There was no testing of the waters to gauge audience appeal and political receptivity.

Perhaps Jesus was just scared, wary of all the complex emotions and high hopes people of the time might read into his mission if he promoted himself as the messiah. Their expectations would have been enormous and varied as we shall see.

Nor was Jesus the only messianic contender. The Essenes looked for two messiahs. One would be a king; the other, a priest. They thought that both human leaders would join forces—an early Justice League perhaps? According to the *War Scroll* of the Dead Sea Scroll Community, these two leaders would combat evil through warfare, help bring about an independent Jewish state under the sovereignty of God, and reform Temple worship. The Zealots, too, entertained their own messianic dreams. Tired of waiting for God to act, this militant group actively fought the Romans with guerrilla tactics, ambushes, and armed skirmishes. Members of this radical Jewish faction were not waiting for God to act: they took matters into their own hands to rid the land of the colonialist occupiers.

Dismay may represent another possibility. Jesus may have been thoroughly disappointed that people didn't think of him in messianic terms, that is, as a king, as the new David. Yes, he had spoken about a Kingdom, but the crowds were not thinking of him as the king of that Kingdom. They just did not perceive him to be royalty, someone who as a sovereign would assist God in the transformation of society. If Jesus thought of himself as a messiah, he may have realized he needed more time to beef up his royal résumé.

That would take some doing. Was he a king? Was he a descendant of King David? What royal credentials could he muster?

There's a serious issue with Jesus's ancestry and it has to do with theology. Writing later in the 1st century than Mark, the authors of the gospels of Matthew* and Luke contend that Jesus had no human father. They advance a virginal conception and virgin birth view of Jesus in order to bolster the theological position that God had become incarnate in Jesus. That theological view holds that Jesus was born of the Virgin Mary, without any male involvement. Joseph played no role in Jesus's conception. So, Jesus had no biological human father.

Virgin birth theology thus jeopardizes any attempt to trace Jesus's lineage back through Joseph to David some 1000 years earlier. Having no human father makes Joseph's ancestry irrelevant. It breaks the family chain, at least through Jesus's paternal lineage. Thus, virgin birth theology undermines Jesus's claims to royalty and thus to being a potential messiah, a descendant of King David.

Maybe ancestry back to David could be established through his maternal lineage. Perhaps his mother, Mary, could trace her ancestry back to King David. That possibility, however, encounters another theological roadblock. According to the 2nd century writing, the *Infancy Gospel of James*, Mary, the mother of Jesus, was also conceived mysteriously, without male involvement.

---

* The author of the Gospel of Matthew in the 80s was the first to suggest this and the author of the Gospel of Luke followed in the 90s. The author of the Gospel of Mark, Paul and the author(s) of the *Gospel of Thomas* do not mention this theological view.

So she, too, had no human father. This contention gave rise to the Roman Catholic and Eastern Orthodox doctrine of the immaculate conception of Mary. This view—Mary having no human father—undermines any attempt to trace Jesus's ancestry through Mary's lineage back to King David, at least through her patrilineal ancestry. So that ancestral link is blocked by theology: no link from Jesus back through Mary's paternal ancestry to David. It leaves open the possibility of matrilineal ancestry back to King David through Mary's mother, Anna. However, we know nothing of the Jesus-Mary-Anna family line.

So, was Jesus connected to King David? Did he have royal credentials? No credible biological lineage is provided. At best, one could argue that Jesus was born under mysterious circumstances into a family descended from David—assuming Joseph's lineage is secure—although he himself was not of royal blood from Joseph's DNA.

Did being a messiah mean rebellion against Rome? If so, how would rulers such as Herod Antipas react, that wily political leader who had already killed John the Baptist simply because he had become too popular? How would Roman authorities in Jerusalem take to someone claiming to be a "King of the Jews?" Perhaps Jesus assessed the mood of the nation and judged that now was not the right time for such a proclamation.

On the other hand, it may be that the author of the Gospel of Mark simply wanted to create suspense, to tease us into wondering how this revelation might play out. In this sense, silence would represent a dramatic artifice: an attempt to get us—the reader—involved in the saga. Perhaps he wanted us to wonder if Jesus might evolve into a messiah and if he would be accepted by the crowds as such. This interpretation does not necessarily mean that Jesus himself urged silence. It would be a narrative device designed by the gospel writer to create suspense for his readers.

Alternatively, Jesus may simply have enjoyed hearing the range of impressions he had stirred up without endorsing any one in particular. Perhaps it was, after all, just a midterm assessment partway through his mission. It's stock-taking, that's all, something to take into account moving forward.

At any rate, midway through the gospel, Mark drops messiah talk. Perhaps the Gospel of Mark is just not the right place to search for messiah.

Let's jump ahead 300 years.

The Nicene Creed Is Silent

But there is another problem and it, too, is a curious one. Jesus as the Messiah is not mentioned as an article of faith in the defining statement of Christian belief, the Nicene Creed. Since 325, Christians are those individuals who affirm the truth of the Nicene Creed. Those who don't, aren't. In many Christian denominations, the Nicene Creed is said or chanted during worship services—at the Catholic Mass, the Eastern Orthodox Divine Liturgy, as well as in Anglican and Lutheran Eucharists. That's 80 percent of all Christians worldwide. Protestants and Evangelicals tend not to recite this ancient creed, although it is typically embedded in their articles of faith as positions to which their denomination adheres.

Here's a portion of the Nicene Creed pertaining to Jesus, using Anglican sources. The wording is from its contemporary Episcopal Church USA expression, with emphasis added:

> We believe in one Lord, Jesus Christ,
> the only Son of God,
> . . .
> For us and for our salvation
> he came down from heaven:
> by the power of the Holy Spirit
> he became incarnate from the Virgin Mary,
> **and was made man.**
> **For our sake he was crucified**
> **under Pontius Pilate;**
> he suffered death and was buried.
> On the third day he rose again . . .

Notice the two phrases:

1. ". . . and was made man."
2. "For our sake he was crucified under Pontius Pilate."

There's an enormous gap between (1) and (2): all of Jesus's life, teachings, and actions. It is as if his human life, his creative parables about the Kingdom of God, and the Lord's Prayer expressing hope for the Kingdom to appear were of no consequence. All that has disappeared. The creed shifts the focus *from* the teachings of Jesus about the Kingdom of God *to* beliefs about Jesus, his divinity, and role in salvation.* It's as if he was born to die, not to teach.

Most noticeably, there is no statement affirming that "we believe that Jesus is the Messiah." That's simply not there, although he is called "Jesus Christ" as if *Christos* were a surname.

The creed's primary claim is that God is manifested as a trinity—Father, Son, Holy Spirit—although the essence of God is one. It goes on to affirm that God became human in the form of Jesus, that Jesus was raised from the dead, and that this resurrection makes possible eternal life. According to the Nicene Creed, these doctrines are the badge of Christian belief.

This creed does not mandate belief that Jesus is the long-promised Jewish messiah. That claim simply is not made in this carefully crafted, authoritative defining statement of what it means to be Christian. So, it would appear that the Creed is not the place to search for messiah.

Again, there is silence.

Overwhelming Silence

So, what we have is sheer silence—by Jesus, the disciples, Peter, the author of the Gospel of Mark, and the Nicene Creed.

Mark leaves us hanging, wondering what Peter's claim means. What constitutes a messiah? Does Jesus qualify? If so, how?

So, we come back to a fundamental question: What did Jews at the time of Jesus understand by the term "messiah"? What was the job description? Until we know that, we cannot evaluate the validity of Peter's insight . . . or even begin to understand what he may have meant.

---

* This is the same shift as with Peter's insight of Jesus as messiah: away from the Kingdom message to the person of Jesus.

So we, the reader of the Gospel of Mark, are left puzzling why there is such silence concerning Peter's insight. Why no follow-up?

As it turns out, there are more problems than sheer silence. There is conflicting evidence concerning what was actually said at Caesarea Philippi on this momentous occasion. As it turns out, the evidence is contradictory.

3

ABOUT THE GOSPELS

———∞∞∞———

The Gospel of Mark is not the only writing to speak of Jesus asking his disciples about his identity. The Gospel of Matthew and the *Gospel of Thomas* present remarkably different versions of the incident. They not only disagree with Mark, but with each other. Hence, we have three varying accounts. Which version (if any) is correct?

In other words, the evidence we have before us as to the accuracy of this encounter between Jesus and his disciples is contradictory.

Before we discuss these radically differing accounts, it is helpful to keep in mind what we now know of the gospels according to modern critical historical scholarship. The gospels differ from each other as much as media outlets such as CNN, Fox, MSNBC, and *Breitbart* do. The latter all have different agendas, messages, and audiences. Perhaps the gospels do as well. So, let's first explore *why* the various gospels are so different. Then we'll examine the differing accounts of the incident at Caesarea Philippi in Matthew and *Thomas* in the following chapter.

Reading any gospel requires bifocals because we are always looking at two different timeframes. One has to do with the time of writing, the late 1st century. That's one layer—what the writer of that gospel is trying to communicate to *his* audience at *his* time of writing. The other has to do with the events about which the gospel writes, things that happened decades earlier. That's another layer, buried deep under the first. This bottom stratum has to do with what Jesus was trying to communicate to *his* audience in *his* era.

Those two time periods are decades apart and that temporal gap plays an important part in interpreting the gospel writings.

As we shall see, some incidents and sayings appear to stem less from the time of Jesus and more from the author's own time. In other words, not everything that is attributed in the gospels to Jesus can actually be from Jesus. Some sayings attributed to Jesus may be just that: utterances ascribed back to Jesus by the gospel writer as *if* Jesus had said them. But it is that "if" we must keep in mind.

So, in a sense, there are two Jesuses: one from the time of writing and one from earlier times. They are significantly different.

As we shall shortly see, there are far more than just two Jesuses. There are four gospels included in the Christian Scriptures/New Testament: Mark, Matthew, Luke, and John. In addition, there are others not included, for instance, the *Gospel of Thomas, Gospel of Peter, Gospel of Philip, Gospel of Mary Magdalene, Gospel of the Hebrews, Gospel of Truth, Gospel of the Savior*, and so on. These writings favored by various groups of early Christians add richness and complexity to perceptions of Jesus, each having agendas and audiences. Only those gospels included in the New Testament will be discussed here.

Background: About the Gospels

Not Transcripts

We should resist the temptation to regard the four gospel writings as transcripts or recordings made at the time in which the incidents and sayings occurred. It is not as if Jesus's students took notes while he spoke. In modern terms, the gospels are not verbatim reports, not meeting minutes, and, above all, they are not instantaneous tweets. So, to speak accurately, one should not say, "Jesus said . . ." but rather "the author of the Gospel of X said Jesus said . . ."

According to the Gospel of Matthew, Jesus was born shortly before the death of Herod the Great, that is, before 4 BCE. The Gospel of Luke places his birth almost a decade later, in 6 CE. He was executed by means of crucifixion in the early 30s, sometime between 30 and 33 (scholars differ here). His mission occurred during the late 20s and early 30s—likely over a three-year period.

According to modern scholarship,[*] the gospels were written in the late 1st century between the years 70 and 100. So, with Jesus dying in the early 30s, there's a significant gap of some 40 to 70 or more years between the time when the events occurred and the time of writing. The gospels are creative writings—not on-the-spot reports—composed in political, religious, and social circumstances vastly different from the environment in which Jesus spoke and acted.

Unknown Authors

The author of the Gospel of Mark was a well-educated individual, writing in Greek, around 70. We don't know who this author was—the gospel is merely attributed in antiquity to 'a Mark.' We're supposed to think that it was Mark, an associate of Paul. But the writing is anonymous: it is not signed and there is no statement in the gospel about the identity of its author. We could equally call it Gospel One, indicating that it was the first in a series of gospels.

Attributing a writing to an ancient figure was common practice in the ancient world. Works were attributed to such individuals as Philip, Thomas, Mary the Magdalene, and even one to the Savior himself. There are also writings attributed to Paul (that is, writings in addition to the ones deemed genuine), John, Peter, Timothy, James (Jesus's brother), Jude (another of

---

[*] See, for instance, a standard contemporary introduction to the New Testament widely used in North American universities such as Bart D. Ehrman's *The New Testament: A Historical Introduction to the Early Christian Writings*, 6th edition. New York: Oxford University Press, 2015.

Jesus's brothers), as well as to Hebrew Bible/Old Testament figures such as Enoch, Solomon, Ezra, Jacob, and many others. Apart from their genuine writings, additional works were attributed in antiquity to the Greek philosopher Plato and to the Roman thinker and statesman, Seneca. According to scholars, there is no good reason to accept any of these attributions. They are meant to lend weight to the views expressed within the writings penned by anonymous authors.

So, according to modern scholarship, these gospel writings are effectively anonymous.

Unknown Sources of Information

Whatever the identity of the author of the gospel we refer to as Mark, he was not present at the time of the original incidents. He himself was not an eye witness to the events about which he writes. He created his document two generations later, some 40 years or so after the events in question. He probably used other peoples' recollections—perhaps many—but no source materials and no witnesses are named. Likely he used various chains of testimony, one of which might have gone as follows: A provides a report to the author of the gospel, having heard it from B, his grandmother, who had heard it from a friend C whose cousin D had heard of it from a friend E who had heard it from the son F whose father G had been present. But we don't know the eye-witness sequences for any specific incident.

Moreover, there are no indications as to the identity of the witnesses or how many there were. We don't know how extensively the writers canvassed people who remembered the sayings and doings of Jesus who were alive at the time they were writing. Nor do we know how carefully they vetted and fact-checked their testimonies. We also don't know if they received conflicting accounts and, if so, how they sifted through different sets of remembrances judging which ones to be more reliable than the others. Basing reports on a string of unidentified—and now unidentifiable—hearsay narratives is faulty historical methodology.

Even firsthand contemporaneous eye-witness testimony can differ significantly, no matter how sincere each person is. What a number of people discern in any event can vary immensely. Think back to a more recent event comparable to the gap in time to what the gospel authors were faced with. Let's go back to events 40 to 70 years earlier. For instance, with the assassination of President John F. Kennedy almost 60 years ago, there were many eye witnesses. Even with live TV and radio coverage, personal film footage such as Abraham Zapruder's, and the extensive Warren Commission investigation, we have a wealth of differing interpretations as to what happened. People dispute who was involved, the number and location of shooters, who might have benefitted from the assassination, and why the incident occurred. That Kennedy was killed is agreed upon, but by whom, why, and how is open to speculation.

Moreover, for events in the life of Jesus, there would have been not just one chain of remembrances, but many. No one source could have witnessed Jesus's whole life, from birth, through Passover in Jerusalem at the age of 12, to his three-year mission in the Galilee, his dramatic entrance into Jerusalem, his trial, and death. There would have been many different witnesses to each of these significant moments in the life of Jesus. Not many, however, would have been available to the gospel writers decades later. This is especially the case since these authors composed their works outside of Israel, in other parts of the Roman Empire.

Not knowing the source of information for many incidents such as Jesus's birth and his trial poses serious questions for the historian. For example, we do not know who might have been present at Jesus's trial who could accurately convey, some 40 or 70 years later, what actually occurred. All the disciples, for instance, had fled.* So who provided this information?

Source analysis is somewhat more complex than just outlined but, for our purposes, this does not have to be probed in detail. While we don't know the sources for the Gospel of Mark, there were sources for Matthew and Luke. They both used the earlier gospel, Mark. Luke may also have used Matthew (scholars disagree). Both Matthew and Luke

---

* When arrested, "all of them [the disciples] deserted him and fled" (Mark 14:50). Peter was in the vicinity of the trial, being "in the courtyard below" (Mark 14:66) where he was denounced as being a follower of Jesus by a servant girl. But Peter was not present where the trial was taking place.

contributed some material of their own. The late Gospel of John used his own traditions. The details here need not concern us, for they simply drive the questions back: we do not know the evidential base for these gospels or any of their source materials—or even if the events and sayings have simply been made up. That's a handicap for any serious historical analysis.

Historical Gap

In addition to not knowing the sources for the gospels (or, in turn, their sources) or the identity of their authors, a huge temporal gap exists between when the events that are said to have happened and when they were written down. Think back in our own society to events some 40 to 70 years ago, in the 1950s to 1980s: the Korean War, the Cold War, the Berlin Wall, the Vietnam conflict, and so on. Pretend that there are no written records between those events and ours, no videotapes, no books, and no TV footage. Imagine having to reconstruct the travels, speeches, and actions of various presidents from this time, Harry S. Truman, Dwight D. Eisenhower, and Ronald Reagan among them. Imagine having to reconstruct this from a chain of disparate remembrances of people alive during that era who may have conveyed what they recalled to others, friends, enemies, family members, journalists, each with their own agendas and political beliefs, before finally coming to you. That's the reality the gospel writers faced.

Their problem, however, was even more challenging. The examples given above are all American: an American event years ago and an American account today. But the gospels were written outside their Jewish environment—perhaps in Syria, Rome, or Alexandria. They were not composed in the same geographical area in which the events took place decades earlier. That is, they were not being written in the land of Jesus,

---

* There is also "Q," the name scholars give for material common to the Gospels of Matthew and Luke not derived from the Gospel of Mark. This may represent an earlier small collection of sayings, a separate written document perhaps. If Luke used Matthew, however, then there would be no Q: there would be just what the author of the Gospel of Matthew contributed over and above what he took from Mark that Luke preserved in his gospel.

in the Galilee, or in Jerusalem where there might be grandchildren or great-grandchildren of people who had encountered Jesus at various points in his life. The gospel writers were living in different parts of the empire in an environment hostile to the new religious movement.

When the gospel writers were working, the Galilee had been decimated by Roman troops and over a million Jews had been killed in Jerusalem. The world had changed dramatically. So, take the problem out of the American context.

Imagine, for instance, having to reconstruct the lives and sayings of a foreigner who lived some 40 to 70 years earlier in a different culture. For example, suppose we are Italian, living today in Rome, Italy. Imagine we are tasked with having to reconstruct there, in that city, the lives of leaders from another culture who lived some 40 to 70 years earlier. We are to do this solely on the basis of oral reports of people who are now living in or passing through Rome—no library or Internet research allowed. Let's say we are trying to reconstruct the Watergate scandal of President Richard Nixon, or the wartime sayings and doings of Winston Churchill in the United Kingdom, or the reforms of British prime minister Margaret Thatcher, or the activities of the Canadian prime minister in the 1970s.

That's the huge challenge the authors of the gospels were faced with: how to write in Greek, about an individual, based on oral recollections passed on over several generations who lived decades earlier, in a different culture, in a region decimated by Roman power.

The "Created Jesus"

Gospel writers had their own beliefs about Jesus and wrote for different audiences. Written for an audience of Jews, or those at least somewhat familiar with Judaism, the Gospel of Matthew positioned Jesus as a new Moses giving his Sermon on the Mount, reminiscent of Moses on Mount Sinai. According to this writer, Jesus cries out in desperation on the cross, "My God, my God, why have you forsaken me?" (Matthew 27:46). For him, Jesus died a disappointed individual, bewildered, angry, and feeling betrayed that the Kingdom of God had not yet materialized.

The later Gospel of Luke puts it differently. Luke was writing for a Roman audience, and his Jesus was like Socrates, dying a noble death. According to this gospel—written after the Gospel of Matthew, around 90—Jesus's last words were: "Father, into your hands I commend my spirit" (Luke 23:46). Here Jesus is serene, composed, and ready for whatever he faces in death.

Each gospel writer has a different version of Jesus and is trying to persuade the reader that his version is the accurate one. Each gospel, in other words, is constructing a "created Jesus," a historical Jesus filtered through later perspectives and interests. It's a take, not pure fact.

So, we really have more than two Jesuses. We have at least five: the historical Jesus, speaking in the late 20s and early 30s about the Kingdom of God and four "created Jesuses" constructed by each of the four gospel authors. There are more as well if we take into account the created Jesuses of the many gospel writings not included in the Christian New Testament.

This applies to all the other figures mentioned in the various gospels, including Peter. In terms of the incident at Caesarea Philippi, is Peter's contention that Jesus is messiah reflective of the historical Peter, or is this part of the "created Peter" by the authors of the gospels decades later, the Peter they needed for theological reasons?

The gospels, then, are all partisan and polemical works, written from a point of view with a specific agenda and audience in mind, much like many media news broadcasts today. While rooted in history, each gospel is overlayered with later concerns, some mythology (as in the birth narratives), some guesswork (as in the genealogies and trial narratives), and each presents a Jesus from a specific perspective. The gospel portraits are as far apart as current television broadcasters.

A Different World

The gap widens, however, when we realize that the world had changed dramatically between the time of Jesus and that of the gospel writers. The authors of the gospels lived and wrote for individuals who were part of a different culture—the larger Roman Empire, not the backwaters of a small Roman province in the Middle East. With the exception of the author of the Gospel of Matthew, they were writing primarily for non-Jews, unlike Jesus's historical audience who consisted mainly of Jewish peasants in and around the Sea of Galilee area.

The gospel writers lived at a time when the central institution of Jewish life, the Temple, had been destroyed; when the cultural center, Jerusalem, had been devastated; and when Jewish leadership and factions such as the Sadducees, Essenes, and Zealots had been swept away so only the Pharisees remained.* The world had shifted dramatically. The first readers of the gospels were not all that familiar with Jewish customs, beliefs, or expectations, nor with the geography of the Galilee. And, in fact, probably few cared. These details were not relevant to *their* religion.

Even more startling, they were not familiar with the writings of the Hebrew Bible, let alone the beliefs and practices of Judaism, which is what Jesus himself would have followed, as he was, of course, Jewish. And, again, probably few cared. It was not as if converts to Christianity had to undergo a series of lectures on the Hebrew Bible as part of their initiation. Again, the Hebrew Bible was just not relevant to *their* religion as it evolved away from Judaism.

The gospel authors were faced with an immense challenge: how to transcend time, culture, and place in order to present a portrait of Jesus, not as he was back there then, but how they thought he should be viewed in the here and now. Each offers us a different portrait of Jesus—a conceptual landscape they would like us to share, a way of populating our minds with the specific ideas and images of Jesus they wished to convey. As already mentioned, Mark, Matthew, and Luke give us very different impressions as to the character of Jesus. They were geniuses at literary composition, especially the author of Mark, who started the process of gospel writing.

---

* For the differences between these various Jewish factions, see Barrie Wilson, *How Jesus Became Christian*. New York: St. Martin's Press; Toronto: Random House, 2008, Chapter 3.

Putting It All Together

So, interpreter beware. Cross-cultural and cross-historical transposition of Jesus's words and actions poses an exceptionally difficult interpretive leap. The shift involves moving *from* Jesus in the Galilee in the early 1st century, speaking in Aramaic for a Jewish audience *to* an entirely different time and place. The gospel authors' audiences were Greek-speaking Romans, in the late 1st century, primarily non-Jews who either did not know much about or did not care about Judaism, but who were all too familiar with the realization that the promised Kingdom of God had not come about.

The gospels had to address that failure while simultaneously presenting the message that it was coming. That in itself was an immense undertaking: how to make the promise of a coming Kingdom of God credible to people who had every reason to believe that the promise had not come true.

Add to this the overwhelming influence of Paul. His teachings stem from the 40s and 50s and overlay the gospels we now have. Paul was not the least bit interested in the Jesus of history. In his writings there is almost nothing about Jesus's teachings or activities. All we would know about the historical Jesus from Paul is that Jesus was born, was Jewish, had brothers, and died. Paul's focus was exclusively on Jesus's death, resurrection, and what they signified for humanity. He referred to Jesus as "Christ." We shall explore later on what this means.

The gospels were written by and for people with Paul's theology in mind. Paul ignored the teachings *of* the historical Jesus, substituting instead teachings *about* Jesus. Paul's "created Jesus" is superimposed on the gospels we possess.

Reading any gospel is therefore a complex matter, requiring us to "see through" the Pauline overlay of Jesus as "Christ" to the Jesus of history underneath. We have to move, if we can, from the created Jesus—that is, the character the gospel authors fashioned to suit their own agendas—to the historical Jesus below. Reading a gospel is akin, then, to an archeological dig, sifting through various layers that come from different times.

Putting it altogether: the disparity between the time of composition and the time when Jesus lived should therefore be visualized as follows:

Us here and now

↓

2000-year gap

↓

The gospels

*Composed anonymously 70–100+CE
in Greek, for Gentiles living in the Roman Empire who
knew little about Judaism and likely cared less,
on the basis of unknown source materials.
Written in the light of Paul's message that
Jesus the Christ is a divine human whose sacrificial
death and resurrection offer the hope of eternal life*

↓

Historical gap: 40–70 years+

*No written records; oral accounts transmitted
over two or three generations by chains of unknown individuals*

↓

Teachings of Jesus

*Spoken in 20s and 30s CE
in Aramaic for Jews in the Galilee and Jerusalem.
Message: Kingdom of God is coming within
your lifetime. Prepare by repenting.*

To repeat an important point already made—but frequently overlooked—the gospel narratives are not factual reports. They are highly creative works written for audiences far removed from the culture and times in which the incidents are alleged to have occurred. Their intent is not historical, that is, not just to say, "this happened." Rather they are persuasive, "you should believe this about Jesus." The gospels are political documents, written from different points of view for different audiences with specific agendas in mind.

With this theoretical background in mind, let us return to the two differing accounts of Peter's insight at Caesarea Philippi, one from the Gospel of Matthew; the other, from the *Gospel of Thomas*.

What are we to make of contradictory evidence?

4

STRANGE INCONSISTENCIES

———✦———

In Mark's account of Peter's declaration at Caesarea Philippi, Jesus is silent about which identification he favors: a charismatic individual like John the Baptist? Elijah returned? A prophet? A messiah? He does not comment either positively or negatively on the disciples' reports. Nor does he endorse Peter's insight. Jesus shuts down messiah talk. That positioning just does not suit his agenda.

In addition to the Gospel of Mark, two other accounts exist. The three versions of the incident do not match. There are major differences. This poses a significant problem.

Matthew's Version

A decade or more after Mark, around 80–85, the anonymous author of the Gospel of Matthew writes in Greek. He has the Gospel of Mark in front of him, which he uses as a base template for his own writing. He adds material: a birth narrative up front; a Sermon on the Mount which groups some of Jesus's major teachings; and an extended narrative about Jesus's trial, death, and its aftermath.

Matthew also omits Mark's contention that Jesus declared all foods to be kosher (Matthew 15:17 *versus* Mark 6:19). For Matthew, Jesus observed the dietary laws. That's important because observing the dietary laws was commanded in Torah as part of the Covenant with God. If Jesus flouted the dietary laws as Mark would have it, say by eating roast pig, this would have been noticed and commented on by his contemporaries. In the context of his time and culture, this act would have been seen as extraordinary, scandalous, and absolutely outrageous. So, it is highly unlikely that Mark's account of Jesus as nonkosher is reliable, although it does represent Christian practice after Paul. As we shall see, Paul denied the validity of Torah, something Jesus never did (at least according to the author of the Gospel of Matthew).

Indeed, in the Sermon on the Mount, Jesus is depicted as commanding his followers to follow the Torah strictly (Matthew 5:17–20), even more so than did the scribes and Pharisees. That would include keeping the Sabbath, observing the dietary laws, honoring the festivals, and being ethical in dealings with other people. In a curious passage, Jesus even seems to endorse the teachings of the Pharisees:

> Then Jesus said to the crowds and to his disciples, "The scribes and the Pharisees sit on Moses' seat; therefore, do whatever they teach you, and follow it . . . (Matthew 23:1, 2)

He also adds:

> . . . but do not do as they do, for they do not practice what they teach." (Matthew 23:3)

According to the Gospel of Matthew, Jesus's issue is with the behavior of the Pharisees, not their teachings. Thus, for the author of this gospel, Jesus is a Torah-observant, traditional Jewish teacher.

Matthew's Jewish Jesus is a very different person from Mark's nonkosher Jesus. Presumably the reason Matthew wrote his gospel was to fix Mark's mistakes, using what he could of Mark that wasn't at odds with his perspective and by adding significant details. In all likelihood, he probably thought that Mark's gospel would disappear over time now that he had set the record straight. The irony is that it didn't and so we have two impressions of Jesus: as kosher and Torah-observant (Matthew), as nonkosher and not Torah-observant (Mark), not a minor discrepancy given the constant biblical injunctions to observe the Law of God given to the Jewish people through Moses.

Matthew's gospel presents the narrative about Peter's insight differently. Like Mark's gospel, Matthew locates Jesus and his students in the district of Caesarea Philippi. His first question, however, is worded somewhat differently: "Who do people say that *the Son of Man* is?" (Matthew 16:13, italics added) rather than, "Who do people say I am?" as in Mark.

In Matthew's account, Jesus has already loaded the question. It represents a different conceptual field, the landscape of a "Son of Man" and the ideas associated with that concept. It's not a blank screen and it is by no means a neutral question. The identity of Jesus has been partially filled in with a Son of Man descriptor. In posing the question in this manner, Jesus has already self-identified with an avatar and, just like Peter's description, it is not an identification that grows out of the disciples' report. Again it is something that arises out of the blue: no one is thinking of him as "Son of Man."

Jesus, however, links his identity to a figure called the Son of Man, not messiah. It's an odd phrase. In either the language of the biblical texts (Hebrew) or in the vernacular of the time (Aramaic, a close cognate language to Hebrew), Son of Man just means a human being. In the Greek text of Matthew, there would be no upper and lower cases as in Son and Man—that's a translator's addition and interpretation. The question Jesus poses really is this: "Who do people say that the human is?" It's a strange question. We'll return to discuss what "the human" might mean later on.

As in Mark's gospel, Jesus's disciples in Matthew report that people think of him either as John the Baptist, Elijah, Jeremiah, or as one of the prophets (Matthew 16:14).

Jesus then inquires, "But who do you say that I am?" Here Peter's answer is a bit longer than in Mark. He says, "You are the Messiah (*Christos* in Greek), the Son of the Living God" (Matthew 16:16).

Here Peter amplifies the idea of messiah and associates it with being a Son of God. That's significantly different from what Mark writes. Again "Son of God" is a phrase which in Hebrew and Aramaic could signify a divine being just as the construction "Son of Man" denotes a human being. More loosely, however, anyone who prays the Christian Lord's Prayer or the Jewish prayer *Avinu Malkeinu* ("Our Father, Our King") is addressing God as "father" and so positions himself or herself as a son or daughter of God. Here there is no implication that the person praying is anything more than a human being who stands in a particular relationship with God.

Matthew continues. He writes that Jesus praises Peter's response:

> Blessed are you, Simon son of Jonah! For flesh and blood has not revealed this to you but my Father in heaven. (Matthew 16:17)

Thus in Matthew, unlike the earlier Gospel of Mark, Jesus strongly endorses Peter's perception of him as messiah and as Son of God. It is nothing less than a divine revelation.

Furthermore, Jesus elaborates:

> And I tell you, you are Peter, and on this rock, I will build my church, and the gates of Hades will not prevail against it. I will give you the keys of the kingdom of heaven, and whatever you bind on earth will be bound in heaven, and whatever you loose on earth will be loosed in heaven. (Matthew 16:18, 19)*

Then, and only then, does Jesus order the disciples not to tell anyone that he is the messiah (Matthew 16:20).

---

* Note the play on words: both the words "Peter" and "rock" are *petros* in Greek. Jesus's followers appear to have had code IDs or nicknames, Peter as "The Rock;" Mary the Magdalene as "The Tower;" James and John, the sons of Zebedee, as "Sons of Thunder."

In Matthew's account, there are two significant elaborations to Mark's version of events: Jesus's endorsement of Peter's response and his intention to create a church.

Why did Mark miss these?

Or, perhaps more to the point, why did Matthew add these?

What's a church got to do with the idea of a messiah and a Kingdom of God? How does that relate at all? That, too, is unexpected, another feature totally out of the blue, something that makes absolutely no sense in the time of Jesus. If Jesus promised us the Kingdom of God, why do we suddenly get a church? That seems like a classic bait-and-switch maneuver, a poor substitute for the real thing.

Is the creation of a church something Jesus in the late 20s could have said? Or is this more likely something the author of the Gospel of Matthew attributed to Jesus some 50 or more years after the event in question in light of new circumstances? Is this perhaps how the author of the Gospel of Matthew accounts for the failure of the Kingdom to materialize? Is the church the substitute for the promised Kingdom?

It was during the latter part of the 1st century that the Christian movement developed its own worshipping centers—a church or an *ekklesia* in Greek—separate from Judaism's synagogues. It took a while for that development to happen. Even in the second half of the 1st century, the Letter of James in the New Testament refers to Christian places of worship as "synagogues" (*sunagoge* in Greek). It is highly unlikely that Jesus himself contemplated creating a new religious infrastructure, especially if he envisaged a Kingdom of God: that is, a new social order occurring within the lifetime of his hearers (Matthew 16:28). A new religion with separate institutions would have been very far from his mind and completely at odds with his central focus. Again, it would be off-message.

The reference to building a church is extremely odd and highly unexpected. It should stop us in our tracks. Jesus proclaimed a coming Kingdom of God, one that would manifest itself on earth within the lifetime of his hearers. He did not come to found a reformed Judaism, far less a religion separated from Judaism with separate places for assembly. He announced something quite different: the time was ripe for God to exercise his power over human affairs. God's sovereign rule over the world was on the doorstep.

So, no, this addition about founding a church on Peter is not from Jesus. Rather the author of the Gospel of Matthew has retrojected this saying back to Jesus in order to support a position he thought his audience in his era needed to hear.

In fact, if Jesus had been right about the Kingdom, there would be no need for a church. The Kingdom of God, after all, is not a church. The existence of the church is an important indicator that Jesus's promised Kingdom did not materialize. The creation of a church reflects later circumstances far removed from Jesus in the Galilee early in the 1st century.

Similarly, there would be no need for gospels. Jesus did not promise a new set of readings—a New Testament—but rather a new social order. It was only decades later, after Jesus's death and the destruction of the Second Temple in 70, when the Kingdom of God had not materialized as Jesus had said it would, that gospel writings began to appear. New writings and a wholly different infrastructure were not what was promised.

The existence of gospel writings along with a church are important indicators that Jesus's core message failed. The gospels represent a strategic move, decades later, to salvage Jesus's message for another generation. They are attempts to transfer and extend Jesus's promise *from* the lifetimes of his audiences *to* the lifetimes of the readers of the gospel writings. Thus the promise of the Kingdom coming soon is extended from the lifetimes of those living in the 30s to those living in the late 1st century. In modern terms we would describe the writing of the various gospels as a "re-boot." The maneuver buys time for the promise to come true.

This elaboration in Matthew shows us clearly the freedom writers after Mark thought they had in adding or changing earlier works. This license extends so far as to change or to add to the words Jesus is said to have spoken. This is remarkable because it makes utter nonsense of the view that scripture is unchangeable. Matthew clearly thinks Mark's gospel is defective in a number of ways.

On Matthew's conceptual tableau we have a Son of Man avatar, Jesus's endorsement of Peter's insight, and a church with Peter as its foundation.

So there it sits: Matthew's version alongside Mark's.

Who's right?

Thomas's Version

We are fortunate to have not only Matthew's alternate account, but also one from another gospel, the *Gospel of Thomas*.*

This gospel was not included in the New Testament, although it is attributed to Jesus's disciple Thomas. The *Gospel of Thomas* likely dates in part from the 1st century.† This writing emanated from the Gnostic Christian community. All their writings—including this gospel—were excluded from the New Testament whose contents were not determined until the mid 4th century.‡

The *Gospel of Thomas* does not give us a location for Jesus quizzing his disciples about audience impressions. The anonymous author of this gospel had no interest in where Jesus made pronouncements. Nor is he interested in Jesus's birth, death, resurrection, or miracles. Interestingly, eternal life is not tied to a sacrificial atonement, but rather to a profound understanding of Jesus's teachings. This gospel portrays Jesus as saying, "Whoever discovers the interpretation of these sayings will not taste death" (*Gospel of Thomas* 1).

The process of understanding is referred to as *gnosis*, that is, "insight," a deep personal understanding of the spiritual message expounded by Jesus. This gospel represents a bare bones listing of Jesus's sayings without any

---

* All references to this writing are to the translation in Marvin Meyer, *The Gnostic Gospels of Jesus*. New York: HarperOne, 2005, pp. 3–25.

† As Marvin Meyer points out, "A reasonable case can be made for a first-century date for the first edition of the *Gospel of Thomas*, though some scholars prefer a second-century date." Marvin Meyer, *The Gnostic Gospels of Jesus*, p. 5.

‡ The contents of the New Testament were determined by Archbishop Athanasius in his Festal Letter of 367. He selected 27 books as authoritative, writings congruent with the Creed of Nicea of 325. Political considerations entered into both the formulation of this Creed as well as in the selection of New Testament writings. Prior to the 4th century there were many Christian communities, each with somewhat different teachings and each favoring somewhat different writings. The Gnostic Christian community was one such group. It was a major force within early Christianity from the 2nd through the 5th century but its teachings—and writings—differed from the faction that was supported by the Roman Emperors. Their beliefs were not represented in the Nicene Creed and their writings excluded in the New Testament. Fifty-two of their writings were discovered in 1945 at Nag Hammadi, Egypt.

context for when Jesus might have uttered these words or any elaboration as to their meaning.

In one saying, Jesus simply instructs his disciples, "Compare me to something and tell me what I am like" (*Gospel of Thomas* 13:1). Peter responds first and says that Jesus is "like a righteous messenger." Matthew compares Jesus to "a wise philosopher." Thomas, on the other hand, addresses Jesus, saying, "Teacher, my mouth is utterly unable to say what you are like" (*Gospel of Thomas* 13:2–4).

Jesus focuses on Thomas. He admonishes him for saying that he is a teacher. He then takes Thomas aside and tells him three things in private. When the others ask him what Jesus had disclosed, Thomas refuses: "If I tell you one of the sayings he spoke to me, you will pick up rocks and stone me, and fire will come from the rocks and consume you" (*Gospel of Thomas* 13:6–8). In other words, we'd both be destroyed if I were to divulge to you what Jesus told me. So whatever Jesus told Thomas presumably died with both of them.

The contrast between the *Gospel of Thomas* on the one hand and Mark and Matthew on the other is astounding. In the *Gospel of Thomas*, Jesus doesn't ask for impressions about how the crowds understand him, but how his disciples do. What insight have *they* achieved? The responses are vastly different from those given in Mark and Matthew: righteous messenger, wise philosopher, teacher. There is nothing that reaches back into Jewish culture, to Elijah the messianic forerunner or to the prophets. There is conspicuously no mention of Peter's startling insight. There is no elaborate staging, no placing the incident at Caesarea Philippi, for instance, against the dramatic backdrop of the divine Roman Emperor and the playful god Pan.

More than that, the correct answer seems to be Thomas's. And his response represents an inability to answer the question.

The Problem of Alternate Accounts

We have three versions of the incident and they differ substantially. They can't all be true. Nor must any one of them be true. They could all be fabrications.

Gospel of Mark

Should we prefer Mark's version? If so, why? Should we choose his account because, according to general scholarly consensus, it is the earliest gospel? Or because, unlike *Thomas*, it is included in the New Testament?

Or should we dismiss Mark's account? Perhaps it is just imaginative staging, locating Peter's insight against the backdrop of an amazing locale. Is that something Mark fabricated to suggest a theological point, that Jesus is greater than the emperor or Pan? Did anything like Mark's version of the events really happen? Is it possible that Mark's narrative concerning Peter's dramatic insight is simply the result of creative crafting in the 70s? In other words, perhaps it could be part of Mark's "created Jesus," the one he wants us to believe.

As we have seen, creative changes are not unknown when it comes to biblical writings. The author of the Gospel of Matthew adds substantially to the words of Jesus, to give the impression, appropriate for circumstances in the 80s, that Jesus had authorized the creation of a church with Peter as its head. That's part of Matthew's created Jesus.

Do the special effects—or fake news—go even deeper? Could it be that the entire incident was made up, first by Mark who created an elaborate backdrop of a city showcasing the Roman emperor and the Greek god Pan? What fantastic staging for this momentous revelation! Could this have then been followed subsequently by Matthew who, liking its heightened drama, elaborated upon the scenario?

As has already been mentioned, we know the author of the Gospel of Mark misrepresented Jesus in at least one important respect. The author of the Gospel of Matthew clearly thought Mark was lying by saying that Jesus set aside the biblical commandments concerning kashrut, the dietary laws (see Leviticus 11, for instance, and compare Matthew 15:17 with Mark 7:19). Matthew corrected Mark. For him, Jesus kept kosher.

The author of the Book of Acts also thought that Mark was lying. Acts was written by the same writer who composed the Gospel of Luke in the

---

* Catholics interpret this passage as referring to the person of Peter who, as first bishop of Rome, became the first amongst equals, that is, pope. Protestants interpret the passage as referring to Peter's belief that Jesus is messiah.

90s or so. In the Book of Acts, Peter goes into a trance. He sees a massive sheet descending to the earth, full of all kinds of animals, reptiles, and birds. A voice then asks him to kill and eat these animals. Peter protests, saying that he has never eaten anything impure (that is, nonkosher). We know from these protestations that Peter, up to that point, observed the laws of kashrut, as did Jesus and all the disciples (Acts 10:9–16). The voice goes on to say, "what God has made clean, you must not call profane." It is on this basis—Peter's trance, as well as the teachings of Paul—that early Christians set aside the Jewish dietary laws. So, eating pork, bacon, and shellfish became acceptable menu items, but not until after Jesus had died.

The result? Mark is the odd person out when it comes to Jesus's diet. Someone is not telling the truth, and for Matthew and the author of the Book of Acts, it would be Mark.

On the other hand, there's always the chance that Mark got it right and that Matthew and Acts are mistaken, although a nonkosher Jesus is highly unlikely in the culture he inhabited.

Gospel of Matthew

Turning to the Gospel of Matthew: should we accept his version of Peter's insight and Jesus's high approval? Matthew, after all, corrected Mark and he likely described Jesus's diet correctly.

But there are problems with some of Matthew's changes. Having Jesus talk about a church built around the personage of Peter is fake. It just doesn't ring true in Jesus's time, although it makes eminent sense in Matthew's era as the church was struggling to define itself by developing an infrastructure divorced from Judaism and by regularizing its leadership around a separate hierarchy of bishops and priests.

Fake News

Matthew makes another extremely serious anachronistic claim, one that has had tremendous and deadly repercussions over the centuries. He changes Mark once again, this time with respect to the issue concerning responsibility for the death of Jesus: he shifts the blame for his death from the Romans to the Jews. We can trace the impact of Matthew's false narrative in how subsequent trial accounts handle the matter.*

Here's what Mark, the earliest gospel, reports. According to the Gospel of Mark, Pilate, the Roman governor, orders Jesus executed, albeit with the urging of the chief priests and crowd. So, for him, the Romans are to blame for Jesus's death—Pilate "handed him over to be crucified" (Mark 15:15). This decisiveness fits with the portrait of Pilate in the writings of the 1st century Jewish historian, Josephus, and in the works of the 1st century Jewish philosopher, Philo. In the writings of Josephus and Philo, Pilate is depicted as an utterly ruthless political appointee of Rome; he would have tolerated no threat whatsoever to Roman authority.

Writing a decade or so later, for an audience who might not take kindly to the view that Roman authorities were responsible for their founder's death, the author of the Gospel of Matthew shifts responsibility. According to him, Pilate wants nothing to do with Jesus's death. His wife informs him during the trial of Jesus, "Have nothing to do with that innocent man, for today I have suffered a great deal because of a dream about him" (Matthew 27:19). Sensing that a riot is about to ensue, Pilate signals his judgment by washing his hands of the whole affair. Note how Matthew shifts responsibility—away from the Romans to the Jews:

> So, when Pilate saw that he could do nothing, but rather that a riot was beginning, he took some water and washed his hands before the crowd, saying, "I am innocent of this man's blood; see to it yourselves." Then the people as a whole answered, "His blood be on us and on our children!" (Matthew 27:24, 25)

According to Matthew, the Jewish mob demands Jesus's death and a weak-kneed Pilate simply turns him over to them. Thus, for Matthew, the Jewish rabble is responsible. This gospel fabricates a tremendous shift

---

* See also Gary Greenberg, *The Judas Brief: Who Really Killed Jesus?* New York: Bloomsbury Academic, 2007.

in responsibility, one that would make more sense in the pro-Roman late 1st century than in the anti-Roman Jerusalem of the early 30s. It makes nonsense, however, of the character of Pontius Pilate, who was removed by Roman authorities in 36 for excessive cruelty and barbarity.

In making this significant change, Matthew became an unfortunate trendsetter. The author of the Gospel of Luke, writing a bit later than Matthew, has Pilate declaring Jesus innocent:

> Pilate then called together the chief priests, the leaders, and the people, and said to them, "You brought me this man as one who was perverting the people; and here I have examined him in your presence and have not found this man guilty of any of your charges against him. Neither has Herod [Antipas], for he sent him back to us. Indeed, he has done nothing to deserve death." (Luke 23:13–15)

Here Pilate exonerates Jesus and in so doing reveals that the charges had been brought forward not by Roman authorities, but by the Jewish chief priests ("your charges"). So, according to the author of the Gospel of Luke, the whole arrest and trial was a Jewish conspiracy. It wasn't a Roman initiative at all. In fact, according to the author of the Gospel of Luke, Pilate declares Jesus innocent three times (Luke 23:22). Then, weakly, he hands Jesus over to the Jewish rabble.

Even later, in the late 90s or early 100s, the author of the Gospel of John has Pilate declare Jesus innocent—"I find no case against him" (John 19:4)—before handing him over to the Jewish people.

Matthew therefore has the dubious distinction of fabricating the vile myth that the Jews killed Jesus. There was no religious crime on the part of Jesus, and he was not convicted of any such wrongdoing. So it is difficult to fathom why Matthew's account would be accorded any credibility. This fake news charge has reverberated throughout history and is responsible for the death of thousands.

The anti-Jewish trend started by Matthew unfortunately escalated. In the 2nd century, the *Gospel of Peter*, a writing not included in the Christian Scriptures, portrays the Jewish leaders as guilt-ridden:

[After Jesus has been crucified] Then the Jews, the elders, and the priests realized how much evil they had done to themselves and began beating their breasts, saying "Woe to us because of our sin. The judgment and the end of Jerusalem are near." (*Gospel of Peter 25*)

Note how the *Gospel of Peter* relates the fall of Jerusalem in 70, not to the overwhelming might of the Romans but to the crucifixion of Jesus. Divine payback is the message of this writing.

In the 3rd century the Christian leader in Carthage, Tertullian, put forward a nonsensical story that Pilate had been so impressed by Jesus that he had sent a letter of commendation on his behalf to the Roman emperor Tiberius.* That letter purportedly mentioned Jesus's miracles and resurrection, noting that people throughout the land consider him to be divine. Tiberius then allegedly referred the matter to the Roman Senate. However, that body refused to acknowledge Jesus as a god. This is sheer fabrication: there was no such letter from Pilate to the emperor in the early 30s, and no such debate in the Roman Senate about the divinity of Jesus.

All this is fake news caused by shifting blame for Jesus's death from the Roman authorities to the Jewish leaders and Jewish mob. Matthew started it and the rest followed, all wanting to exonerate the Romans whom they were trying to recruit as members in their new religion.

Manipulating the facts and creating fake news is not a unique 21st century preoccupation. So having Jesus talk about creating a church represents more disinformation. It's all part of Matthew's created Jesus. It suits his agenda to portray Jesus as separating his movement from Judaism. It's a polemic.

Gospel of Thomas

If we reject both Mark and Matthew's accounts of the incident, then perhaps the *Gospel of Thomas*'s version should be accepted. After all, it comes

---

* Tertullian's account is provided by Eusebius, *Ecclesiastical History*. Translated by C. F. Cruse. Peabody, Massachusetts: Hendrickson Publishers, 2001, Book 2, Chapter 3, Sections 1–3.

from a gospel writing which simply lists sayings attributed to Jesus, without place settings or elaboration. It does not support the role of Peter, however, nor the claim that Jesus is the messiah. It is simply an affirmation of Jesus's mysterious nature.

Or maybe the *Gospel of Thomas*'s narrative should be rejected as historically accurate. After all, it comes from a writing not included in the New Testament, although parts of this work are equally the product of 1st century writing.

This point of view—rejecting the *Gospel of Thomas* account simply because it was not included in the New Testament—ignores all the political factors that went into the selection of the contents of the Christian Bible. There was no conference of early biblical scholars assembled around a table with dozens of manuscripts judged suitable for possible inclusion into a set of Christian readings. That never happened. There was no assembly of scholars, no vetting process, and no due consideration given to the merits of each possible writing for inclusion into the new biblical canon.

There were, moreover, many denominations in the first four centuries—Pauline Christians, several varieties of Jewish Christians, Marcionites, and various Gnostic Christian groups amongst many others. Each had their own favored set of writings supporting their respective theologies. No one group was mainstream or normative with the rest being deviant any more than that's the case today. Is Eastern Orthodoxy mainstream today because it is the oldest? Or is Catholicism mainstream because it is the largest? Or is Anglicanism mainstream because it combines Catholic worship with Protestant theology? What about Mormonism? Is it mainstream because it has had the benefit of a second revelation? Without a basis on which to judge "normative-ness" or "mainstream-ness," these questions make no sense now or then.

The contents of the New Testament were not compiled until the mid-4th century when Archbishop Athanasius listed the 27 books he considered authoritative, thus bringing the Christian writings into alignment with the already agreed upon Christian creed, the Nicene Creed of 325. The bishops who attended the Council of Nicaea did not include leaders from the Gnostic Christian perspective. Hence their theology and writings were excluded. So the church's belief system determined the list of acceptable writings. Thus belief determined Bible; not the other way around. The shape of the Christian New Testament is thus a 4th century creation.

∽

So we have several versions of the insight at Caesarea Philippi. They do not correspond and there is no clear-cut way of determining which, if any, is accurate.

Did Peter really make that claim, that Jesus is messiah? The critical historical questions keep piling up.

Should we be combing gospels such as Matthew, Luke, *Thomas*, or *Peter* in order to search for messiah? Or are these the wrong places to look?

But there is a far bigger problem.

5

GOING INCOGNITO

※

Where's the Evidence?

The disclosure at Caesarea Philippi faces a much greater problem than simply the existence of three different versions of the incident. After Peter utters his earth-shattering insight that Jesus is the messiah, we would expect the author of the Gospel of Mark to back up this claim. Why did Peter think Jesus was one? On what basis? What was his evidence?

In other words, convince us. Don't just leave us dangling.

But that's exactly what the author of the Gospel of Mark does: he leaves us hanging.

More than that, he has Jesus running for cover.

After Mark 8:30, where Peter says Jesus is "the messiah," virtually nothing is said about Jesus as messiah. There's nothing in the gospel that demonstrates how he merits this distinction.

After Chapter 8, there are four very brief mentions of Jesus as *Christos* (messiah) in Mark. There's one where Jesus seems to dismiss the view that the messiah is the son of David (Mark 12:35). That's strange since, as we shall see, one of the criteria for being a messiah is to be a king from the lineage of David.

In another passage Jesus cautions his followers about the possibility of false messiahs (Mark 13:21–22). This, too, is strange, because without knowing the job description of a messiah, it is impossible to judge who is and who is not an authentic one.

Moreover, who are these other false messiahs? Who else was running around Galilee as a possible candidate for this title in the late 20s?

Or is talk about false messiahs something that would pertain more to the time of the author of the Gospel of Mark and his audience in the 70s rather than the time of Jesus and his? Also who might these false messiahs be even in the 70s? Who had such stature?

In another passage, the high priest asks Jesus if he is the messiah. Mark says that Jesus replies, "I am" (Mark 14:61). Here, again, we would expect backup. We would expect Jesus would go on to recite a litany of actions that would make one believe that he is the messiah. It's his one big chance to set the record straight, to win over the high priest and the religious establishment. There is, however, no recital of messianic accomplishments. Moreover no massive world changes are taking place that would corroborate Jesus's claim.

Note that claiming to be a messiah is not a religious crime, so Jesus would be of no real interest to religious authorities on this account. The Romans, however, might interpret a messianic claim as signaling a potential revolt. If there were evidence that he was amassing a huge following, collecting arms, and mobilizing troops, then Jesus would be of interest to them. But was Jesus really positioning himself to lead an armed rebellion comparable to those of Simon of Peraea or Judas the Galilean? Was there any evidence to this effect?

Finally, there is a passage where Jesus is mocked as he is dying upon the cross (Mark 15:32). While mocking is cruel, in context, such ridiculing behavior is not unexpected, especially since the Kingdom Jesus had talked about had not come to pass. Pestering Jesus as he was dying as to the whereabouts of the Kingdom would be predictable. Moreover, would a true messiah be put to death before the Kingdom of God had appeared? Or, for that matter, ever put to death?

None of these passages provides any indication why Jesus might be considered a candidate for messiah status. Peter does not defend the claim. Neither does Jesus. Nor does the author of the Gospel of Mark.

Very strange.

Jesus as the Son of Man

Even more curiously, immediately after verse 30 of Chapter 8, Mark goes on to talk about Jesus in terms of another image: Son of Man. There are seven mentions of Jesus as Son of Man after Chapter 8. There is, however, no tie-in linking Jesus as messiah to Jesus as Son of Man. Nowhere is there a statement to the effect that "the messiah" is also known as "Son of Man." There are no linkages, no connection.

That's amazing.

It's as if there are really two Gospels of Mark. One document goes from Mark 1:1 to Mark 8:30 where Jesus is touted to be the messiah. Perhaps that was the high point of some original version of Mark. Then another document about Jesus as the Son of Man figure seems to be pasted on, extending from Mark 8:31 until the end of the writing. Thus we have two different titles and job descriptions. Perhaps two separate writings were attached to each other in antiquity.

This split can be pictured as follows:

Mark 8:27–30
... he [Jesus] asked his disciples, "Who do people say I am?" And they answered him, "John the Baptist; and others, Elijah; and still others, one of the prophets." He asked them, "But who do you say that I am?" Peter answered him, "You are the Messiah." And he sternly ordered them not to tell anyone about him.

—SPLIT—

Mark 8:31–33
Then he began to teach them that the Son of Man must undergo great suffering, and be rejected by the elders, the chief

priests, and the scribes, and be killed, and after three days rise again. He said all this quite openly. And Peter took him aside and began to rebuke him. But turning and looking at his disciples, he rebuked Peter and said, "Get behind me, Satan!"

The contrast between Jesus as messiah and then Jesus as Son of Man, without any intervening links, appears to represent a splice line in the gospel. A Jesus as messiah writing seems to have had attached to it a different account, that of Jesus as a Son of Man figure.

It's as if a book about a doctor suddenly shifts midway through to one about a hedge-fund manager. We would stop and say, "What's going on here? Is the hedge fund manager the same individual as the doctor?" We would have every right to wonder how these two narratives connect. There is nothing said that would connect the idea of Son of Man to that of a messiah in Mark's writing. Nothing at all.

The context indicates that Jesus seems to be talking about himself. Talking about himself as "Son of Man" is odd behavior for a number of reasons.

First of all, the disciples have not indicated that anybody thinks of Jesus as Son of Man. That descriptor isn't included in their report about his public persona. This title, therefore, does not emerge organically from the exchange. It's again something that comes out of the blue.

Secondly, unlike the characterization of messiah, Jesus does proceed to explain the task of the Son of Man. The Son of Man—that is, he himself—must undergo suffering, rejection, and, ultimately, redemption by being raised from the dead by God.

Peter protests. Clearly, he did not think a messiah would be killed. He did not associate the idea of death with the idea of messiah. There's no conceptual linkage between death and messiah. This is a sharp jolt out of nowhere. Perhaps Peter expected—as we might—some discussion of the kind of world that messiah would help bring about. Perhaps something about their role as his disciples in it. Instead Jesus lambasts Peter as "Satan" (Mark 8:33), all within four verses of his identification of Jesus as messiah. These are indeed harsh words and an abrupt turn of events.

Thirdly, speaking of oneself in the third person is odd. We do not normally do that. It represents a weird way of speaking. This manner of speech would have sounded as awkward to his original hearers as to us. We have already indicated that the phrase "son of man" simply means "the human" or "the man" (generic) in Hebrew and Aramaic. So here's how Jesus speaks about himself: instead of saying, "I am going to do this or that," Jesus says, referring to himself, that "the human is going to do this or that." Small children sometimes refer to themselves in the third person, for instance, three-year old Johnny saying of himself, "Johnny would like to go to the park." But adults do not.

Bearing in mind that Jesus doesn't explain his use of this expression, there are several ways of understanding this awkward phrase. All of them are conjecture.

Son of Man as an Old Testament Reference

One possibility is the phrase may harken back to some usage of the "son of man" phrase in the Hebrew Bible, or the Christian Old Testament. There is, however, no obvious linkage to a specific passage. In fact, there is no passage in which "*the* son of man" phrase occurs in the Hebrew Bible/Old Testament, nothing with the definite article denoting a specific human being.

There are, however, 107 uses of "a son of man" meaning just a human being or humanity in general. It's a generic word. A typical usage occurs in the following psalm:

> What is man (*'enosh*) that You have been mindful of him,
> Mortal man (*ben adam*) that You have taken note of him,
> That you have made him little less than divine
> And adorned him with glory and majesty (Psalm 8:5, 6)

Here the phrase *ben adam* or "son of man" is simply a poetic synonym for "man" (generic) or "humanity." The JPS version translates what is literally "son of man" as "mortal man" because of the context. Psalm 8 emphasizes the immense contrast between majestic divinity and frail humanity. Similarly, God addresses the prophet Ezekiel as, "O mortal," literally, "O son of man," (*ben adam*) (Ezekiel 2:1, 3). Here, too, the passage emphasizes the prophet's lowliness before the Almighty. So the phrase "son of man" connotes a frail, vulnerable human being, lowly in stature before the almighty God.

Another possibility is that Jesus is harkening back to the Book of Daniel, Chapter 7, in which the figure of a human being appears. That chapter, written in Aramaic, relates how Daniel has a nighttime vision:

> One like a human being (*kbar 'anash*, literally like a son of man)
> Came with the clouds of heaven;
> He reached the Ancient of Days
> And was presented to Him.
> Dominion, glory, and kingship were given to him;
> All peoples and nations of every language must serve him.
> His dominion is an everlasting dominion that shall not pass away,
> And his kingship, one that shall not be destroyed. (Daniel 7:13, 14)

In this passage, a being who looks human comes before God, called here "the Ancient of Days." That human lookalike receives sovereignty from God. It will be an everlasting monarchy to which all peoples will be subject.

It is doubtful, however, that the author of the Gospel of Mark had this particular passage in mind. For one thing, the phrase is not the same: the passage reads "*like a* human being." It's simply saying that the figure resembles a human; it is not referring to a specific human, that is, it does not say "*the* human being." Secondly, it links the human being lookalike to the themes of kingship and universal rule, not to death and dying as Jesus does.

Moreover, the author of the Book of Daniel is speaking about an earthly kingdom, not a spiritual one—a Jewish monarchy that he hopes is imminent.

A bit of background. According to most scholars,* the Book of Daniel was written around the time of Antiochus Epiphanes in the mid 2nd

---

* See, for instance, Barry L. Bandstra, *Reading the Old Testament: An Introduction to the Hebrew Bible*. Belmont, CA: Wadsworth Thomson Learning, 2004, third edition. The evolution of the Book of Daniel is discussed on pp. 476–486. Christian Old Testaments include Daniel among the Prophets; in the Jewish Hebrew Bible the Book of Daniel is found in the section called Writings, not in Prophets.

century BCE. The ruthless persecutions of this foreign ruler threatened to wipe out Judaism—especially during three years of intense brutality, 167 to 164 BCE. The Book of 2 Maccabees describes these atrocities in great detail: death for practicing circumcision, destruction of biblical writings, desecration of the Temple, and compulsory eating of nonkosher foods. The times are so dire that 2 Maccabees gives us one of the clearest expressions of belief in personal resurrection. As her seven sons are being tortured in front of her for refusing to eat pork, their mother cries out:

> [Addressing the king] You accursed wretch, you dismiss us from this present life but the King of the universe will raise us up to an everlasting renewal of life, because we have died for his laws . . . But for you there will be no resurrection to life. (2 Maccabees 7:9, 14)

For her, fidelity to the commandments is what counts for resurrection to eternal life. Note that it is not the Torah that saves, it is a person whose life is lived in accordance with the requirements of the Torah—all of that person's decisions and actions—who is saved by God.

The Book of Daniel is written with a specific group in mind. Its author is concerned with infusing a group he calls "the holy ones (or "the saints") of the Most High" with courage and enthusiasm. This group represents one faction of a broad-based resistance movement fighting to overthrow the regime of Antiochus Epiphanes. The writing makes it clear that "the holy ones of the Most High" will inherit the kingdom:

> The kingship and dominion and grandeur belonging to all the kingdoms under Heaven will be given to the people of the holy ones of the Most High. Their kingdom shall be an everlasting kingdom, and all dominions shall serve and obey them. (Daniel 7:27)

The promise is to a group of people who will rule, not a specific individual. The resistance movement against Antiochus Epiphanes achieved success, liberating Jerusalem and parts of Judea, cleansing the Temple, and instituting the Festival of Hanukkah. Theirs was not an everlasting kingdom, however, although the Maccabean or Hasmonean dynasty that emerged did rule Israel for over a hundred years.

Consequently, there is no good reason to suppose that Jesus or, for that matter, the author of the Gospel of Mark, is thinking of any specific Old Testament passage by appealing to the Son of Man image. No clues are given which would entitle us to select one passage out of the 107 that contain this phrase. The intended reference could easily be this one from the Book of Job:

> How much less man, a worm,
> The son-of-man (*ben adam*), a maggot. (Job 25:6)

It could just be that by "Son of Man," Jesus has humility rather than messianic grandeur in mind.

Son of Man as Perfected Humanity

In his identity as "the human," perhaps Jesus is indicating that he is not a fragmented person, a being divided by lack of integrity or completeness. He is the integrated human being, the perfected human, made the way God intended humans to be. He is the fulfillment of our humanity, whole and complete.

While this view may seem strange to some readers, the *Gospel of Thomas* has many passages promoting the view that Jesus is the unity of all that divides us, the person who helps us overcome our fragmented selves.* The following passages are typical:

> Jesus said to her, "I am the one who comes from what is whole. . . .
> For this reason I say, if one is <whole>, one will be filled with

---

* For an excellent discussion of the *Gospel of Thomas* and Jesus as the integrated human being, see Robert W. North, *The Messiah's Unrealized Revolution*. New York: CreateSpace, 2017, Chapter 2 "Jesus' Gospel: Become Fully Human."

light, but if one is divided, one will be filled with darkness."
(*Gospel of Thomas* 61)

Jesus said, "When you make the two into one, you will become
children of humankind (literally, sons-of-men)." (*Gospel of
Thomas* 106)

The idea of an integrated human as a perfected human being harkens
back to Genesis Chapters 1 and 2, the two accounts of creation. The first
version—Genesis 1:1–2:4a—is a stately, majestic account of creation, with
the action taking place orderly over seven days. It culminates in the creation
of humanity on day six and the Sabbath on day seven. The passage dealing
with the creation of humanity goes as follows:

And God created man (*ha-adam*, the man) in His image, in the
image of God He created **him**; male and female He created
them. (Genesis 1:27. Emphasis added)

So how many human beings did God create on day six? Looking at the
last phrase with the word "them," it would seem that there was a simul-
taneous creation of two beings, one male and one female. Looking at the
phrase containing "him," however, referring to "the man" (generic), it would
appear to be one composite being. The next verse seems to disambiguate
the passage with God blessing "them," plural, and instructing "them" to
reproduce and fill the earth (Genesis 1:28). That only makes sense if there
are two beings.

There is another version of creation immediately after the first (Genesis
2:4b–3:24). This is the story of the wonderful Garden of Eden, the creation
of woman, some rules, temptation, sin, a talking serpent, a blame game,
and expulsion from the garden. After creating a beautiful ideal Paradise,
God observes that it is not good for "the man" (*ha-adam*) to be alone. This
would imply that "the man" is one entity, one composite being who is alone.
It would be better to translate *ha-adam* as "the human," since this being
is dually gendered, encompassing both female and male attributes. In this
account, "the woman" is created out of the side (or rib, as it is sometimes

translated) of "the human," resulting in two gender-specific individuals from the one gender-composite primal being.

That's the picture in Genesis 2. It is not as if a biological male gives birth to a female. It is rather a composite being with both genders (a male-female) becoming severed into two separate entities. This is a very different picture of the creation of humanity that has profound consequences for understanding what it means to be human.

To see this, we need to explore what some call "the fall of humanity," that is, the expulsion from the original mythical world God intended for people. One way of interpreting this is to see the fall as involving disobedience and sin, with the serpent persuading the female who entices the male to eat forbidden fruit. This is an interpretation often found in Christian circles, with the sin of humanity traced back to the original mistake made by Adam (first male) in the garden and transmitted biologically to subsequent generations.*

The fall of humanity can be interpreted, however, quite differently. According to this alternate reading of Genesis, the real fault—the root cause of the ensuing catastrophe—is the bifurcation of humanity. Once a composite being, this human entity is split, resulting in two separate genders.† That separation is the root cause of human tragedy. It precedes the act of disobedience.

The author of the Book of Genesis seems to prefer this reading in the second story of creation. Yes, humans are at fault for disobedience and are expelled from Paradise as a consequence. But they are also fragmented beings, not the integrated persons they were intended to be. Genesis goes on to promote marriage as a reunification of the genders: "Hence a man leaves his father and mother and clings to his wife, so that they become

---

* This view—that the fall of humanity is an historical event, the consequences of which are transmitted biologically—underlies the Christian theology of redemption, that people are born sinful, in need of salvation, and that this is achieved through Jesus's act of atonement which undoes the effects of the fall.

† Given the modern view of the fluidity of gender and gender identification, the Gnostic position could perhaps be restated that all humans are incomplete and need to seek their counterpart, whatever the gender of each person. The emphasis is upon becoming a whole integrated human being, not a fragmented self.

one flesh" (Genesis 2:24). That's the punch line of the second account of creation. Genders can be restored to wholeness, as God intended.

Jesus, moreover, seems to share this view as well. He quotes the passage from Genesis just cited and adds: "So they are no longer two, but one flesh. Therefore what God has joined together, let no one separate" (Matthew 19:6). Again the union of the genders restores wholeness.

On this view, the idea that sin was the main fault in creation ignores that this act of disobedience is a consequence of something much deeper. The main rupture is within the human being itself: the split into separate genders and the failure of each individual to be a whole person. It is only when humans are so divided that disobedience or sin enters into the world. Fragmented, incomplete humans are conflicted internally and at war with others externally.

This concept—that the main disruption to God's plan was human bifurcation—was prominent within Gnostic Christianity, a form of the religion that lasted until well into the 5th and 6th centuries. For these Christians, overcoming the rupture of wholeness and integrity was what was meant by redemption. Unlike Christians whose theology was informed by Paul and his followers, Gnostic Christians celebrated the sacrament of the bridal chamber as the means of reunification and redemption. This large and influential community of Christians did not interpret Jesus's death as a sacrificial atonement for sin. Instead they understood Jesus as the teacher who provided the way forward to a reunited human being. He was truly "the human."

As the *Gospel of Thomas* indicates, Jesus saw himself as "the human."

By calling himself "the human," Jesus may be signaling that he is the prototype for a new humanity, the integrated human, the one whose teachings can restore wholeness to humans the way God intended them to be.

It may go farther. According to some Gnostic Christians, the ultimate redemptive sacrament was the rite of the bridal chamber, a celebration of the sacred marriage between Jesus and Mary the Magdalene. This sacred

---

*   Again, given the modern view of the fluidity of gender and gender identification, Jesus's position could perhaps be restated that all humans are incomplete and need to seek their counterpart, whatever the gender of each person. The emphasis is upon become a whole integrated human being, not a fragmented self.

union was viewed as overcoming the fault within creation, the real reunification of the two genders into one flesh. This idea is explored in depth in *The Lost Gospel.**

Whether or not we think of Jesus as married, let alone agreeing with the Gnostics that the bridal chamber sacrament signifies the means of redemption, Jesus referring to himself as "the human" may mean he considers himself to be the exemplar of the undivided self.

Son of Man as Dismissive

Jesus injects his own preferred descriptor just after reports that he is perceived as like John the Baptist, Elijah, a prophet, or even as messiah. It may be that by referring to himself as "the Son of Man," Jesus is rejecting all these other titles. It could be a way of saying, they don't fit. If so, then Jesus has seriously miscommunicated his identity and mission to the audiences to whom he has been speaking . . . and to his students. No one thinks of him as "Son of Man" and the disciples do not endorse this impression. Jesus is out there, alone on a limb, with this description.

Perhaps he is simply saying, "You have no idea who I am. I'm going to die and suffer." In addition, "I'll be raised from the dead."

The first two—suffering and dying—are not surprising. Dying is the lot of all mortals and suffering is the fate of many. The last one—being raised from the dead—is also not surprising. Many people of his time would have expected that, as a righteous Jew, Jesus would be raised by God to eternal life. By the time of Jesus, resurrection of the righteous was a well-established Jewish view, as the passage from 2 Maccabees quoted earlier makes clear. Some but not all Jews of the time believed that God would resurrect the faithful after death to eternal life. Some probably thought resurrection occurs immediately after death; others, perhaps later, at the end of time when the earth will be restored to its true form as Paradise.

---

* See Simcha Jacobovici and Barrie Wilson, *The Lost Gospel: Decoding the Ancient Text that Reveals Jesus's Marriage to Mary the Magdalene.* New York: Pegasus; Toronto: HarperCollins, 2014. See also "(PDF) The Lost Gospel—the Manuscript Tradition—ResearchGate."

Resurrection is still a fundamental Jewish belief. The *Amidah*, the central prayer of Judaism, includes the following phrase: "Blessed art Thou, O Lord, who callest the dead to life everlasting."

The idea of resurrection takes the reality of death seriously: people do die. On this view, there is no immortal soul that flits effortlessly from corpse to bliss. That view emanates from ancient Greek thought, amongst other ancient religions. In Judaism, as in Christianity, only God has the power to reconstitute the person after death. Paul echoed this view of resurrection in 1 Corinthians 15, and tried valiantly to explain it. But this was not a new development with Paul: the idea of resurrection was part of the belief structure of Judaism centuries before him.

It is also clear that Jesus did not self-resurrect. Passages referring to his resurrection are often expressed in the passive voice, "was raised from the dead" (1 Corinthians 15:4, Matthew 28:7). Only God can resurrect.

Moreover, that Jesus was resurrected, as Christians believe, is in no way proof of his divinity. It is simply a testament to his righteousness as a Torah-observant Jew and the power and grace of God. Eternal life in both Judaism and Christianity is seen as a gift of God.

If Jesus is dismissing all the conventional ways of understanding him, then perhaps his disciple Thomas was closest to the truth. After all, he was the one who said that he was unable to provide a description. That, for the author of the *Gospel of Thomas*, seems to have been the right answer.

Going Incognito: Son of Man as Disguise

Jesus uses "the Son of Man" phrase to refer to himself 14 times in Mark; 32 times in Matthew; and 26 times in Luke.* One possibility is that Matthew and Luke simply copied Mark in this respect. Maybe it reflects something that was characteristic of Jesus's linguistic behavior. As always, when reading the gospels, interpreters have to be careful with what is attributed to Jesus several generations later and what might have stemmed

---

* Marius Nel, "'Son of man' in the Gospel of Mark," 2017. See http://www.scielo.org.za /scielo.php?script=sci_arttext&pid=S2305-08532017000300004.

from the actual person who roamed the Galilee and Jerusalem in the early 1st century.

What "Son of Man" ("the human") means represents one issue and there are a variety of approaches as we have seen. Another issue has to do with third person speech in general.

For an individual to speak about himself in the third person is extremely odd. Instead of saying, "I do this or that," Jesus prefers to say, "The Son of Man (or "the human") does this or that" referring to himself. As mentioned previously, this pattern of speech might be prevalent in young children who don't understand the nuances of self-referential pronouns, but it's not a speech pattern common in adults, today or in Jesus's time.

In medical terms, this condition is called illeism. What it denotes is open to question. The phenomenon has been studied by psychotherapist Kim Schneiderman who notes that "viewing your life as an objective observer can help you see yourself through gentler, more compassionate eyes." She adds:

> It is also aligned with narrative therapy techniques that put emotional distance between people and their storylines so they don't overidentify with their problems.[*]

Talking about oneself in this fashion is a distancing technique. It would appear that by speaking of himself in an obscure, third-person way, Jesus is distancing himself from other descriptors, perhaps especially with the inflated popular understandings of messiah. He has chosen a unique term to create his own identity. Recall it is one not found in the Old Testament—there is no "*the* son of man" there. Nor was it part of any public perception. It is his own *persona*, and it is mysterious. He typically, but not exclusively, uses the phrase when he wishes to speak of his own mortality—suffering, dying, and being resurrected.

One possibility not suggested in the Son of Man scholarly literature is that Jesus is assuming a disguise. Perhaps he thinks of himself as a prophet, a teacher, perhaps even as a messiah. We really don't know how Jesus

---

[*]   Kim Schneiderman, *Step Out of Your Story*. Novato, CA: New World Library, 2015. See "Introduction."

himself perceived his own identity—we know much more about how the later gospel writers constructed his identity. Instead of identifying himself in conventional terms, Jesus creates a new identity for himself, one that allows him to distance himself from customary ones such as prophet, teacher, or messiah. His self-effacing designation provides him with a cover that allows him to escape all the baggage associated with the more traditional descriptions.

Perhaps Son of Man represents Jesus's Clark Kent move, just like Superman hiding behind the persona of Clark Kent, reporter. He can pop out of hiding whenever he wishes, without anyone suspecting who he might really be along the way. As "the human," he can move freely, simply as a human being without his true identity constantly on public view . . . or his superhuman powers on call.

Moreover, as "the human," he can allow other people to project onto him whatever they think he is or want him to be. That way he can be anyone they desire.

No wonder there are so many impressions of Jesus's identity.

He turned on "incognito."

No Evidence for Peter's Claim

But if we move away from Jesus being the "Son of Man," what we are then faced with is Jesus as "messiah." It was Peter who claimed Jesus to be "the messiah." Recall that this was an identification Jesus himself shied away from: In the Gospel of Mark Jesus immediately shifts the focus over to "Son of Man," his preferred descriptor. He explains the latter (Son of Man) but not the former (messiah). There's no discussion, no evidence presented why one would think of Jesus as a messiah.

So, what's a messiah? How did this idea take shape? Can we find out what Jews at the time of Jesus understood a messiah to be? What was the job description? Does Jesus measure up?

II

HOW DID THE IDEA OF THE MESSIAH COME ABOUT?

6

MESSIAH AS ANOINTED LEADER

⁓

It is not difficult to find a messiah in the Hebrew Bible. Typically all we have to do is look for an ancient king or priest. In the time of Moses, for instance, some 3,200 or more years ago, Aaron the priest was anointed along with his sons. As the Hebrew text reads (Leviticus 8:12), Moses poured "shemen haMishchah" on Aaron's head. *Mishchah* derives from the Hebrew verb, *mashach*, to anoint, the same root as *mashiach*, messiah. So the phrase *shemen haMishchah* means "anointing oil." The root concept of a messiah, then, is one who has been anointed.

Several centuries after Moses, Israelite kings were anointed, that is, messiahed. The prophet Samuel anointed Saul as the first king (1 Samuel 10:1). Saul's successor, David, was also anointed—several times, in fact, as we shall see. David's son, Solomon, was anointed by Zadok the priest (1 Kings 1:39). Later on, Elisha anointed Jehu king over Israel (2 Kings 9:3).

The king was spoken of as "the Lord's anointed" (1 Samuel 16:6; 1 Samuel 24:6), that is, "the Lord's messiah." Just to be clear, "Lord" here denotes God; "messiah" refers to the king who has been anointed. The messiah is not God. In the 6th century BCE, the last king of David's dynasty, Zedekiah, was also said to be "the Lord's messiah" (Lamentations 4:20). This ruler suffered a terrible fate, with his children killed before his eyes and he himself blinded before being taken into exile. Being a King-Messiah does not guarantee success, or even, as we shall see, the assurance of righteousness.

Even a prophet can be anointed, although this is rare. The 9th century BCE prophet Elijah anointed or "messiahed" Elisha as his successor (1 Kings 19:16). Elisha went on to perform some remarkable miracles, twice the number of his famous predecessor, Elijah. His miracles included helping a widow pay off debts by miraculously creating a huge supply of oil she could sell; bringing a dead child back to life; and feeding 100 people with just 20 loaves of barley bread and some grain (2 Kings 4).

So there have been many biblical messiahs, primarily kings and priests. Zadok the priest anoints or messiahs Solomon as David's successor (1 Kings 1:39), and the people of the land anoint or messiah Jehoahaz king (2 Kings 23:30). God's prophets are collectively said to be "messiahs" or "anointed ones" (Psalm 105:15). Even Cyrus, king of Persia, a non-Jew, was said to be a messiah for his role in allowing the Israelites in exile to return to their homeland (Isaiah 45:1).

It is sometimes difficult, however, to spot all these references to messiah in our English Bibles. The Hebrew word for messiah, *mashiach*, is often translated as "anointed," not as "messiah." Also, unlike English, the concept is sometimes expressed as a verb, "to messiah," that is, "to anoint," rather than just as a noun. Individuals are thus said to be "anointed" or "messiahed."

Perhaps these references to messiah or individuals being messiahed are not translated as such for theological reasons so as not to detract from what Christians see as Jesus's uniqueness as "*the* Messiah." By not translating all these other biblical references to messiah, Jesus would appear to stand out as the one and only messianic figure. Such a practice, however, is misleading. As mentioned above, there have been many messiahs or individuals who have been messiahed. Plus nowhere in the Hebrew Bible does the phrase "*the* messiah" appear. It is not a unique descriptor.

A messiah, then, is a divinely designated leader who has been anointed—smeared with oil—and singled out to perform a task, typically that of being a ruler or priest. That's the root concept. It denotes a political or priestly role and it embraces three ideas: selection by God, being anointed, and given a task.

King David: The Prototypical Messiah

Creating a Messiah

For all his faults—and he had many—the prototypical messiah is the colorful King David who lived some 3,000 years ago, roughly around 1000 BCE. We encounter the saga of David in the Books of 1 and 2 Samuel. These writings vividly bring to life the ups and downs of this remarkable ruler.

A later biblical writing, 1 Chronicles (Chapters 10–29), rewrites David's history using the two books of Samuel as a base along with some other sources. Chronicles's revisionist account whitewashes David's wrongdoings, such as his affair with Bathsheba, and so presents a sanitized version of his heroic rule.

Even later, a 2nd century BCE Jewish writing, Sirach* extols David in a song, "Let us now praise famous men" (Sirach 44:1–50:24). When the hymn comes to David, it celebrates his many achievements, reaching a huge crescendo:

> The Lord took away his sins and exalted his power forever; he gave him a covenant of kingship and a glorious throne in Israel. (Sirach 47:11)

As these various records indicate, David was a figure of popular imagination, romanticized as the ideal king, feted as the champion of Israel, and

---

* Sirach is also known as "Ecclesiasticus" or the "Wisdom of Jesus, Son of Sirach." This writing is included in the Septuagint version of the Old Testament used in Catholic, Orthodox, and Anglican faith communities. It is not found in the Jewish Hebrew Bible or in the Protestant/Evangelical Old Testament. The Septuagint version includes such additional writings as Judith, Tobit, Sirach, and Wisdom of Solomon as well as additions to the Books of Esther and Daniel. The NRSV translation is used for these writings not found in the Hebrew Bible or Protestant/Evangelical Old Testament.

celebrated as the one with whom God made a covenant regarding kingship over Israel in perpetuity.

Not to be outdone by these writings, many psalms are attached to the name of David. We should not imagine that all these psalms or songs were necessarily composed by David personally. Some were written by others either for David or about an event in his reign. Still others were simply about David, extolling his virtue or his immense standing with God.

These various writings trace the rise of David in the latter years of King Saul's turbulent rule; his friendship with Saul's son, Jonathan; his growing popularity; his marriage to Michal as well as other marriages; his successes . . . and his flaws.

In the Books of Samuel, the earliest account, David is presented as a complex person. This biblical portrait allows for many interpretations as to his true character. He is a shepherd, a skilled musician, a composer of songs, a ruler, a warrior, a husband of many wives, an adulterer, a murderer . . . and, also, the Lord's messiah. Josephus eulogizes him,

> This man was of an excellent character and was endowed with all virtues that were desirable in a king. (*Jewish Antiquities*, Book 7, Chapter 15, section 2)

He praises David for his piety, righteousness, fortitude, and obedience (*Jewish Antiquities*, Book 7, Chapter 8, Section 1).

> 1 Samuel simply says that David is "a man after His [God's] own heart" (1 Samuel 13:14).

So who is David and how is he the prototypical messiah?

More importantly, how does an adulterer, a schemer, and a murderer fit into the picture of the Lord's messiah, a man after God's own heart?

David as Messiah

As already mentioned, David is anointed three times. The first takes place in the latter years of King Saul's reign when the country was beset by constant warfare. According to 1 Samuel, Saul had displeased God by failing to provide effective leadership. As 1 Samuel puts it,

> The word of the Lord came to Samuel: "I regret that I made Saul king, for he has turned away from Me and has not carried out My commands." (1 Samuel 15:10, 11)

Samuel is directed by God to go to the house of Jesse, in Bethlehem, and there to select one of his sons as king-designate.

One by one, Jesse's sons are paraded before Samuel. Suspense is heightened as Samuel suspects that Jesse's oldest son, Eliab, might be "the Lord's anointed," that is, "the Lord's messiah." But he is not, and the text notes that God sees into a person's heart.

Seven of Jesse's sons are rejected. The eighth, the youngest, is out looking after the sheep. That one—named David—is summoned. God says to Samuel, "rise and anoint (messiah) him, for this is the one" (1 Samuel 16:12). Consequently Samuel takes the oil and anoints (messiahs) him in the presence of his brothers. The text adds that "the spirit of the Lord gripped David from that day on" (1 Samuel 16:13).

Saul is still king, but his reign is waning. David is the heir apparent, the King-Messiah in waiting.

Sometime thereafter, David engages in his famous battle with the Philistine giant, Goliath, killing him with a stone fired from his slingshot. His fame and popularity grow with this amazing victory and 1 Samuel records that women chant: "Saul has slain his thousands; David, his tens of thousands!" (1 Samuel 18:7). In so doing, David becomes a household name.

A while later, David hears of the death of Saul and his son Jonathan on Mount Gilboa. King Saul had attempted suicide but didn't quite succeed. At his request, an Amalekite warrior puts an end to Saul's life. This individual brings Saul's crown and armlet to David. Rather than being praised for his action, David asks him how he dared "kill the Lord's anointed (*mashiach*)." With that, David kills him for having said, "I put the Lord's anointed (*mashiach*) to death" (2 Samuel 2:17). Then David begins a lament, singing "The Song of the Bow" from a collection of songs no longer in existence, the *Book of Jashar*.

David settles in Hebron, some 20 miles south of Jerusalem. There the leaders of Judah messiah him (2 Samuel 2:4) and he becomes king over the tribe of Judah. Meanwhile another claimant to the throne, Ish-bosheth [Ishbaal], son of Saul, is made king (but not messiahed) in the north, over all Israel. Civil war breaks out and after two years of fighting, David's army is victorious and Ish-bosheth killed.

A momentous event then takes place: all the Israelite tribes flock to David in his capital city, Hebron, recognizing him as the divinely chosen "shepherd" and "ruler." The tribal chiefs messiah him as king over Israel (2 Samuel 5:3). As we now know, this means that they anoint him with oil and proclaim him their leader.

Thus David becomes King-Messiah in three phases: first as king-in-waiting as Saul's rule splutters to an end; as king of only one tribe, Judah; then as king of all 12 tribes.

David's Monumental Achievements

David is 30 years old when he becomes king of all Israel. He reigns for 40 years (2 Samuel 5:4). Three main accomplishments stand out. First David manages to unify all the Israelite tribes into one nation. Then he extends the borders of Israel north, east, and south. Finally David succeeds in capturing an enclave in between the northern and southern tribes—the city of Jerusalem controlled by the Jebusites. He ingeniously uses the complex water cistern system to infiltrate the city.

Jerusalem thus becomes the national political capital of the 12 tribes. David moves the Ark of the Covenant from Kiriath-Jearim to Jerusalem and makes plans to build a temple to God there, thus proposing to make Jerusalem the national religious capital as well. The Temple was not built during his reign. Instead Solomon, who ruled from approximately 970–931 BCE, carried out the project. The Temple survived for over 450 years, being burned by the Babylonians in 587 BCE. After the Babylonian Exile it was reconstructed, surviving until the year 70 when it was destroyed by the Romans.

David marries Saul's daughter, Michal, thereby establishing a link to the former dynasty and giving his claim to the throne enhanced legitimacy. He also has seven additional wives, various concubines, and at least 18 children.

The song in praise of David in Sirach notes other achievements. It says that David permanently crushed the power of the Philistines, encouraged singers and arranged the schedule of festivals (Sirach 47:7–10). The author of Sirach extols David's faithfulness:

> In all that he did he gave thanks to the Holy One, the Most High, proclaiming his glory; he sang praise with all his heart, and he loved his Maker. (Sirach 47:8)

Perhaps David is best known for the writings that have as a superscription "a psalm of David," especially Psalm 23, beginning "The Lord (*YHVH*) is my shepherd" and concluding "and I shall dwell in the house of the Lord for many long years" (Psalm 23:6). The King James version translates the last phrase as "for ever."

David's Notable Flaws

In spite of a stellar résumé crowned with impressive national accomplishments, many flaws are exhibited in David's character. These account for much of the chaos during his later years.

He runs afoul of his wife, Michal. When the procession brings the Ark of the Covenant into Jerusalem, David appears to have gone into a euphoric dance, leaping and dancing wildly before the cart carrying this precious religious artifact. Wearing only a short ephod, or skirt, in his frenzy he exposes himself to the crowd. Michal thought this was highly inappropriate and unseemly, despising him for appearing naked before the people. They argue. David defends himself by saying he was dancing before the Lord. The upshot? Punishment for Michal—no children.

In the lead-up to another incident—the affair with Bathsheba—2 Samuel faults David:

> At the turn of the year, the season when kings go out [to battle] . . . David remained in Jerusalem. (2 Samuel 11:1)

Clearly no good can come from this apparent royal dereliction of duty. He should have gone out with his troops instead of remaining behind. Sure enough, trouble ensues. David starts an affair with Bathsheba which changes the course of history: their son, Solomon, becomes his successor as King-Messiah rather than one from David's other wives.

The illicit affair begins innocently enough. David spies Bathsheba bathing on the roof of her residence in Jerusalem. She is very beautiful, and David lusts after her. Married to Uriah the Hittite, she is nonetheless summoned to David's palace. Uriah is away, fighting in David's army. He is where David should have been. Bathsheba becomes pregnant. To cover up his actions, David asks his commander, Joab, to send Uriah back home from the battlefront, hoping that he would take the opportunity to sleep with his wife, thereby confusing fatherhood. These plans fail to materialize. Being on military duty, Uriah preferred to stay with the garrison near the palace and did not return to his house.

Frustrated in his attempt to conceal his liaison with Bathsheba, David orders Joab:

> Place Uriah in the front line where the fighting is fiercest; then
> fall back so that he may be killed. (2 Samuel 11:15)

Uriah dies in battle. After a period of mourning, David brings Bathsheba into his household, making her his wife.

That, of course, is not the end of the matter. Adultery, political cunning and murder—such actions have consequences. Nathan, a court prophet, goes to David and poses a problem. Consider, he said, this situation. A rich man possesses huge flocks of sheep, and a poor man has only one lamb, a precious animal who was part of the household and "like a daughter to him" (2 Samuel 12:3). One day a visitor comes to the rich man's estate. The wealthy owner is reluctant to take any of his sheep to be slaughtered for a banquet. So he takes the one lamb from the poor man. Enraged by this outrageous act, David responds that the rich man should die and should reimburse the poor man four times the value of the lamb. Nathan simply replies, "That man is you."

Nathan condemns David's actions. He reminds him that God has anointed him (2 Samuel 12:7), giving him the throne of the Houses of Israel and Judah. And yet, Nathan continues, David chose to displease God by arranging for Uriah's death in battle and taking his wife (2 Samuel 12:9). David acknowledges his sin and Nathan reassures him in the following manner:

> The Lord has remitted your sin: you shall not die . . . [but] the child about to be born shall die. (2 Samuel 12:14)

Nathan also predicts that disasters will cloud the latter part of his reign.

Nathan is right: disasters do ensue. David and Bathsheba's son dies, but the next child born of their union survives. A rape occurs in his household: David's daughter, Tamar, is attacked by her half-brother, Amnon. Amnon would likely have succeeded David as king, being the oldest son. Absalom, however, the next in line for the throne, kills Amnon and leads a revolt against David. During the civil war that follows, Absalom forces David to abandon Jerusalem and uses the opportunity to engage in an orgy with David's concubines, in public. In accordance with the views of the times, some 3,000 years ago, this act would not have been viewed as just sexual in nature. It would have been seen as representing a political statement, signifying his takeover of David's possessions and status. Absalom, however, dies in an accident. On top of all this, there is a three-year famine.

The portrait of David's latter years as king is marked by unrest, all caused, in the view of the author of the Books of Samuel, by David's complicity in murder and adultery. From a literary perspective, the account of David's reign is written as an inverted V—a brilliant upward rise to power with consolidation and expansion of the kingdom; then downward actions that precipitate a fall. The latter are all attributed to David's bad judgment and poor choices.

Theology of David, the King-Messiah

Call it theology, mythology, romanticizing, or fantasizing—David the heroic King-Messiah of the United Kingdom of Israel and Judah is viewed as having a special relationship with God, despite his many personal sins.

The King-Messiah as Son of God

There are a number of psalms that praise the king, either David directly or one of his royal successors. These psalms represent coronation songs chanted in religious ceremonies as the king is messiahed or on other special royal occasions. They would likely not have been written by David about himself but by others wishing to honor him and to convey his exalted stature to the people.

The context for making a king over Israel is that God himself is king. The country is a theocracy. The Israelite king is, in a sense, a regent, a lesser being, ruling within the framework of the Covenant with God. Psalm 47, for instance, makes it clear that God is king, not only of Israel, but of the whole world:

> Sing, O sing to God
> Sing, O sing to our king;
> For God is king over all the earth;
> Sing a hymn.
> God reigns over the nations;
> God is seated on His holy throne. (Psalm 47:7–9)

Even though he rules over the whole world, God and the king of Israel are said to enjoy a special relationship. Some of the psalms are written antiphonally, that is, as an exchange between various people. It could include the leader (perhaps the composer himself, or a priest or a Levite), the congregation and even God himself. Psalm 2 is such a dialogical song, likely chanted back and forth by different choirs. It imagines the nations of the world gathered against Israel. The lead singer poses a question:

> (leader)   Why do nations assemble,
> And peoples plot vain things;
> Kings of the earth take their stand,
> And regents intrigue together
> Against the Lord and against his anointed (his *mashiach*)? (Psalm 2:1, 2)

The question is this: Why do other nations dare to make war against the King-Messiah of Israel? The implication is that these foreign leaders do not know with whom they are dealing.

This question then sets up a verbal exchange between God, the king, the people, and the nations. God answers the questioners:

> (narrator) Then He [God] speaks to them in anger
> terrifying them in His rage,
> (God) But I have installed My king
> on Zion, My holy mountain! (Psalm 2:6)

The king of Israel is "My king"; that is, the king God has installed in Jerusalem (Zion). As the song continues, the king interjects:

> (King) Let me tell of the decree:
> The Lord (*YHVH*) said to me,
> "You are My son,
> I have fathered you this day." (Psalm 2:7)

The Lord is God, and the king is quoting something God has said to him as his son. As the composer of this song sees it, the Israelite king is like a son to God.

This thought—the king as a son of God—is echoed in other places in the Bible. In 2 Samuel, for instance, we find God telling David that when he dies, the following will happen:

> I will raise up your offspring after you, one of your own issue, and I will establish his kingship. He shall build a house for My Name, and I will establish his royal throne forever. I will be a father to him, and he shall be a son to Me. (2 Samuel 7:12–14)

The passage here is speaking about David's son, Solomon, who was his successor. David and all the kings who followed him are, metaphorically, speaking, "sons of God."

Even all the people of Israel are referred to as "sons of God" (and presumably also as "daughters of God"):

> I fell in love with Israel
> When he was still a child;
> And I have called [him] My son
> Ever since Egypt. (Hosea 11:1)

The King-Messiah, like all Israelites, enjoys a special bond with God, that of being one of God's children. It does not mean that the King-Messiah is divine, just that he enjoys a special relationship with God.

David's Dynasty is Everlasting

Psalm 89 focuses on another theme, that the royal dynasty of David will endure forever. It begins as follows:

> (God)   I have made a covenant with My chosen one;
> I have sworn to My servant David:
> I will establish your offspring forever,
> I will confirm your throne for all generations.
> (Psalm 89:4, 5)

The song continues, with the congregation praising God for his faithfulness, righteousness, and justice. God again speaks, and here he sets forth four main themes regarding David. First of all, he singles out David as King-Messiah:

> (God)   I have exalted one chosen out of the people.
> I have found David, My servant;
> anointed (messiahed) him with My sacred oil.
> (Psalm 89:20, 21)

Secondly, he sets forth David as son of God. Noting that he will crush all David's enemies, God continues, imagining what David would say of him:

(God) He [the king] shall say to Me,
    "You are my father, my God, the rock of my
    deliverance." (Psalm 89:27)

Thirdly, he represents David as a divinely guided victorious king:

(God) I will appoint him first-born,
    highest of the kings of the earth. (Psalm 89:28)

Finally he mandates that David's dynasty will continue forever:

(God) I will maintain My steadfast love for him always;
    My covenant with him shall endure.
    I will establish his line forever,
    his throne, as long as the heavens last.
    If his sons forsake My Teaching (*Torah*)
    and do not live by My rules;
    if they violate My laws,
    and do not observe My commands,
    I will punish their transgression with the rod,
    their iniquity with plagues.
    But I will not take away My steadfast love from him;
    I will not betray My faithfulness
    . . .
    I will not be false to David
    His line shall continue forever. . . .
    (Psalm 89:29–34, 36, 37)

This is not a conditional covenant. As the verses above make clear, even if David's King-Messiah successors violate the requirements of Torah, the agreement God made with David would not be nullified.

This passage makes clear that King-Messiah descendants of David are expected to follow Torah. Torah, sometimes translated as "Teaching," "Law," or "Instruction," refers to the human side of the Jewish covenant with God. Torah sets forth a lifestyle, a set of teachings that embrace values, choices, decisions, and actions relating to building a relationship with God and with other people.*

This psalm reiterates what was said in 2 Samuel about God's covenant or agreement with David: "Your house and your kingship shall ever be secure before you; your throne shall be established forever" (2 Samuel 7:16).

The promise is quite clear: there will always be "a David" on the throne of Israel. History, however, didn't unfold this way. The royal lineage from David to Zedekiah died out some time during the Babylonian Exile. Since then there has been no king of Israel descended from David ruling in Jerusalem. While there were Hasmonean kings in the 2nd and 1st centuries BCE, they were not considered to be descended from David.

Messiah as Anointed Leader

A messiah is a leader who has been anointed. In the case of David, he is a king operating under the sovereignty of God. As king, the messiah enjoys a special relationship with God, described variously as a "son of God" or God's "first-born." King-Messiahs are expected to observe the commandments of Torah and to function within the framework of the Jewish covenant with God. In addition, as per God's specific, additional covenant with David, his dynasty will endure throughout all generations. The concept of a messiah is fundamentally political in nature.

The story of King David is one of the most inspiring and comforting in the entire Bible. It is comforting, because, for one thing, it portrays God's favor as not dependent on exceptional merit on the part of a person. David is not especially pure, virtuous, or upright. He has many strengths: he has wisdom and valor in battle, he is an accomplished musician, a poet, and a wily leader. But he also exhibits many flaws—murder and adultery included—which, surprisingly, do not count against him. So ordinary people, with failings, and with repentance, can stand before God, even

---

* See especially Deuteronomy 29:1 to 30:20. Deuteronomy 30:15–20 urges people to "choose life" by loving the Lord your God [attitudes], walking in his ways [actions] and keeping his commandments [lifestyle choices].

finding favor with him. Sinfulness does not block out access to God so long as that person repents.

So a King-Messiah is a charismatic leader who, like all humans, is flawed. He is not divine, although said to be a "son of God," a term that describes a relationship, not status of divinity. A King-Messiah is simply an individual tasked with being a ruler and anointed by God to fulfill this mandate. He sins, repents, is punished, and continues to find favor with God.

7

BIBLICAL SUPERHERO
SAVIORS—MALE
AND FEMALE

———

The Old Testament portrays key individuals who come to the fore to save the community from some looming disaster. This injects the idea of savior or rescuer into the messianic profile. These heroes are not said to be "messiahs," that is, they are not anointed for the task. Rather, they are individuals who through their own resources perform actions that manage to save the community. They are saviors who emerge to meet a serious challenge that threatens the existence of the community.

These persons are biblical superheroes. They arise typically in time of crisis or threatened disaster. They are successful in meeting the challenges of their time. Biblical superheroes are rescuers or fixers who deal effectively with a crisis. Their decisions and actions result in better conditions for the people—not the ideal world, not Paradise restored, just better circumstances.

The idea of superhero rescuers surfaces from time to time throughout history, not just in biblical times, but also in modern history. In our era there have been fictional superheroes who have emerged during times of trouble—Superman, Batman, and Wonder Woman, for example, all originated around World War II.

Joseph the Israelite, Esther the Persian Queen, and Judith the widow are three examples of biblical superheroes who saved their community.

Joseph the Israelite:
The Savior Who Went on Ahead

It began innocently, with a gift. It was a present of a lifetime that changed the course of history. Thirty-five hundred years or so ago, an aging father gave his son a wonderful long coat of many colors. It was spectacular. In his day and age, it would have stood out against drab one-color garments as a very special item. The father was Jacob, and the young man, Joseph. Jacob and Joseph were nomads living in Canaan, modern-day Israel, along with Jacob's wife, Rachel, and Joseph's 11 brothers.

The story of Joseph (Genesis Chapters 37–50) has been made famous by Andrew Lloyd Webber's musical, *Joseph and the Amazing Technicolor Dreamcoat*. The biblical saga is filled with intrigue—rejection and acceptance, plots, attempted seduction, revenge, forgiveness, and reconciliation. There are unexpected turns of events that reveal a divine plan behind the circumstances of history . . . and, most importantly, salvation for people in peril of death by starvation.

As the story unfolds, the gift is the catalyst for life-altering and history-changing events. While the coat is treasured by Joseph, this sign of parental favoritism sparks envy and jealousy amongst his siblings. Rather than confronting their father, they gang up on Joseph. Fueled by a dream that seems to indicate that Joseph is destined to rule over them, the brothers conspire to get rid of him. Things rapidly turn for the worse for Joseph and he endures many years of hardship.

One calamity turns into another. Joseph is sold into slavery by his jealous brothers who develop a cover story that he had been killed. That is what they tell their father, Jacob, who is heartbroken at the loss of his favorite child. Joseph winds up in Egypt, eventually becoming the personal attendant of Potiphar. But, just as things are looking up for him, he runs afoul of Potiphar's wife. She accuses him of rape because he resists her sexual advances. He is thrown into prison and languishes there for years.

A while later, Pharaoh has two dreams which neither he nor his advisers can interpret. A court cupbearer who had been in prison remembers a fellow inmate who was a skilled interpreter of dreams. That individual—Joseph—is ushered into the palace where he successfully decodes Pharaoh's mysterious and troubling dreams. There will be seven good agricultural years followed by seven years of crop failure and famine. Instantly Joseph's fortune changes and his rapid rise to power is ensured. He becomes second-in-command to none other than Pharaoh himself.

Savior of the World

Pharaoh gives Joseph a wife, Aseneth, daughter of the priest of On. Pharaoh also bestows a new name on Joseph: "Zaphenath-paneah" (Genesis 41:45). Josephus said this Egyptian name meant "revealer of secrets" on account of Joseph's great wisdom and ability to interpret dreams (*Jewish Antiquities*, Book 2, Chapter 6, Section 1). The JPS translation of the Hebrew Bible provides a footnote saying that the Egyptian phrase means "God speaks; he lives," or "creator of life." That's a modern interpretation of what the name means.

Jerome was the 4th century Christian translator of the Bible into Latin. He translated this name as "Salvator Mundi"—"Savior of the World."* Whether or not this Egyptian name means what Jerome says it meant, it is an apt description for Joseph: he is a savior figure.

At Pharaoh's behest, Joseph oversees food operations for the next 14 years, storing up grain in the first seven and then dispensing it from the storage containers in the following seven years. This prudent policy saves the Egyptians from starvation.

---

* See Jerome's Commentary on the Book of Genesis. C. T. R. Hayward (trans.), *Saint Jerome's Hebrew Questions on Genesis*. Oxford: Clarendon Press, 1995, p. 78.

Famine also strikes those in Canaan, and Jacob sends his sons to purchase food from the Egyptians. Joseph recognizes his brothers—although they fail to recognize him. He also understands, of course, their discussions amongst themselves.

After several delays and a journey back to Canaan to bring Benjamin, the youngest son, back to Egypt, Joseph dramatically reveals himself to his brothers. He forgives them for having sold him into slavery, saying that it was all part of a divine plan: "it was to save life that God sent me ahead of you" (Genesis 45:5). God, through Joseph, saved his people. Without this event, the House of Jacob would have perished and, with it, the history of the Israelite people. The family is reunited and the brothers, along with their father and other relatives settle in a delta area of Egypt called Goshen.

Thus Joseph saves two communities from starvation, despair, and suffering—the Egyptians as well as the household of Jacob. He did not set out to do this: his life just unfolded that way, the right person at the right time in history.

Joseph comes to the realization that his personal history was not just a random sequence of events. There was more to it than that. The moral of the story is Joseph's theological interpretation of the course of his life: God is behind world events and his plan for individuals eventually comes to light, creating good out of evil. While Joseph is a savior figure, it is God, behind the scenes, who saves by arranging events so as to rescue people from terrible misfortune: death by starvation.

Joseph is a charismatic person with a gift of discerning the true meaning of dreams, a planner, an implementer, a person who forgives, a revealer of secrets. More than that, he is not just a revealer of his own personal secrets but of the hand of God in human affairs.

No wonder the author of Sirach exclaims, "Nor was anyone ever born like Joseph" (Sirach 49:13).

While not said to be a messiah or anointed, readers of the Hebrew Bible would have regarded Joseph as a savior figure. In particular, the characterization of Joseph as a savior was not lost on early Christians. They saw some of the incidents of Joseph's life as parallel to those in Jesus's life: betrayal, vindication, forgiveness, and redemption. Sermons noting similarities between Joseph and Jesus were a favorite in antiquity.* Joseph as a savior figure does not mean he was divine: just a gifted ordinary person who helped shape world history. Hence, as Jerome put it, he was "savior of the world."

Queen Esther—The Savior Who Finds the Courage to Speak Up

The powerful Book of Esther presents the challenge of Jew hatred.†

The situation is as follows: roughly 2,500 years ago, the Jews represent a minority within the vast Persian Empire. This Middle Eastern world power stretches from India to Ethiopia, 127 provinces in all. The evil protagonist is Haman. He's an Agagite, a descendant of Amalek.

This is not an innocuous description. The Book of Exodus records how the Israelites escaping Egypt were attacked by the Amalekites, a tribe living in the Negev in southern Israel (Exodus 17:8–16). Because of their actions—the first group to attack the Israelites—Amalek became the prototype of all Jew-haters, the surrogate name for the anti-Semite who arises in each generation. Amalek is thus the Grand Inquisitor, Stalin, Hitler, and other powerful anti-Semites. As we shall see, the Amalek of some 2,500 years ago, Haman, pursues a course of action which ultimately results in his downfall.

Against Haman stand two Jews. Esther is a very beautiful woman who rises to power as the queen. She seems quiet at first, demure, and totally overshadowed by the immense power of the king. Her foster father, Mordecai, is her faithful advisor and mentor. He is a savvy politician and seems to have his ear to the ground as plots swirl around the court.

There are two versions of the Book of Esther, a short one and a longer one. The shorter version is the original one and it is found in the Hebrew Bible. In this version, the Hebrew word for "God" does not appear. That

---

* See, for instance, Simcha Jacobovici and Barrie Wilson, *The Lost Gospel*, Chapter 7 where parallels between Joseph and Jesus are traced in sermons from early Christianity.

† For a recent study on anti-Semitism, see Deborah E. Lipstadt, *Antisemitism Here and Now*. New York: Schocken Books, 2019.

silence seems intentional. We are likely supposed to discern that God lies behind the events of world history even when he is not explicitly mentioned.

The longer version comes from the Greek translation of the original Hebrew—the Septuagint—and it is the one found in Christian Old Testaments. That version inserts some additions, to make Queen Esther seem more observant of Jewish beliefs and practices. An example of this additional material occurs when Mordecai gives her instructions upon becoming queen. Esther, Mordecai urges, should continue:

> To fear God and keep his laws, just as she had done when she was with him. So Esther did not change her mode of life. (Esther 2:19, 20, NRSV version only).

That passage is not to be found in the Hebrew original. Clearly the Greek translators of the Septuagint did not understand the hidden message within the book. Or perhaps they wished to make God's sovereignty more explicit for the less-than-discerning.

The NRSV translation of the Bible helpfully identifies the later Greek additions to the original Hebrew text of the Book of Esther.

The Persian king is called Ahasuerus in the JPS version, Artaxerxes in the NRSV, as well as in Josephus's account. The king holds an over-the-top festive banquet for all his administrative officials in the city of Shushan (Susa). This powerful monarch is likely either Xerxes I (ruled 486–465 BCE) or one of his successors. Esther is chosen by King Ahasuerus to be queen. His former wife, Vashti, was displaced because of her refusal to participate in a drunken exhibition, although she was ordered to do so by the king.

Ahasuerus seems to know little about Esther other than that she is very beautiful. On Mordecai's advice, she does not reveal her ethnicity (Esther 2:10, 20). Consequently, the king does not appear to know that she is Jewish.

Mordecai overhears two of Ahasuerus's eunuchs plotting to kill the King and conveys this information to Esther, who warns her husband. An investigation ensues and the charges are verified. The two conspirators are impaled (JPS) or hanged (NRSV) (Esther 2:21–23). Although Mordecai is not honored for providing this vital information, his position and Esther's seem secure. Events, however, soon take a turn for the worse.

Sometime later the king promotes Haman, putting him in charge of all the other officials of his court. In this exalted position Haman expects everyone to bow to him, but Mordecai refrains from doing so (Esther 3:2). Presumably this was because, as a Jew, he did not feel he could give such recognition to a descendant of Amalek. Enraged, Haman finds out that Mordecai is a Jew and plots to take revenge, not just on Mordecai, but on all Jews throughout the whole kingdom (Esther 3:6).

Notice the shift here in Haman's thinking, from *a* Jew to *the Jews*. A perceived slight on the part of one individual is transferred onto a whole ethnic group.

Haman proceeds to advise the king:

> There is a certain people, scattered and dispersed among the other peoples in all the provinces of your realm, whose laws are different from those of any other people and who do not obey the king's laws; and it is not in Your Majesty's interest to tolerate them. If it please Your Majesty, let an edict be drawn for their destruction, and I will pay ten thousand talents of silver to the stewards for deposit in the royal treasury. (Esther 3:8, 9)

The charge is that the Jewish people are different and a threat to social order, obeying laws that are said by Haman to differ from civil laws.

The king replies to Haman that "the money and the people are yours to do with as you see fit." The order is given:

> To destroy, massacre, and exterminate all the Jews, young and old, children and women, on a single day . . . and to plunder their possessions. (Esther 3:13)

This order is sent by courier to officials in all 127 Persian provinces, from India to Ethiopia. The sentence is scheduled for the 13th day of the month of Adar, this date having been determined by lots (*purim*).

After deciding the fate of the Jewish people throughout the empire, the king and Haman sit down to eat.

Reaction, however, is swift. Ordinary citizens are confused—as the JPS translation puts it, "the city of Shushan was dumfounded" (Esther 3:15). But that's all: just confusion. There is no hint that non-Jews were about to come to the aid of this imperiled minority. Mordecai goes into mourning, wearing sackcloth. Jews throughout the empire fast and weep, knowing that disaster is about to befall them.

Note that when two Persian officials are accused of a serious crime—the plot by two eunuchs to assassinate Ahasuerus—an investigation ensues. When Haman accuses Jews of being different, however, his charge is simply believed. There is no investigation, no corroboration, and no evidence.

The king does not stop to ask the obvious questions: In what way are Jews different? How does Jewish law correspond to Persian law? Have there been any instances where Jews have not obeyed the king? Moreover, why should these differences require complete elimination of all Jews everywhere throughout the empire? Are they that huge of a threat?

The anti-Semitic slur is simply believed, accepted, and acted upon swiftly. Jews everywhere throughout the vast empire are condemned without evidence. Anti-Semitism is the big lie. And it succeeds in being believed.

Queen Esther finds out about the decree and wonders how to approach the king. Developing a plan, she instructs Mordecai to tell the Jews who live in Shushan to fast for three days. On the third day Esther puts on her royal apparel and enters the inner court of the king's palace. This is a daring move since it was forbidden to enter the presence of the king without having first been summoned. Risking death, this superheroine bravely sallies forth. The king graciously puts her at ease. She invites him to attend a party she has prepared. Haman is also on the guest list. At that party the king tells Esther that he will grant her a wish, even if her request, he boasts, is half his kingdom. She simply invites the king and Haman to attend another feast on the following day.

Haman is happy as he leaves the palace and tells his wife, Zeresh (Zosara in the NRSV), of his good fortune, being invited to a feast alongside the king and queen. He also confides that this contentment pales in comparison with the greater joy of seeing "that Jew Mordechai sitting in the palace gate" (Esther 5:13), dressed in sackcloth and in mourning. Zeresh suggests building a huge stake (or gallows, NRSV), 50 cubits, or about 75 feet, high, and to ask the king on the following day to impale Mordecai upon it (to hang Mordecai on it, NSRV). Zeresh clearly shares her husband's anti-Semitism. Haman agrees with his wife and has a stake (or gallows) erected.

Before the feast takes place, King Ahasuerus has a sleepless night. He recalls that Mordecai had warned him through Esther of a threat against his life and that he had not been rewarded. Seeing Haman, Ahasuerus asks him, how should we honor a person that the king wishes to recognize? Thinking that the king was speaking of him, Haman suggests that that person should be dressed in royal robes which the king himself has worn and that person should be paraded through the city square on a horse the king himself has sat upon. The king orders Haman to fetch "Mordecai the Jew"—note that he is now not just Mordecai but Mordecai the Jew—and to exhibit him publicly in the manner Haman had suggested.

Upset by this unexpected turn of events, Haman runs home and confides in his wife. His advisors and wife warn him,

> If Mordecai, before whom you have begun to fall, is of Jewish stock you will not overcome him; you will fall before him to your ruin. (Esther 6:13)

The struggle is now clearly defined. It is not merely a quarrel between two individuals, two rivals. It's not simply a feud between Haman and Mordecai. It has escalated into something far more powerful. The confrontation pits a malevolent person against an entire ethnic group; evil *versus* good; a force bent on destruction contending with a group who is somehow mysteriously protected.

The promised feast hosted by Queen Esther takes place, with the king and Haman in attendance. Esther takes the opportunity to respond to the king's invitation to state a wish. She says,

> If Your Majesty will do me the favor, and if it pleases Your Majesty, let my life be granted as my wish, and my people as my request. (Esther 7:3)

She explains,

> For we have been sold, my people and I, to be destroyed, massacred, and exterminated. (Esther 7:4)

The king inquires as to the identity of the enemy and Esther singles out "the evil Haman." Enraged, the king leaves the feast while Haman throws himself upon the couch on which Esther is reclining, begging for mercy. Upon reentering the room, the king accuses Haman of assault and orders Haman executed.

The king gives Haman's property to Esther and elevates Mordecai to Haman's position in court. Esther continues, asking the king to annul the order he had sent to all the provinces, ordering the killing of all Jews. The king does not cancel the command, explaining that his former decree cannot be revoked. He gives instructions, however, that if attacked, the Jews have every right to defend themselves (Esther 8:11). So self-defense has royal approval.

> There was gladness and joy among the Jews, a feast and a holiday. And many of the people of the land professed to be Jews. (Esther 8:17)

Some citizens attacked the Jews and they were met with resistance. Those who sided with Haman's attempted pogrom were decimated.

The festival of Purim was instituted, to be observed forever as a time to reflect upon these events. The name Purim derives from the Persian word for "lots," the methodology by which the day of death was decreed for the Jews.

Thus Queen Esther, with the help of Mordecai, saves the Jewish people.* Both are superhero saviors. She finds the courage within herself to speak out and to confront the evil of anti-Semitism. She persuades her husband,

---

* Mordecai is also a savior and plays an important role behind the scenes advising Esther what to do.

a non-Jew, to act. And she empowers her people to act, with the consent of the law, to defend their lives.

In all this, we are expected to see the hand of God acting in history, arranging circumstances to save the people of Israel. God is the savior of Israel. Esther and Mordecai are his instruments in helping to bring this about.

The additions in the Septuagint version of Esther—the one found in the Christian Old Testament but not the Hebrew Bible—elaborate on this theme for those who might miss the message. According to this version, Mordecai has a dream in which he and Haman appear. He decodes these figures as two nations. Haman represents those nations who would destroy the Jews; Mordecai is the surrogate for the nation of Israel. The upshot of the dream is salvation:

> The Lord has saved his people; the Lord has rescued us from all these evils; God has done great signs and wonders, wonders that have never happened among the nations. (Esther, NRSV, addition F)

Esther—a female savior, an ordinary woman who becomes extraordinary. She uses what she had: beauty, the advice of an insightful mentor, a strong sense of ethnic identity, position, connections, power, courage, and her voice. She is a superhero who saves millions.

The Book of Esther points out some of the salient features of anti-Semitism: seeing the Jew as "other;" interpreting Jews collectively as a threat; and proposing death as the way of dealing with the perceived problem. Perhaps more than anything else, anti-Semitism relies on belief in the big lie, that whatever untruth is said about Jews collectively is just to be accepted as truth, with no evidence and no rational examination. Any vilification is accepted without debate. The Book of Esther positions anti-Semitism not as rational but as emotional, a passion to do away with a specific group simply because they are who they are.

And that's the problem: How can anti-Semitism, as it existed then and how it exists now, be challenged when it is not amenable to rational inquiry or rebuttal?

Judith:
The Savior Who Seduces a General

This story of Judith has all the elements of a great story: a horde of bad guys, a community facing disaster, a beautiful widow, clueless leaders, a plan, a bit of piety, seduction, and a murder.

The Book of Judith is fiction, a short novel or folktale about a Jewish heroine. This amazing writing is included in the Catholic, Eastern Orthodox, and Anglican Old Testament based on the Septuagint, but not in the Protestant or Evangelical one. Nor is it included in the Hebrew Bible. It highlights a heroine who singlehandedly saves the people of Israel. The writing possibly dates from the mid to late 2nd century BCE when the Jewish people were being persecuted by Antiochus Epiphanes. Its intent, however, is not to mirror history, but to teach a lesson: how to withstand the threatened extinction of a community.

So, once upon a time, the story goes, 132,000 enemy soldiers led by General Holofernes arrive at the gates of a mythical Israelite city—Bethulia—the gateway to Jerusalem and the center of Jewish life. This vast army encircles the city and takes over the water supply. The citizens of Bethulia huddle together and are sure that they will have to surrender. Uzziah the Israelite leader urges the desperate citizens to hold out for five additional days, to see if God will send help.

Enter Judith, a widow. The Book of Judith describes her as follows:

> She was beautiful in appearance and was very lovely to behold. Her husband Manasseh had left her gold and silver, men and women slaves, livestock, and fields; and she maintained this estate. No one spoke ill of her, for she feared God with great devotion. (Judith 8:7, 8)

So she is beautiful, wealthy, and pious. As it turns out, she is also resourceful and smart. She confronts Uzziah and the elders of the town, arguing that they were wrong to put God to the test by imposing a five-day limit for him to act. She recognizes that the situation is dire: if Bethulia is conquered, then Jerusalem would fall, the city plundered, and there would be massive death and destruction throughout the land. Fearlessly she proclaims that they should set an example for their people: "for their lives depend upon us" (Judith 8:24). She contends, moreover, that it is God who is putting them to the test.

She rises to the challenge, saying that what she is about to do "will go down through all generations of our descendants" (Judith 8:32). "The Lord," she says, "will deliver Israel by my hand" (Judith 8:33). She prepares with prayer; wears festive attire with beautiful jewelry; and packs food, some wine, oil, grain, figs, cakes, bread, and her dishes (in other words, she keeps kosher). She passes into the enemy camp and is allowed to meet Holofernes who urges her to stay with him. He boasts about sleeping with her and on the fourth day he holds a banquet at which he drinks huge amounts of wine. He passes out—as the Book of Judith succinctly puts it, "he was dead drunk" (Judith 13:2). She courageously cuts off his head, places it in her food bag and praises God. She observes, in a now familiar refrain, that the enemy has been defeated "by my hand, this very night" (Judith 13:14). The enemy takes flight and Bethulia is saved, along with Jerusalem and the Temple.

The story concludes with Judith's song of praise, shouting that "the Lord Almighty has foiled them [the enemy invaders] by the hand of a woman" (Judith 16:5). Extolling the greatness of God, she cautions that nations who rise up against Israel "shall weep in pain forever" (Judith 16:17). And so the story ends.

Judith the widow is a savior seductress, not shy of committing murder in pursuit of a good cause. While this raises ethical issues, the book celebrates Judith's cunning and courage by saving not only her city, but also Jerusalem and the Temple, the center of Jewish worship and life. Hers is a fantastic victory.

Biblical Saviors

We see in these three stories accounts of leaders who rise to meet extreme challenges—death of a community through famine, anti-Semitism, or invasion. In all instances, while heroic individuals play the role as savior, we are expected to see the hand of God controlling the outcome of history. God is the true savior standing behind historical events who uses individuals to accomplish his objectives.

We should note carefully the role played by these individuals. It is not as if God acts independently of human agents: humans are the instruments by means of which God achieves a righteous result. People are not expected to remain passive, banking on faith, waiting for God to swoop in and dramatically change the course of history.

As these narratives indicate, people are expected to use their own resources, intellect and insights, physical capabilities, connections to other people . . . in short, whatever abilities they possess in order to achieve a desired outcome. This theme will be echoed in some of Jesus's parables. Biblical superheroes are not angelic beings, divine humans, magicians, or miracle workers.

The message of these books is that ordinary people should act with what they possess: their intelligence, skills, and resources. The hope for a savior in such circumstances should not be "someone else" but one's self, however difficult it might be to rise to the occasion. Hoping for someone else to come to the rescue is simply magical thinking.

8

A SAVIOR, A MESSIAH, AND A REDEMPTION

───⊗───

Some heroic people reach the status of savior. Joseph saved Israelites and Egyptians; Esther saved Jews throughout the vast Persian empire; Judith saved the Jewish inhabitants of Judea and Jerusalem. They were all individuals whose actions resulted in salvation. Ultimately, however, it is God who saves. He lurks behind the scenes in all these accounts.

Salvation here, it should be noted, has everything to do with individuals who rescue a community. It has nothing to do with life after death. There is no mention of what happens to Joseph, Judith, or Esther after they have saved their people. One can assume they lived out the rest of their lives uneventfully. There is nothing about heavenly rewards or eternal life.

One book of the Bible portrays the mission of a redeemed community and its actions, not just that of a single heroic individual. What should we expect from such a national entity? What are its responsibilities? Obligations? Opportunities? What role does community play in helping to ensure a better world?

The Isaiah of Chapters 40 to 55 addresses what a redeemed community can do. This prophet is absolutely euphoric, and Isaiah is one of the most remarkable books of the Bible. It is nothing less than a startling manifesto.

Isaiah Chapters 40–55:
A Savior, A Messiah, and A Redemption

Referred to by scholars as "Second Isaiah," this prophet proclaims his message just as the Babylonian Exile of the Jewish people is nearing its end. He addresses the community—the people of Israel—and lays out before them a tremendous vision for the future. It's a charter document—a proclamation of a new national identity, a social mission that gives purpose and meaning to the Jewish people throughout history.

The Isaiah scroll is divided by scholars into three parts, reflecting the voices of prophets who lived at different times:*

- Chapters 1–39 reflect the 8th century BCE prophet Isaiah.
- Chapters 40–55 embody the message of a later 6th century prophet who speaks just at the end of the Babylonian Exile, around 539 BCE. ("Second Isaiah")
- Chapters 56–66 address the situation a few decades later, around 510 BCE. This is either a "Third Isaiah," or possibly a continuation of Second Isaiah but later on in his career.

The introductory chapter to Second Isaiah—Chapter 40—is intriguing. The prophet is speaking just as the city of Babylon is about to fall to the Persian armies led by Cyrus. He's breathless, he's so excited. He senses that a new international power is about to emerge on the world stage, and he writes with this insight in mind. Ironically, the new international power he envisages is not the emerging Persian empire, but a restored Israel.

---

* See, for instance, the brief Introduction to NRSV translation of Isaiah. Also consult Barry L. Bandstra, *Reading the Old Testament*, Chapter 10, for a fuller discussion.

Second Isaiah begins by portraying God telling the community of Israel that its period of punishment for sins is over—in fact, the people have paid double the penalty for sin (Isaiah 40:2)! They have suffered immensely for their sins. The failure of the community to uphold the Torah and to be faithful to God's covenant was regarded by some (for example, Lamentations 1:5) as the reason for the Exile—not, oddly enough, the overwhelming might of the Babylonian empire. Blame the victim seems to be this theology . . . but that's another story.

Captives from Jerusalem and the surrounding region had been living in Babylonia for four or five decades—deportations occurred periodically, in 597, 587, and 582 BCE. Some had fared well in their new environment, but others, like those whose views are expressed sadly in Psalm 137, had a profoundly different experience: "By the rivers of Babylon, there we sat and wept, as we thought of Zion."

The bitter tone of Psalm 137, however, is not the mood of Second Isaiah. He's the Wolf Blitzer of his generation, the ecstatic presenter of "breaking news." Something fantastic is about to happen, something that has tremendous significance for the beleaguered exiles. He wants people to sit up and take notice.

The prophet is interrupted. Immediately a voice rings out. It says:

> Clear in the desert
> A road for the Lord!
> Level in the wilderness
> A highway for our God!
> Let every valley be raised,
> Every hill and mount made low. (Isaiah 40:3, 4)

The voice is announcing tremendous metaphorical changes that will happen out in the wilderness. It is saying that the way home from exile in Babylonia will be made easy by God—a pleasant journey over flat land.

Moreover, the return of the exiles will be an international event:

> The Presence of the Lord shall appear,
> And all flesh, as one, shall behold. (Isaiah 40:5)

That's the headline, the lead story, front-page news for the nations of the world.

The suspense builds. What's this all about? When will it happen? How? Who will bring it about? The subsequent chapters of Second Isaiah go on to reveal the mystery piece by piece. A whole drama is unfolding on the world stage, and this prophet is letting the community in on the secret.

The message is a communal one, intended for the people of Israel—specifically those who have been held hostage in Babylonia for more than a generation. The community is identified throughout this work as "God's servant":

> But you, Israel, My servant,
> Jacob, whom I have chosen,
> Seed of Abraham My friend—
> . . .
> To whom I said: You are My servant. (Isaiah 41:8, 9)

The equation of Israel with God's servant is reiterated a number of times:

> This is My servant, whom I uphold,
> My chosen one, in whom I delight.
> I have put My spirit upon him,
> He shall teach the true way (*mishpat*)* to the nations.
> . . .
> I the Lord, in My grace, have summoned you,
> And I have grasped you by the hand. I created you, and appointed you
> A covenant people, a light of nations. (Isaiah 42:1, 6)

So the servant is a community—the people of Israel—not a person. The community has an important teaching mission to the nations.

---

* The NRSV translates *mishpat* as "justice."

A Savior

God is the savior, and this is repeated many times. The prophet speaks about God's role as redeemer of Israel.

> *I* will help you
> —declares the Lord—
> *I* your Redeemer, the Holy One of Israel. (Isaiah 41:8, 14)

> But now, thus said the Lord
> Fear not, for I will redeem you;
> I have singled you out by name,
> You are Mine. (Isaiah 43:1)
> . . .
> Thus said the Lord,
> Your Redeemer, the Holy One of Israel (Isaiah 43:14)
> . . .
> And all mankind shall know
> That I the Lord (*YHVH*) am your Savior,
> The Mighty One of Jacob, your Redeemer (Isaiah 49:26)

Redemption entails the restoration of the community back to the land of Israel, now with a huge new international mandate, as we shall see. It is depicted as a startling new creation and God is portrayed as actively bringing about something unique in human history. It will be nothing less than a leadership society that all the nations of the world will come to acknowledge. Recalling the original exodus out of Egypt centuries before (Isaiah 43:16), the prophet declares that God is about "to do something new" for "the people I formed for Myself (Isaiah 43:19, 21).

What is that new creation? The prophet is specific: the Babylonians will be defeated (Isaiah 43:14); the returning exiles will flourish (Isaiah 44:3, 4); Jerusalem will be reinhabited (Isaiah 44:26); the towns surrounding Jerusalem rebuilt (Isaiah 44:26); and the Temple will be restored (Isaiah 44:28). Most importantly, the community will be given a highly important new mandate.

In other words, the exiles are going home, to forge a new national identity with a renewed sense of mission on the world stage. They have been liberated for a reason. And what is that reason? We will soon find out.

A Messiah

But, first, who says they can go home?

After five chapters of exciting buildup about the glorious future that awaits the returning exiles, the moment of truth is reached. Who is the catalyst who will bring about this return? It's none other than Cyrus, the Persian king, described as God's messiah (*mashiach*):

> Thus said the Lord to Cyrus, His anointed one (*mashiach*)
> . . .
> For the sake of My servant Jacob,
> Israel My chosen one,
> I call you [Cyrus] by name,
> I hail you by title, though you have not known Me.
> (Isaiah 45:1, 4)

Cyrus, of course, would not have known he was messiah. But he was an external rescuer, someone who, unbeknownst to himself, threw a lifeline to a community that needed rescuing. Isaiah recognized this and saw the hand of God weaving the texture of world history.

The exiles would have experienced captivity in various places throughout the Babylonian empire. Now, two generations later, they hear that return is possible.

The experience of the Babylonian Exile is book-ended by two biblical writings. The first one is the Book of Lamentations, written just at the beginning of the Exile after the deportations of 587 BCE. It's a short writing, just five very sad poems that portray a horrible situation of devastation and despair. Picturing Jerusalem as a widow, the poet mourns her immense suffering, her children taken away into harsh servitude. She is mocked, there's famine, and foreigners have invaded the Temple. The poet asks the question,

All who pass along the road—
Look about and see:
Is there any agony like mine,
Which was dealt out to me
When the Lord afflicted me
On His day of wrath? (Lamentations 1:12)

Even "the Lord's anointed" (*mashiach*), King Zedekiah, was captured (Lamentations 4:20). The Davidic monarchy had come to an end (Lamentations 5:16). That wasn't supposed to be. God had said there would always be "a David" on the throne of Israel.

The dirge continues, describing in vivid terms the suffering of those who remained in Jerusalem—famine, rape, destruction, death. The city has been humiliated on the world stage, and so has God. The nations rejoice in the destruction of Israel. As we shall see, Lamentations is similar to a later work, *Psalms of Solomon.** That work likewise laments the fate of Jerusalem when captured by the Roman general Pompey in 63 BCE—but it ends on a positive note, unlike Lamentations.

The last verses of Lamentations are bitter as the poet tries to understand Jerusalem's plight in theological terms. While acknowledging sinfulness at all levels of society, the question still remains, why has it happened? The poet poses a question to God:

Why have You forgotten us utterly,
Forsaken us for all time? (Lamentations 5:20)

Then, a plea, a ray of optimism:

Take us back, O Lord, to Yourself
And let us come back;
Renew our days as of old! (Lamentations 5:21)

---

* These are not the Psalms found in the Bible, many of which are attributed to David. The *Psalms of Solomon* are a 1st century BCE composition. This important writing will be discussed in Chapter 10.

But the work concludes on a sour note:

> For truly, You have rejected us
> Bitterly raged against us. (Lamentations 5:22)

Clearly the Book of Lamentations is not a work for the faint-hearted.

A Redemption and a Mission

The Bible is often best understood as a dialogue between various writers rather than as a lengthy monologue expressing the same perspective. Here we see contrasting points of view in action. Second Isaiah is the answer to Lamentations at the tail end of the Exile. The restitution Lamentations hoped for is not just a restoration "as of old": it will be an entirely new undertaking. Excitement replaces despair.

With God as savior and Cyrus as messiah, the community of Israel is the redeemed people. Their course is clear: return. Make the trek homeward back to Jerusalem and the surrounding areas. They have been given a roadmap of the return. Of course, two generations have passed since they left, so not everyone remembers former good times in the "old country" when it was an independent state. Some exiles left Babylonia; some did not.

The Books of Ezra and Nehemiah describe the situation on the ground as the exiles returned and the serious social and political realities that had to be faced. Nation-building was hard work—securing houses, shoring up defenses, rebuilding the Temple, coping with intermarriage and foreign customs, and so forth. But the Realpolitik of Ezra and Nehemiah has nothing to do with the magnificent landscape painted by Second Isaiah.

Israel = God's Servant Nation
Four Servant Community Songs

How should the mandate for the restored community be proclaimed? The author of Second Isaiah unveils a sequence of four "servant community songs." Interestingly, the servant community is personified as if it were an individual, similar to what Lamentations did picturing Jerusalem as a widow. A later work, as we shall see, the *Psalms of Solomon*, will also depict Jerusalem as an individual. Portraying a collective as an individual is a familiar biblical narrative device. So the servant as depicted in Second Isaiah is not a specific individual: it's a community.

The servant community has endured terrible historical trauma. The people had sinned and the kingdom had been brutally conquered by the Babylonians in the 6th century BCE. Exiles had suffered and languished for decades. Now the community has been restored to wholeness, in other words, saved. That's the theological outlook of Second Isaiah as he interprets the world in which he lived.

The identification of the community of Israel as God's servant is made clear right from the outset in this writing. Recall a passage already quoted:

> But you, Israel, My servant, Jacob, whom I have chosen, Seed of Abraham My friend. (Isaiah 41:8)

This theme is reiterated throughout the four songs.

"This is My servant, whom I uphold" begins the first servant song (Isaiah 42:1–4). The gist of this song is the community's mission: to "bring forth justice" (NRSV) to the nations of the world. It will do so steadily and gradually. The community will not grow weary until this objective of establishing justice has been accomplished.

The song is not specific: no details are provided about how this will take place or how justice will be instituted throughout the world. It's a visionary objective.

The second servant song is a memo: from Israel, to the world (Isaiah 49:1–6). "Listen," the song begins—in other words, nations of the world, take note. Personified as an individual, the community proclaims that it was present in God's mind long before it came into being. God, the personified nation contends, has made its teachings "like a sharpened blade," that is, strong and effective. Israel has a special mission, different from that of other nations.

What is this mission? The prophet portrays God as saying to the servant community, Israel:

I will also make you a light of nations,
That My salvation may reach the ends of the earth.
(Isaiah 49:6)

The NRSV translates "a light of nations" as "a light to the nations." Either way, God's servant nation is to be a model community.

Teaching on an international scale, bringing justice to the world and being the light of/to the nations—these are awesome responsibilities. No other nation has these obligations.

What more is required of the servant community?

Be confident in standing up for what's right and continue to observe God's Law. So proclaims the third servant song (Isaiah 50:4–11), again positioning the nation as an individual. Israel faces challenges confidently. The servant does not flinch in the face of physical abuse. In vivid language, the song proclaims, "I offered my back to the floggers, and my cheeks to those who tore out my hair" (Isaiah 50:6). These abuses undoubtedly mirror experiences many of the members of the community had endured during captivity in Babylonia.

Nor did the servant feel shame when verbally mocked—"I did not hide my face from insult and spittle"—further reminiscences from the exile when the community, its king and its God were mocked for seeming to have been defeated. Going forward, the song urges the community to rely on God as vindicator. This defeat is only temporary.

Trust in God is the message. The song concludes by castigating those who light their own fires, that is, those who prefer to follow their own lifestyle, ignoring God's teachings. Those individuals will fail. As the song says to such people, "you shall lie down in pain."

So God's teachings as expressed in Torah are presented as the successful way of living, a kind of Waze system for getting along in this world.

From abject subjugation and brutality to triumph and vindication is the theme of the fourth servant song (Isaiah 52:13 to 53:12). It begins: "My servant shall prosper." Good times ahead for the servant community, a welcomed message in light of what the community had just gone through in the Exile.

This song envisions the exaltation of the community, imagined as being lifted up for the whole world to see. This is Israel on the world stage. Rulers of other nations will be astonished at what the people of Israel have achieved and how far they have come. The song writer envisages how absolutely amazed these rulers will be, wondering how this destitute enslaved group really could become a unique nation, one that paves the way for all humanity? The poet asks: Who would ever believe such a startling turn of events? The author of Second Isaiah goes on to trace the community's rise from a young plant into that of a huge tree. Who would ever have imagined this could happen? The transformation of the community is immense.

At one time, the community had been despised. Israel as God's servant had suffered tremendously, suffering for the sake of its sins. Here Second Isaiah is referencing the plight of suffering experienced by the exiles during the Babylonian captivity. They had been beaten, mistreated, abused, and rejected. As with the other three servant songs, the community of Israel is personified as an individual, but it is the collective that is meant. The personified community is further described as follows:

> But he [the community of Israel] was wounded because of our sins,
> Crushed because of our iniquities.
> He bore the chastisement that made us whole,
> And by his bruises we were healed. (Isaiah 53:5)

The "he" here is the community, the people of Israel. It has been wounded *because of* its own sins. The passage says literally that it was wounded *from* (the Hebrew is the preposition "*mem*," meaning "from" or "due to") its own sins.

The NRSV translates this passage differently: "But he was wounded *for* our transgressions." This translation is potentially misleading. As noted, the Hebrew preposition is *mem* ("from"), not *lamed* ("for"). There is no sense that the servant community was being punished for the sins of others. It's not a punishment on behalf of others. It is not an atonement. So there is no sense that Israel as the suffering servant—or any individual—atones for the sins of others. Rather it represents a self-inflicted wound and the punishment is the consequence of the community's own actions. The point is that the generations of the people in exile were being punished for their own sins.

But that's not the end of the story. As this servant song sees it, during those decades of brutal punishment, their sins had been expiated, and the community had been healed, made whole again. That reinforces the point of view Second Isaiah mentioned right off the bat, in the very first verse of his writing: Israel has come through the captivity experience, having paid the price of sin, doubly (Isaiah 40:1). That time of expiation and punishment is over and now a new reality has emerged onto the international scene.

Israel is God's suffering servant, the light of/to the nations, the bearer of justice, the teacher, the one who has endured the punishments and disgrace of the exile, the one who remains faithful to the commandments of God in spite of abuse and challenges, the one who steadfastly refuses to "light its own fires," the one who has been redeemed. This is Israel's manifest destiny, as Second Isaiah sees it. The servant community has been liberated to serve a great cause in world history. Nations will see the turnaround as exiles flock back to the land from which they came.

What does being a model community entail? As the servant songs mention, the community is to teach justice to the nations of the world, patiently and gradually. It is to be confident in its message, relying upon fidelity to the Torah, not "lighting their own fires." The nation will be exalted on the world stage. It will be a "light"; that is, a trendsetter for the rest of the world.

More than that, the exiles are to return and restore the nation. Returnees will be welcomed from the north, west, and from Egypt (Isaiah 49:12). Moreover, they are to demonstrate to the world that the Lord (*YHVH*) is the savior (Isaiah 49:26). Furthermore, they are told to remember "the quarry" from which they were dug. In other words, they are to recall their origins as children of Abraham and Sarah and the promise God made to them that they would grow into a mighty nation (Isaiah 51:1, 2).

In addition, this newly reconstituted community, "My nation," is to be the base from which God's commandments will be shared with the world:

> . . . give ear to Me, O My nation,
> For teaching (*Torah*) shall go forth from Me,
> My way for the light of peoples. (Isaiah 51:4)

That's the light: the "way" or "teaching" of Torah.

Some Christians interpret Jesus as a suffering servant of God, building on selected themes in Second Isaiah, and notably on Isaiah 53. This is, at best, a secondary application. The primary meaning of Second Isaiah, which he makes very clear, is that the *community* of Israel is God's servant. It's not an individual, although poetically portrayed as such.*

Moreover, the four servant community songs highlight the role of the restored nation on the world stage. Detaching the fourth song from the other three and from the words of Second Isaiah taken as a whole completely ignores and distorts the message of the prophet.

The author of Second Isaiah is speaking to *his* community in *his* era, that it should teach justice to the nations of the world, follow the dictates of Torah, be a model community on the world stage, and bear witness to God as savior. It is the Israel of the 6th century BCE which has an international mandate coming out of the experience of the Babylonian Exile. That's the focus of his proclamation.

The community around Jesus did not adopt the mission of Israel's servant community, following the Torah, or patiently and persistently teaching justice to the nations of the world. In fact, the community that grew up around Jesus's teachings led by Paul abandoned the Torah and preferred, as Second Isaiah would put it, to light their own fires. The secondary application of these texts to Jesus just doesn't fit: no Torah observance by Jesus's community and no mission to teach justice to the nations of the world. This is not, however, to minimize the sufferings of Jesus on his last two days or the pain he endured because of his unjust execution by the Romans. It's simply to say that Second Isaiah is not referring to him.

---

* Moreover, Jesus was not despised and rejected but, by all accounts, was a popular preacher. Nor was Jesus executed because of his sins. It was rather the community of Israel that was despised and rejected, because of its sins which were expiated during the Babylonian Exile.

A better secondary application would be to the modern state of Israel, post 1948. The Jewish community had come through the worst of all possible times, both from the Holocaust in Europe and by the expulsion of 750,000 Jews from the Arab states—the combined historical experience was many times worse than the experience of the Babylonian Exile. Does the 20th century Israel share in Second Isaiah's vision of the restored community of the 6th century BCE, a new creation, a light to the nations of the world, a model high-tech multicultural community? A nation which excels in medical, scientific, agricultural, and environmental achievements? A time when Jews from the Diaspora have returned from around the globe to Israel to contribute to building an advanced society? How far do secondary applications extend? Applying Second Isaiah's mission statement to the modern state of Israel at least has the merit of being applied to a community, not an individual.

Let's return to Second Isaiah's message to the people of *his* own time, however, not to possible secondary applications. The point here is, as the prophet views *his* world, the Israel of his era is God's servant, the light of/to the nations, the bearer of justice, a teacher, the one who endured the suffering of the Babylonian Exile, the one who has been redeemed. This is Israel's manifest destiny, as the writer of Second Isaiah interprets it. The servant community having suffered dreadfully in exile for its sins has now been liberated to serve a great cause in world history. Nations will see the turnaround as exiles flock back to the land from which they came.

Israel—A Catalyst for Change

Second Isaiah is a magnificent writing. It can be seen as a public relations document, an enthusiastic cry for the captives in Babylonia to pack up their bags and make the long trek home to Jerusalem. Or it can be seen as an aspirational writing, something that the Jewish people can aspire to as a new community is formed. Reading Ezra and Nehemiah, however, is sobering in the light of Second Isaiah: the returning exiles face a number of social, political, and religious challenges. Reality on the ground enters the picture.

Just as Second Isaiah dialogues with Lamentations, so, too, Ezra-Nehemiah converses with Second Isaiah.

Second Isaiah can also be read in modern terms as a "mission statement," the purpose of the Jewish community throughout history, to be a covenant community, witnesses to the redemptive power of God and the teachings of the Torah, a model leadership community mirroring justice to the world, the servant community of God. From a redeemed community, much is expected.

As Second Isaiah sees it, a better world will come about when the exiles return and reconstruct their society. The community is a kind of catalyst for world improvement. All people will benefit as Israel acts as a beacon for all humanity. The world will not be perfect and there will still be suffering and disasters. The future, however, is bright as God and people work cooperatively to bring about better conditions on earth.

Second Isaiah laid out the mission of Israel as he saw it in his era some 2,500 years ago. Israel will have an important task on the world stage spearheading social development. The idea of a nation with a divinely sanctioned world mission contributes to the growing sense that the world at some point in the future will be better than it is now.

It's important to note, however, that it is the community that is the agent: it's a collective that has to do this work. It's not up to one special individual. That would be radically "off message." God as savior has already done his work: the community has been redeemed. Now world transformation is up to this new fledgling nation, freed from subjugation and exile in the Babylonian empire and nestled as a small semi-independent entity within the vast Persian empire.

How will the future unfold?

9
WORLD TRANSFORMATION

W ith Second Isaiah, optimism reigns. A transformed—and transforming—society looms on the horizon. These are heady times. Israel is on the move and this community is nothing less than God's new creation. What a fantastic development on the world stage!

Unfortunately, euphoria has a way of crashing down. Historical circumstances changed. After the Babylonian Exile, the Jewish community fell under the shadow of Persian, Greek, and Roman empires. People lived under relentless occupation, with brutal overlords who did not value the Jewish way of life and who oppressed faithful individuals just trying to survive in a hostile world. These were dark times, breeding desperation and despair. Jews looked for relief and longed for a new era in human history, one where God would reign supreme.

In the mid-2nd century BCE, the Jewish community in Israel underwent an intense persecution by Antiochus Epiphanes. As already mentioned, under his regime Jewish religious practices were outlawed; scrolls destroyed; the Temple in Jerusalem desecrated; people compelled to forego circumcision and to consume nonkosher foods. It was an all-out attempt to eradicate Judaism. Noncompliance meant death.

Enforced Hellenization was the objective. As Antiochus and his followers probably saw it, it was an attempt to align Jewish practices with
mainstream culture, to bring it into "modern" times, by embracing Hellenistic religions and values shared by millions around the empire. Those
who wished to remain faithful to the teachings of the Torah, however, did
not see "globalism" that way. In 167 BCE various militant Jewish resistance
groups arose that were successful in liberating Jerusalem and surrounding
areas.

A reflection of these events occurs in the Book of Daniel. The author
of that writing anticipates the day when God's kingdom will be given to
a specific faction of the Jewish resisters, a group he calls "the holy ones (or
"saints") of the Most High." Recall, too, that the Book of 2 Maccabees,
also from this era, describes a horrible atrocity. A mother witnesses her
sons tortured and killed for their religious practices. She expresses the hope
that "the King of the universe will raise us up to an everlasting renewal of
life, because we have died for his laws" (2 Maccabees 7:9).

In such a time, could one dare to hope for a *perfect* world? Perhaps not
the resolution of one crisis but of all crises? Maybe not just the elimination
of one evil colonial empire but the eradication of all such conquerors? It's
in the context of this brave hope that the desire arose, not for a short-term
solution to problems but for an ultimate restoration of the world as it was
intended to be.

How could such a world come about? When?

King-Messiahs guide the fortunes of the Jewish community. Saviors in
the form of heroic individuals overcome such threats as starvation, ethnic
hatred, and warfare. A redeemed community plots a new path in history.
All these developments reset social conditions: the community survives,
and the world is somewhat better, for a moment anyway. These were short-
term fixes, however.

What about something genuinely different? What if the future held
out the possibility of a *perfected* world—some new ultimate, ideal state-of-
affairs? Perhaps Paradise restored? Maybe the Garden of Eden recreated
on earth? How might this occur? Would it be by direct intervention by
God? Might God make good on his promise that there will always be "a
David" on the throne in Jerusalem? Would it appear by supernatural means,

a sudden divine zap for instance? Or would such a transformation require a designated agent? Perhaps a messiah? All these exciting possibilities were in the air.

That was the hope and it focused, for the most part, on "the what." *What* will a better, perfect world look like? That was clear: a time when there would be no occupying troops, no oppression, freedom to live the life of Torah undisturbed, a Davidic king on the throne, and an independent Jewish state. And perhaps much more.

What was less clear was the when. Or the how. Or the by whom.

A Better World:
God Alone Will Act

The Zechariah scroll contains the writings of two prophets, a 6th century BCE author (Chapters 1 to 8) and a later Hellenistic voice (Chapters 9 to 14).* Only the latter is relevant to our purposes here. This portion will be referred to as "Second Zechariah." This writing bears none of the optimism of Second Isaiah: only terrible warfare on the immediate horizon . . . but, eventually, triumph and better times ahead.

Second Zechariah's 1st Pronouncement:
War, Peace, Return of Diaspora

The first pronouncement talks about a time of warfare followed by peace (Chapters 9 to 11). The author of Second Zechariah envisages some interesting developments. Non-Jews, such as the inhabitants of Philistia on the Mediterranean coast, for instance, will adopt Jewish dietary laws (Zechariah 9:6, 7) becoming like a Jewish clan.

Moreover, at this time a king will emerge who "is victorious, triumphant, yet humble, riding on an ass, on a donkey foaled by a she-ass" (Zechariah 9:9). This king shall call on the warring nations to surrender and his rule

---

* See Barry L. Bandstra, *Reading the Old Testament*, pp. 387–388.

shall extend "from sea to sea."* So this is an earthly ruler, a king over Israel, ruling a vast kingdom. It will usher in a time of peace, with God redeeming and causing his people to prosper.

During this era Jews will return from the Diaspora. Second Zechariah colorfully depicts God "whistling" to them (Zechariah 10:8 JPS translation) and gathering them from amongst the nations—from Egypt, Assyria, and Lebanon. Time to return home.

So several major events are to happen when this king appears: some non-Jews will adopt Jewish dietary regulations; nations will be called upon to cease warfare; and Jews in the Diaspora will flock back to Israel.

When all this will happen is not made clear.

The author of the Gospel of Matthew construed Jesus's entry into Jerusalem in light of Second Zechariah's pronouncement. He applied the anticipated king imagery to Jesus (Matthew 21:1–5). Jesus enters Jerusalem on a donkey: "Look, your king is coming to you . . . mounted on a donkey and on a colt." In fact, Matthew pictures Jesus riding astride on "them," that is, on two animals—a donkey and a colt—clearly not understanding Hebrew poetic parallelism and creating an image hard to imagine. That gaffe aside, the point Matthew is making is that Jesus is the anticipated king of Zechariah, hopefully heralding world-transforming events.

The original context of a king entering Jerusalem on a donkey, however, does not refer to Jesus. The context makes this clear. This is another secondary application which does not fit. The other events predicted by Second Zechariah didn't happen in Jesus's era. There is no mention of the inhabitants of Philistia adopting Jewish dietary laws and they did not become like a Jewish tribe when Jesus lived. Jesus was not a ruler over a kingdom that stretched from sea to sea. Jews from the Diaspora did not flock back to Israel. Even worse, the Jewish people did not prosper after Jesus but rather suffered a devastating war in the 60s with Rome—the Galilee was decimated; 1.1 million Jews killed in Jerusalem; 97,000 taken as captives (Josephus, *Jewish War*, Book 6, Chapter 6, Section 3).

Perhaps Jesus or his followers hoped that this ritual reenactment of entering Jerusalem in a dramatic fashion would prod God in bringing about

---

* Said also of King Solomon in Psalm 72:8.

the changes outlined by Second Zechariah: the Philistines converting, the Jews from returning from the Diaspora, the king ruling a large kingdom in peace. Maybe it represented a bold attempt to force God's hand. If so, then clearly that maneuver did not work. None of these events transpired.

So, as Second Zechariah sees it, the stage is set for some future time. A better world is coming. Warfare will end. Some groups will turn to Judaism. A king will emerge who will call for peace. Nothing else is said about the king and he is not said to be messiahed. Jews will return from the Diaspora. God is the agent through whom this peaceful world will emerge. But the all-crucial question—the when—is not made clear.

Second Zechariah's 2nd Pronouncement:
"On That Day"

Second Zechariah's second pronouncement (Chapters 12 to 14) is thunderous, a solemn warning punctuated with the repeated solemn phrase, "on" or "in" "that day." This is the great Day of the Lord. Dramatic warfare will usher in the supreme rule of God over all the earth. The transition will be dreadful.

Focusing just on Chapter 14, it turns out that all the nations of the world will wage war on Jerusalem. Jerusalem will be captured, houses looted, women raped, and part of the population sent into exile (Zechariah 14:1, 2). Then "the Lord" will stand on the Mount of Olives east of Jerusalem. "The Lord" is *YHVH*, God. This mountain will split into two, one part northward and one part southward, thus allowing the inhabitants to escape from Jerusalem east through the passageway so created.

Moreover, on that day fresh water will flow from Jerusalem east to the Dead Sea and west to the Mediterranean (Zechariah 14:8). And, on that day:

> the Lord (*YHVH*) shall be king over all the earth; in that day there shall be one Lord (*YHVH*) with one name. (Zechariah 14:9)

The nations that fought against Jerusalem will be defeated by a plague.

The oracle concludes that in this era, the survivors of the nations that fought against Israel will go up annually to Jerusalem "to bow low to the King Lord of Hosts and to observe the Feast of Booths (Zechariah 14:16). Those who don't will be punished. The Festival of Booths, or Tabernacles, is called Succoth, a fall event, one of the three major pilgrimage festivals in ancient Israel, Passover and Shavuot (Pentecost) being the other two.

As this passage makes clear, in this time, the world will experience peace. The world will acknowledge and worship the one God under his true divine name (*YHVH*). Everyone will observe the festival of Succoth. Zechariah adds a few more curious details. Every metal pot throughout the country, for instance, from those in the Temple to ordinary households, will be holy to the Lord of Hosts. Moreover, there will be no more traders in the Temple—there would be no need since all items and food will be pure. Note, too, that on that day, Second Zechariah envisages that the Temple will still be standing and its rituals observed.

The world as we know it is to be transformed, changed into one of universal peace and harmony. This is the hope that Second Zechariah holds out: God will act directly and decisively in human history—after terrible bloodshed and suffering—to put the world into a better state. There is no mention here of any human agency—no messiah, no savior, no anointed person—just God acting alone to dramatically shape the world according to his design.

For Second Zechariah, after a horrendous bloodbath, the future world will be a peaceful Torah-observant Jewish community enjoying life in harmony with other nations. Everyone will honor and worship the one God.

That doesn't mean that everyone will convert to Judaism, only that God and God alone will be worshipped. It seems, however, that everyone will observe the festival of Succoth.

Is this the End Time when Paradise will be recreated? When the righteous dead will be resurrected? Second Zechariah doesn't mention these events. Just future peaceful coexistence is his vision.

When would this peaceful time come about? How? By whom? Just by God acting alone, as Zechariah suggested? Or might there be the need for other players—perhaps some supernatural beings like archangels or powerful human agents? Would these peaceful times exist forever? These are questions that naturally arise. Things clearly were not getting better with Greek and then Roman occupation and oppression. These world empires saw no signs of weakening and no successor to King David was on the horizon.

1 Enoch:
Judgment and Reward

The author of *1 Enoch* is much more radical than Second Zechariah. Chapters 37 to 71 of *1 Enoch* focus on various End Time matters. This writing is attributed to Enoch, the great grandfather of Noah. Of course he did not write it: the title represents an attribution to Enoch, to lend its message antiquity and weight.*

1 Enoch is thought by scholars to have evolved over time, with numerous unknown authors at different times adding to the text. The translator suggests that the date of Chapters 37 to 71 is likely 105–64 BCE, so this writing is somewhat later than Second Zechariah. One passage goes as follows:

> When the congregation of the righteous shall appear,
> sinners shall be judged for their sins,
> they shall be driven from the face of the earth,
> and when the Righteous One shall appear before the face of the righteous,
> those elect ones, their deeds are hung upon the Lord of the Spirits,
> he shall reveal to the righteous and the elect who dwell upon the earth,
> where will the dwelling of sinners be,
> and where the resting place of those who denied the name of the Lord of the Spirits?
> It would have been better for them not to have been born. (*1 Enoch* 38:1, 2)

---

* A translation of *1 Enoch* can be found in James H. Charlesworth (ed.), *The Old Testament Pseudepigrapha, Volume 1*. New York: Doubleday, 1983, pp. 29–50. Translated with Introduction by E. Isaac.

The End Time will start to emerge when "the congregation of the righteous" appears. So, where is this congregation of the righteous?

It is possible that this passage played a role in the formation of the Dead Sea Scroll Community (perhaps the Essenes). This group emerged sometime during the late 2nd century, after the brutal rule of Antiochus Epiphanes, or in the early 1st century BCE. They congregated at Qumran, down by the shores of the Dead Sea, about 25 miles east of Jerusalem. There they dedicated themselves to living a life of righteousness in a harsh desertlike setting, following Torah strictly as interpreted by their inspired leader, the Teacher of Righteousness.* Copies of *1 Enoch* were found at Qumran, so they were familiar with the writing.

Perhaps they considered themselves to be the "congregation of the righteous" that *1 Enoch* talked about. They may even have thought that their Teacher of Righteousness was "the Righteous One." Perhaps they were also familiar with Second Zechariah's contention that the Mount of Olives would someday split in two and water would flow from Jerusalem west and east. Water flowing east would land fresh water emptying into the Dead Sea near Qumran, their home. Perhaps they fantasized that in the End Time they would enjoy some of the best real estate in the world.

The formation of the congregation of the righteous heralds the death of sinners:

> At that moment, kings and rulers shall perish,
> They shall be delivered into the hands of the righteous and
> holy ones,
> And from thenceforth no one shall be able to induce the Lord
> of the Spirits to show them mercy,
> For their life is annihilated. (*1 Enoch* 38:5, 6)

1 Enoch introduces a complex set of agents involved in the divine plan to change the course of history. In the passages cited above, we encounter:

---

* An intriguing historical reconstruction of the formation and beliefs of this reclusive group can be found in Michael O. Wise, *The First Messiah: Investigating the Savior Before Jesus*. New York: HarperOne, 1999.

"the Righteous One," "the elect," and "the Lord of the Spirits." Later on, other actors are introduced: a "Chosen One" (*1 Enoch* 48:6), an "Elect One" (*1 Enoch* 45:3), a Son of Man or human (*1 Enoch* 46:3, 4; 48:2), the "Lord of the Spirits and his Messiah" (*1 Enoch* 48:10).

Much of *1 Enoch* is tremendously obscure, especially when it comes to the "by whom" the End Time world will occur. It is not clear what each entity mentioned in *1 Enoch* is responsible for. The Lord of the Spirits is the most powerful supernatural being and a major player in world change. The Lord of the Spirits is likely a major angel, perhaps Michael, the Archangel. This being is subordinate to God who is called "the Antecedent of Time," that is "the [Being] Before Time" (for example, *1 Enoch* 55:1).

While many of the details are obscure, the overall message of *1 Enoch* is clear: when the congregation of the righteous appears, evil people will be destroyed and the righteous rewarded. This is a time of reckoning.

The scenario envisaged by the author of *1 Enoch* is much more radical than that of Second Zechariah. This is the End Time, not just a future time of peaceful coexistence among nations. This is when the righteous dead will be resurrected (*1 Enoch* 51:1). They will come back to life, having been dormant waiting for the End Time. Sinners, on the other hand, will perish eternally (*1 Enoch* 56:8). The fate of the righteous, however, is glorious:

> Blessed are you, righteous and elect ones, for glorious is your portion. The righteous ones shall be in the light of the sun and the elect ones in the light of eternal life which has no end, and the days of the life of the holy ones cannot be numbered. They shall seek light and find righteousness with the Lord of the Spirits. Peace to the righteous ones in the peace of the Eternal Lord! (*1 Enoch* 58:1–4)

This theme of the blessings of the righteous is picked up in *The Community Rule* of the Dead Sea Scroll Community, another 1st century BCE Jewish writing. Those who walk in a spirit of humility, goodness, and understanding, along with other virtues, will experience:

healing, great peace in a long life, and fruitfulness, together with every everlasting blessing and eternal joy in life without end, a crown of glory and a garment of majesty in unending light.*

So, according to the author of *1 Enoch* and the members of the Dead Sea Scroll Community, the future is bright for the righteous.

Thinking about the Future

We have examined future thinking in writings that cover over a thousand years: King-Messiahs such as David and Solomon emerged along with biblical superhero saviors and a national community tasked with a world-changing mission. Now there are further future developments in these two Hellenistic writings: a community of nations living in peace, acknowledging the one true God (Second Zechariah); an ultimate End Time with the restoration of Paradise (*1 Enoch*).

In imaging the future, a cluster of complex political and religious ideas have surfaced: King-Messiah, community survival, world re-creation, universal peace, the elimination of evil, resurrection of the righteous dead, and eternal life. Various players have been identified: extraordinary individuals, kings, God, and world-transforming agents such as a "Lord of the Spirits."

There was not only one correct Jewish way of conceptualizing what the future holds. There were many scenarios. Ordinary people likely entertained a confusing mix of ideas about the future.

Thinking about the future can be laid out along a temporal continuum of short, medium, and long-term outlooks. Not all future scenarios have the same temporal horizon.

Short-term outlook: In the short-term there are King-Messiahs and superhero saviors. These individuals function as catalysts for changes to our

---

* "The Community Rule" in Geza Vermes, *The Complete Dead Sea Scrolls in English*. New York: Penguin, 1997, p. 102.

present world and help to bring about better living conditions for people at that time.

Second Isaiah also presents a short-term perspective. He speculates what a redeemed community will do once it finds itself restored to its homeland and begins to discharge its mandate on the world stage. Israel as light to/ of the nations should make a difference to the world's wellbeing.

Medium-term outlook: an intermediate perspective is represented by Second Zechariah. His focus is on a future peaceful world. It's not now and not soon. It will happen, sometime in the future. It will be a better world, but not the perfected one: the world living in harmony with the nation state of Israel. The whole world will benefit from this future peaceful era. This period in human history, Second Zechariah thought, will be brought about by God intervening in world affairs.

As we shall see, a later work, the *Psalms of Solomon*, also presents a medium-term perspective in which King-Messiahs act along with God to bring about a better world for all humanity.

Long-term outlook: For the author of *1 Enoch*, however, the future is nothing less than the ultimate restoration of the Garden of Eden for humanity. Amazing world-transforming events will take place: universal peace under the sovereignty of God, then return of Jews from the Diaspora, divine judgment, the resurrection of the righteous dead, eternal death for sinners, and eternal life for all the righteous. God and possibly other agents, such as an archangel, will bring it about this new and everlasting set of circumstances.

For *1 Enoch* this future time represents the end of history. At that point there will be no conflict and no struggle, just endless eternal life for the righteous in a restored Paradise brought about by God.

Importantly, in the long-term outlook, a messiah is not connected to these wonderful future times. That is true also for the *Psalms of Solomon*, as we shall see. The changes envisaged are far removed from the abilities of a mere mortal. A messiah is clearly thought to be just that, a human being, a gifted person, but nonetheless a human. The catalyst for change of universal magnitude is God and God alone as in the case of Second Zechariah; or, in the case of *1 Enoch*, God with the possible assistance of other cosmic entities.

Hebrew Bible/Old Testament
and Messiah

No Description of Messiah

There is in the Hebrew Bible/Old Testament no sustained discussion of what constitutes a messiah—not one book, not even one chapter. Other ideas are dealt with at length: for example, creation, the lives of the patriarchs, kosher *versus* nonkosher foods, festivals, Temple furnishings, priestly garments, obligations towards God and fellow human beings, and so forth. There is, however, no chapter on what a messiah is or how to identify a true one from a false one. Even identifying and treating skin diseases, from rashes to boils, gets more press (Leviticus 13, 14).

Looking for a messiah is clearly not one of the main topics in the Hebrew Bible. It ranks well below living a Torah-centered life, the central preoccupation of the first five books of the Bible as well as the Prophets. That's the main focus of most of the Hebrew Bible/Old Testament. Jesus, Mary his mother and his entire family, Mary the Magdalene, and all the disciples and their families would have viewed the commandments of the Torah as central to daily life.

The Torah is essentially a system for righteous living, embracing a whole lifestyle, one oriented towards honoring God and acknowledging God in all human activities. It honors the presence of God in time through the observance of Sabbath and various festivals such as Passover, Succoth, and Shavuot. It emphasizes ethics as the way of interacting with others in a righteous manner. The religious injunctions of the Torah embrace diet, marriage, and other aspects of daily living. Moreover, it involves being merciful, forgiving, and doing righteous deeds that help others. As the Book of Deuteronomy makes clear, the path of Torah is all-encompassing, embracing attitudes, choices, decisions, and actions. It's a religious lifestyle based on doing as a result of values.

That's the focus of the Torah and much of the Hebrew Bible/Old Testament: righteous living. Not messiah.

No Focus on Eternal Life

The emphasis of the Hebrew Bible/Old Testament as a unifying theme is on how to live this life righteously. It is not focused on discussing life after death or the world to come. There are brief mentions of resurrection in writings such as Daniel, 2 Maccabees, and Sirach. Even here the references are spotty and the two latter writings are found only in versions of the Old Testament based on the Septuagint, that is, in bibles favored by the Eastern Orthodox, Roman Catholic, and Anglican Christian communities.

Outside the Hebrew Bible/Old Testament there is some attention to the idea of eternal life in *1 Enoch* and in the writings of the Dead Sea Scroll Community. But just that: brief mentions. Life after death is God's business, resurrecting the righteous to eternal life whenever, wherever, and however he sees fit (or if he sees fit).

The focus of the Hebrew Bible/Old Testament is on the here and now, not, for the most part, some remote far-off period in world history and certainly not on an afterlife conceived of as some heavenly realm. With respect to life after death, most Jews then and now take comfort in Psalm 23—that the righteous will enjoy a life dwelling in the house of the Lord forever. The psalm expresses trust in God to guide life, whether in good times—envisaged idyllically as "green pastures" or beside "still waters"—or in the "valley of the shadow of death." God, the psalmist declares, anoints the person's head with oil (reminiscent of being messiahed), with goodness and mercy following in its wake.

According to Jewish belief, the righteous of all the nations of the world have a share in the world to come (*Tosefta Sanhedrin* 13:1). The *Tosefta* records Jewish discussions from the 2nd and 3rd centuries. The 12th century Jewish philosopher, Maimonides, concurred with this position, stating that "righteous Gentiles have a share in the world to come" (*Mishneh Torah, Laws of Kings* 8:11).

Thus, for Judaism, there is eternal life for all the world's righteous, whatever their religion. This inclusivist position contrasts with one prominent extremist Christian view, first articulated by Cyprian of Carthage in the 3rd century, that "extra Ecclesiam nulla salus," that is, "outside the Church there is no salvation."

So, while Jews have a covenant with God that requires all Jews to observe the Torah—that's what is meant by "chosen," that is, chosen to observe the

Torah—this does not preclude other agreements between people and God. Non-Jews are not obligated (or "chosen") to follow the commandments of the Torah. The requirement for non-Jewish righteousness is to honor the seven universal laws that are incumbent on all humanity. These are the Noahide Laws: not murdering, exercising justice, and refraining from such actions as idolatry, blasphemy, theft, or sexual immorality.

As a result, whatever Psalm 23 means by "dwelling in the house of the Lord," it is multicultural. God's redemption is not limited simply to righteous Jews. This is one reason why Judaism does not seek to convert—there is no advantage to being Jewish when it comes to life in the world to come. Jews have been "chosen" to follow the Torah, not because there is anything special about being Jewish. The chosen-ness is task-oriented; the task being to carry out that lifestyle. But, according to Judaism, any righteous person, Jew or non-Jew, can benefit from God's redemption after death.

The idea of a world to come—however it is conceived—is not tied into the notion of a messiah. It is tied to individual righteous action, whether it's following the Torah or Noahide Laws. As in Second Zechariah and *1 Enoch*, the agent who creates a future better world is God. Typically the idea of a world to come—the ideal world, Paradise restored—is thought of as an event on this planet, not in some supernatural realm somewhere else. It is a transformed earth that is envisaged.

The idea of an immortal soul going at point of death to meet God is more of a Greek view of immortality rather than a biblical view of resurrection which takes death as a fundamental reality. On the biblical view there is no natural immortality: death is real. Only God can restore life to those who have died.[*]

∽

So if there is no biblical definition of messiah, where can we find a job description?

Without such a criterion we cannot evaluate the credentials of any messianic claimant, including Jesus.

---

[*] See, for instance, Oscar Cullmann, *Immortality of the Soul or Resurrection of the Dead?* Eugene, OR: Wipf & Stock, reprint edition, 2000. Original: London: Epworth, 1958.

III

WHAT'S A MESSIAH?

10

A MYSTERIOUS, NEGLECTED, ANCIENT MANUSCRIPT

---

ortunately, an exciting ancient manuscript tells us what Jews understood by "messiah" some 2,000 years ago, just prior to the birth
of Jesus. This very important writing gives us the fullest, most
complete job description.

This manuscript is called the *Psalms of Solomon* by the few scholars who
know about it.

Dates from Just Before Jesus

The *Psalms of Solomon* are not the psalms found in the Bible. These psalms
are attributed to Solomon, although he had nothing to do with them
whatsoever. It's a 1st century BCE writing, whereas King Solomon reigned
over 900 years earlier, around 950 BCE.

Psalms of Solomon were likely attributed to this great Israelite king
because of his legendary wisdom . . . or perhaps, more mundanely, to

give added weight to their contents. Living some 950 years before Jesus, Solomon was said to have composed other works, for example, Ecclesiastes (also known as Koheleth), Song of Songs, Proverbs, and the Wisdom of Solomon. None of these attributions are considered historical.

The *Psalms of Solomon* mirror events that took place in Jerusalem in the 60s BCE, many centuries later than the reign of the wise King Solomon. Thus scholars date the writing to that time or shortly thereafter—so from the 50s or 40s BCE, just a few decades before the birth of Jesus and shortly before the death of Herod the Great (4 BCE).

The author of this remarkable work is an eye witness to the devastation and atrocities that the Romans inflicted on Jerusalem and its inhabitants. Surveying the damage, the poet yearns for the day when the Romans would be swept away, and the Lord's Messiah would usher in a new era in human history. It is likely the work of a Pharisee or devout Jew living in Jerusalem.

A few Old Testament Pseudepigrapha* specialists know about this writing, but it has received very little general attention.† That's curious because *Psalms of Solomon* represent our best source for identifying the Jewish understanding of messiah at the turn of the Common Era. People who heard Jesus speak about the coming Kingdom of God likely entertained some of the hopes and dreams reflected in this work.

The *Psalms of Solomon* survive in a few Greek and Syriac manuscripts, the earliest one dating from the 10th century. The songs were probably originally written in Hebrew or Aramaic and then translated into Greek and Syriac. Syriac was a form of Aramaic used by Christians in the eastern Roman and Persian empires. A Hebrew/Aramaic version no longer exists.

Influential in their day, the *Psalms of Solomon* are mentioned as having been included in some ancient compilations of authoritative Christian

---

* The phrase "Old Testament Pseudepigrapha" refers to important Jewish writings composed from roughly 200 BCE to 200 CE that are not included in the Hebrew Bible/Old Testament. They are anonymous works which are falsely attributed to ancient figures and which relate to biblical themes. For a translation of over 60 such writings, see James H. Charlesworth (ed.), *The Old Testament Pseudepigrapha, volumes 1 and 2*. New York: Doubleday, 1983.

† For recent scholarship on the *Psalms of Solomon*, see Selected References at the end of this book.

biblical writings. They formed part of the Greek Septuagint version of the Hebrew Bible. They were included in the Peshitta Bible used by Syriac-speaking Christians. They were also found in the Codex Alexandrinus, one of the earliest and most complete manuscripts of the Bible dating from roughly 400–450. So some Christians thought the work to be biblical.

Why *Psalms of Solomon* were not included in the Hebrew Bible whose contents were finalized likely by the year 100 (Council of Jamnia) is not known.

Rediscovered in the 17th century, a Latin translation was published in 1626. There are several English translations from both Greek and Syriac manuscript traditions, and these are mentioned in Selected References.

The Situation

The *Psalms of Solomon* have to do with events in Jerusalem after the death of Queen Salome Alexandra. A remarkable leader, she was the last ruler of an independent Jewish state until its rebirth in 1948. She survived the turbulent reigns of two royal husbands, King Alexander Jannaeus and King Aristobolus I. Her reign as sole monarch was a relatively peaceful period, 76–67 BCE.

Upon her death, however, the country convulsed into civil war. Her two sons, Hyrcanus II (high priest and successor as king) and Aristobolus II, vied for power. Both turned to the Roman general Pompey for help. That wily military leader saw an opportunity to take control and, in 63 BCE, he set up siege around Jerusalem. Building a ramp over a ditch to the city walls, he brought up a battering ram which penetrated the walls. Over 12,000 Jews were killed, while the Romans experienced few casualties (Josephus, *Jewish Antiquities*, Book 14, Chapter 4, Section 4).

Upon seizing the city, Pompey entered the Temple. He also entered the Holy of Holies, which only the high priest was allowed to enter, and then, only once a year. Apart from that action, he left the Temple treasures intact and ordered the sacrifices to resume. Hyrcanus II was reinstated as high priest, but not as king. The state enjoyed semi-autonomy but was dependent upon Roman administration in Syria and forced to pay an annual tribute.

Psalms of Solomon reflect the immediate aftermath of Pompey's conquest.

Psalms of Solomon: A Messiah Is Needed Now

In the Situation Room

There are 18 songs in the *Psalms of Solomon* and they systematically set forth a scenario of devastation, hope, and remedy.* The songs are not haphazard but are arranged in a logical order. Here's the narrative they set forth.

The song writer begins by giving an overview of the political and social situation. Portraying the city of Jerusalem as himself, he sets forth the political situation:

> I cried out to the Lord when I was severely troubled,
> To God when sinners set upon [me]. (*Psalm* 1:1)†

The "I" here is the city of Jerusalem which the author has personified.‡ "The Lord" is God. Jerusalem has been invaded by the Romans: the latter are the "sinners" who have set upon her. These are terrible times and Jerusalem is suffering, crying out to God for relief.

The Romans are described as wealthy, powerful, and arrogant. They do not acknowledge God. Furthermore they have "completely profaned the sanctuary of the Lord," that is, the Temple (*Psalm* 1:8).

So *Psalm* 1 introduces the situation on the ground: invasion, devastation, destruction, social upheaval. The situation is dreadful.

Psalm 2 enumerates the specific atrocities committed by the Romans. They "broke down the strong walls with a battering ram" (*Psalm* 2:1). Foreigners entered the Temple. Citizens of Jerusalem also "defiled the

---

* For an English translation of the *Psalms of Solomon* see R. B. Wright's translation in James H. Charlesworth (ed.), *The Old Testament Pseudepigrapha, Volume 2*, pp. 651–670.

† All psalm references here in italics are to the *Psalms of Solomon*, not the psalms found in the Bible.

‡ A common biblical maneuver: recall the personification of Jerusalem as a widow in Lamentations and the personification of the community of Israel as a suffering servant in Second Isaiah.

sanctuary of the Lord, they were profaning the offerings of God with lawless acts" (*Psalm* 2:3). God rejected these disgraceful sacrifices. Prostitution was rampant—females were available to all—and people defiled themselves "with improper intercourse" (*Psalm* 2:13). The writer is sickened by these developments and his pain shows forth in the vivid language he has employed. Religiously and socially these are dark times for Jerusalem and its inhabitants.

Daringly, the composer challenges, perhaps even accuses, God—"you did not interfere" (*Psalm* 2:1). Like Job, he wonders in the midst of immense suffering why God had not intervened to relieve his people of their misery. He asks the age-old question: Why are these atrocities happening to us here now? It's a question that resonates amidst genocides, wars, and horrors. And, with him, we wonder: Why aren't the righteous rewarded and the evildoers punished? Is God really in charge? Is he standing behind his Covenant with Israel?

Josephus had placed the blame for the devastation of Jerusalem not on Pompey, but on the political consequences of the civil war led by the two feuding brothers, Hyrcanus and Aristobulus:

> Now the occasions of this misery which came upon Jerusalem were Hyrcanus and Aristobulus, by raising a rebellion one against the other; for now we lost our liberty and became subject to the Romans. (*Jewish Antiquities*, Book 14, Chapter 4, Section 5)

Unlike Josephus, the composer of *Psalms of Solomon* is living in the moment of devastation and he raises a thorny theological problem—how to understand the plight of Jerusalem in light of the framework of Jewish religion. He sets himself an immense task:

> I shall prove you right, O God, in uprightness of heart: for your judgments are right, O God. (*Psalm* 2:15).

So how is the psalmist going to vindicate God's honor? As he points out, God's reputation seems in tatters. Jerusalem has been devastated. The righteous are suffering. There seems to be no end to evil. He implores God—"Let it be enough, Lord" (*Psalm* 2:22)—adding, perhaps a bit impertinently, that God should not delay.

Immediately, he sees a spark of hope. He recalls that Pompey died off the coast of Egypt (48 BCE)—a detail that helps date the writing. This gives him confidence: clearly Pompey "did not understand that it is God who is great, He is king over the heavens" (*Psalm* 2:26–30). This is divine payback, with God acting in human history to set things right.

What is likely to happen? How can God be vindicated?

The Way Forward

With the death of Pompey, the composer concludes *Psalm* 2 with one of his signature themes, the sharp contrast between the righteous and the sinners. God will separate the righteous and the sinner, he says, and "will repay the sinner forever according to their actions" (*Psalm* 2:34, 35).

Psalm 3 picks up on this theme and introduces the notion that the righteous merit eternal life; sinners, eternal death. The righteous should be confident of their hope because it stems "from God their savior" (*Psalm* 3:6). Those who fear the Lord "shall rise up to eternal life, and their life shall be in the Lord's light, and it shall never end" (*Psalm* 3:12). On the other hand, "the destruction of the sinner is forever" (*Psalm* 3:11).

In other words, vindication will take place in the future, in the world to come, as God rewards the righteous. The righteous are those who have followed God's law as expressed in Torah. They receive eternal life, rising up from the dead as resurrected human beings. Not so, the sinner. They remain dead.

The theme of the fate of the righteous *versus* that of the sinner continues on for several songs. Likely these poems were intended to encourage the righteous to remain faithful to the teachings of Torah in spite of tremendous adversity. Remember what's at stake seems to be the message: nothing less than eternal life. This theme of tying Torah observance to eternal life is reminiscent of the mother in the Book of 2 Maccabees who witnessed the torture and death of her seven sons.

In *Psalm* 9, the composer shouts: "God was proven right in his condemnation of the nations of the earth" (*Psalm* 9:23). With the death of Pompey construed as retribution, the inhabitants of Jerusalem are now able to discern that God does indeed act in human affairs. The death of Pompey is proof positive of the righteousness of God. He sings triumphantly: "We have proven your name right" (*Psalm* 9:26).

He adds a few admonitions—don't neglect us, God, "lest the Gentiles devour us as if there were no redeemer" (*Psalm* 9:30). And he assures God that the people will be faithful:

> And we will not leave you, for your judgments upon us are good. May [you] be pleased with us and our children forever; Lord, our savior, we will not be troubled at the end of time. (*Psalm* 9:32–34)

After several more songs that contrast the misery of sinners *versus* the joy of the righteous, the psalmist comes to a conclusion: "the Lord is faithful to those who truly love him" (*Psalm* 14:1), that is, "those who live in the righteousness of his commandments, in the Law, which he has commanded for our life (*Psalm* 14:2).

Devout individuals are described as "trees of life" and as a "planting . . . [who] shall not be uprooted as long as the heavens shall last" (*Psalm* 14:4). Those who persist will "inherit life in happiness," while sinners will know only "Hades, and darkness and destruction" (*Psalm* 14:9, 10).

Psalms 15 and 16 provide a transition, a plea to God to help the righteous stay righteous. This is a time of immense challenges for the faithful, how to remain faithful to God in the midst of dreadful circumstances and suffering. Like Job, the situation seems to make no sense: the righteous should not be suffering this way and Jerusalem should not be devastated. This raises questions about the Covenant with God: How should we understand the current situation? The writer encourages the devout to hang tight. Don't let temptation lead you astray. Know that "if the righteous [person] endures all these things, he will receive mercy from the Lord" (*Psalm* 16:15). So his recommendation is to look to the long-term for vindication, not the short-term pain.

By the end of *Psalm* 16, the composer has systematically described the situation, outlined two choices in life, and encouraged the righteous to remain faithful to the framework for good living, the Covenant. Those that do so will inherit eternal life; those that don't merit eternal death. The choice is clear. How to survive the crisis of devastation and destruction is evident: observe the path of the Torah. Your life, your eternal life, depends upon it. He reassures the faithful that God is just and is in charge of history, so the righteous should not fear.

So the message of *Psalms of Solomon* is one of hope in spite of terrible historical circumstances. Moreover, it's a call to action—fashion your life around what the Torah says. Things will change for the better . . . eventually. God's in control.

But that's not all.

There's a surprise announcement: there's a better future looming on the horizon.

What Must A Messiah Do?

The last two psalms in the collection—*Psalms* 17 and 18—hold out the hope that maybe God will send a messiah. These two psalms provide a much more extensive description of what a messiah must do than any passage in the Bible.

The songwriter very carefully lays out the theological framework. First of all, God is king (*Psalm* 17:1). Secondly, God is a merciful savior (*Psalm* 17:3). Thirdly, God's kingdom is forever (*Psalm* 17:3). Fourthly, God's Covenant with David (2 Samuel 7) ensures there will always be a descendant on the throne of Israel:

> Lord, you chose David to be king over Israel,
> and swore to him about his descendants forever,
> that his kingdom should not fail before you. (*Psalm* 17:4)

The psalmist knows very well that this line has been broken. It sounds like a guilt trip—why hasn't God kept his promise? He reminds God of

Pompey's brutal actions, massacring "young and old and children at the same time" (*Psalm* 17:11). Moreover, Pompey:

> did in Jerusalem all the things
> That Gentiles do for their gods in their cities.
> And the children of the covenant [living] among the gentile rabble
> Adopted these [practices].
> No one among them in Jerusalem acted [with] mercy or truth.
> (*Psalm* 17:14, 15)

God, the writer urges, open your eyes to our plight. Jerusalem has been ravaged. Many have been killed. There's no legitimate king on the throne. Synagogue attendance is down: as the songwriter picturesquely puts it—"Those who loved the assemblies of the devout fled from them as sparrows fled from their nest" (*Psalm* 17:16).

So now what? What should God do? Here's the psalmist's bold suggestion:

> See, Lord, and raise up for them their king,
> The son of David, to rule over your servant Israel
> In the time known to you, O God. (*Psalm* 17:21)

While the timing is up to God, what is needed is a restoration of the Davidic monarchy, another messiahed king.

The composer tells us what this new King-Messiah has to do, outlining a twofold strategy: one aimed at sinners, another one at the righteous.

First, against sinners, the King-Messiah must bring about the following (*Psalm* 17:22–25):

- Destroy unrighteous rulers
- Purge Jerusalem of Gentiles
- Drive out sinners
- Smash the arrogance of sinners
- Shatter all their substance
- Destroy unlawful nations

That's a massive political undertaking. Discharging these requirements would involve taking on the might of the Roman Empire,
changing the political structure of all the nations of the world, and
removing foreigners from Israel. So when the King-Messiah is raised up
by God, the world will become a vastly different place. Gone would
be the Romans—their soldiers, government officials, and citizens of the
many Gentile colonies in Israel. This represents a huge transformation
of the political landscape.

So that's "the what." *Psalm* 17 does not address "the how"; that is, the
manner in which the King-Messiah will bring all these far-reaching
changes to pass. Will the king undertake these massive upheavals by himself? Or will he rely on the power of God to bring about a transformed
world? Clearly, as the psalmist envisages the scenario, the King-Messiah
will be an active participant in world transformation.

The task before the King-Messiah raises other questions. What is meant
by the King-Messiah's foreign policy, destroying unrighteous rulers and
unlawful nations? It does not mean complete eradication or annihilation
because, as we shall see, foreign countries still exist but are subservient to
the Jewish kingdom.

Next, turning to the righteous—essentially, his domestic policy—the
King-Messiah must do the following (*Psalm* 17:26–31):

- Gather a holy people
- Lead them in righteousness
- Judge the tribes who have been made holy by God
- Not tolerate any unrighteousness amongst the people
- Distribute them on the land according to their tribes, making sure that no alien and no foreigner live near them
- Judge peoples and nations
- Ensure that Gentile nations will serve under his rule
- Glorify the Lord in a place prominent above the whole earth
- Purge Jerusalem and make it holy
- Ensure that nations come to Jerusalem to see the glory of the Lord

These are all action verbs. Again, the King-Messiah has a huge task in transforming society. The hoped-for monarch will be a righteous king, taught by God. The psalmist has already explained what he means by righteousness; that is, following the law given by God as the Jewish part of the Covenant.

The King-Messiah will rule from Jerusalem, developing a land distribution policy, reforming the religion and judging peoples. During his reign, "there will be no unrighteousness among them [the people] in his days, for all shall be holy" (*Psalm* 17:32). The king shall be "the Lord Messiah." This does not imply divinity for the messiah, just that he is the anointed one of God, God being "the Lord."

So, as the psalmist sees it, the new King-Messiah of Israel will get rid of the Romans and will rule all the nations of the world from Jerusalem. He will restore proper worship of God in the Temple. He will be a human being, a descendant of King David, subservient to God and righteous.

Moreover, a messiah is not a savior who resurrects people. As the *Psalms of Solomon* emphasize, God alone is the savior and the dispenser of eternal life to the righteous. The King-Messiah is an instrument of God—just as David and his successors were—fulfilling his purpose in human history.

Not all the details are clear. For one thing, to whom is the land distributed? Is it for the existing inhabitants of Israel? Is it an attempt to create 12 states or provinces corresponding to the geographical boundaries of the ancient 12 Israelite tribes? Or is it also to accommodate the Jews in the Diaspora, returning individuals who would need resettlement in Israel? Does the composer envision the return of the Jews from the Diaspora during this time in history? The latter seems to be what he has in mind by "gathering" a holy people. He appears to envisage the reestablishment of the entire Jewish nation.

The King-Messiah doesn't rely on "horse and rider and bow" in purging the land of foreigners, for "the Lord himself is his king" (*Psalm* 17:33). Does this mean that the transformation of the nations of the world will be carried out peacefully? If so, how? Will the occupying and powerful Romans just pack up their bags and leave? Will the other nations simply adopt peaceful ways? What does the phrase that he will treat the nations of the world compassionately who will "reverently stand before him" mean? (*Psalm* 17:34). How should we imagine this taking place?

The King-Messiah will not weaken, "for God has made him powerful in the holy spirit and wise in the counsel of understanding, with strength and righteousness" (*Psalm* 17:37). So the King-Messiah will have stamina in the face of tremendous obstacles. He himself will be free from sin (*Psalm* 17:36) and will shepherd a holy people (*Psalm* 17:40)—both curious details. This, the psalmist extols, "this is the beauty of the king of Israel" (*Psalm* 17:42).

What the songwriter hopes for is clear: a great new era when Israel will once again be an independent nation, the envy of all other nations who will marvel in the glory of God's kingdom led by a King-Messiah, descendant of David. As he says,

Blessed are those born in those days to see the good fortune of Israel. (*Psalm* 17:44)

This is a portrait of a changed world and he ends *Psalm* 17 with the stirring proclamation, in case anyone should be in doubt, "The Lord Himself is our king forevermore" (*Psalm* 17:46). Here we have the Kingdom of God. The world is a theocracy: God as sovereign with the King-Messiah as his royal agent presiding over the nations of the world.

In *Psalm* 18, the last in his collection of songs, he praises God for his mercy and goodness, adding a blessing upon the righteous:

May God cleanse Israel for the day of mercy in blessing, for the appointed day when his Messiah will reign. Blessed are those born in those days, to see the good things of the Lord, which he will do for the coming generation. (*Psalm* 18:5, 6)

He concludes his collection of songs with a warning. He notes that God is a great and glorious, a being who has ordered the stars in their orbits. They have not veered off course . . . except when God has directed them (*Psalm* 18:10–12). The implication is that the people of Israel likewise should not wander off course, either.

11

MESSIAH
JOB DESCRIPTION

⚬⚬⚬

T hanks to the *Psalms of Solomon*, we now have the job description for messiah. These psalms are far more informative than any passage contained in the Hebrew Bible/Old Testament. This document represents a stunning, breakthrough writing. We now know what Jews living at the time of Jesus expected by way of a Jewish messiah. Some combination of these ideas would have informed the outlook of such Jews of the time as Hillel, the Jewish sage and scholar who lived just prior to Jesus; Jesus's disciples including Peter; Mary the Magdalene; Paul; James; the Essene Teacher of Righteousness; Josephus; and many others. We finally have a check list against which prospective messiahs can be measured.

What's a Messiah?

According to the *Psalms of Solomon* there are six requirements a person must fulfill in order to be counted as a genuine messiah.

A messiah . . .

1   will appear in the midst of desperate times;

2   is a human being, a descendant of King David;

3   is an anointed king, that is, a King-Messiah, who governs in Jerusalem, under the sovereignty of God;

4   is Torah-observant, encouraging and ensuring that his people are likewise Torah-observant;

5   is a catalyst for world transformation. These changes include:
- expelling non-Jews from Jerusalem
- overseeing the return and resettlement of Jews from the Diaspora
- destroying unlawful nations
- ruling non-Jewish nations;

6   presides over a time of universal peace when non-Jewish states live in harmony with Israel.

The composer of *Psalms of Solomon* could have ended his lyrical meditation at the end of *Psalm* 16, encouraging people to remain faithful to the law, pointing out that "if the righteous [person] endures all these things, he will receive mercy from the Lord" (*Psalm* 16:15). In other words he could have simply said that in the present times of deep distress, stick with following the laws of Torah.

But he didn't. He wanted a way out. He looked for a rescuer, a fixer. These were desperate times, and under such conditions that the hope for a messiah emerges. The author of the *Psalms of Solomon* wanted a better future and out of sheer powerlessness—that driver of messianic hopes and ambitions—he dared to imagine the advent of a messiah, a catalyst for the creation of a vastly different era in human history.

So, messiah must be a powerful political figure—a King-Messiah, a leader who restores the Davidic monarchy. He is a strong, charismatic human being who reigns in Jerusalem, looking after and protecting his people, settling them in various political jurisdictions corresponding to the old tribal boundaries, reforming the religion, and ensuring that the nations of the world respect Israel. He is by far the most powerful political agent on the planet. He acts under the sovereignty of God, the world becoming a theocracy.

How much the King-Messiah must do personally is not clear. Somehow, he is the catalyst for world transformation. As already mentioned, the *Psalms of Solomon* reveal the what but not the how of world transformation. Presumably God would have to engage in the big picture changes, destroying unrighteous rulers and nations for example.

Moreover, the King-Messiah must be a righteous individual who follows the Torah lifestyle. Indeed, his mandate is to ensure that all the people do so. Thus he becomes not only the political leader but the religious embodiment of the Jewish nation observing the commandments of Torah within the framework of the Covenant with God.

The reign of the King-Messiah will usher in a time of universal peace. There will be no more unrighteousness. Foreigners will be peaceful and will reverently honor Israel—its king and God. The people of Israel will follow the path of Torah, led by the righteous king. Israel thus becomes a holy nation dedicated to God. Presumably the other nations will honor the laws which pertain to non-Jews, the Noahide Laws which have to do with the acknowledging one God, practicing justice, avoiding sexual immorality, and being merciful.

In short, the world will be dramatically altered in ways that will profoundly impact the lives of everyone living at the time. Existing social, political, economic, and religious arrangements will be severely disrupted as peoples and nations adjust to the new reality of universal peace. It will also require adjustment on the part of Jews living at the time, to become fully compliant with Torah requirements. So, massive changes are envisaged that will affect everyone then alive.

Such is the theocratic hope of the author of *Psalms of Solomon*. A new world, coming soon—"for the coming generation" (*Psalm* 18:6). A new era is dawning, spearheaded by the King-Messiah. People throughout the world of all ethnicities and religions will benefit. It's a universal vision: a time of peace for all the peoples of the world. The righteous will see "the good things of the Lord" (*Psalm* 18:6). He thinks this will happen in the next generation . . . that soon!

An important finding is that King-Messiah is not tied into the idea of an End Time with the world restored to perfection. The messiah is not the creator of the ultimate ideal world—only God is. While the *Psalms of Solomon* mention End Time themes in his collection of songs (for instance, *Psalm* 3), they are not articulated in relation to the era of the King-Messiah. Like *1 Enoch*, for the author of the *Psalms of Solomon*, these ultimate hopes and dreams lie somewhere down the road, at a time known only to God.

A messiah, then, is not the agent of End Time transformation. In that ultimate time, the end of history, God will act to restore the Garden of Eden, resurrect the righteous dead, ensure the universal worship of the one God, and give eternal life to those living when Paradise is restored. But that's entirely God's doing. It's not the task of the King-Messiah.

What A Messiah is *Not*

We now have a check list, a set of job requirements, against which we can measure any possible messiah, whether Jesus, Simon bar Kokhba, Rabbi Menachem Schneerson, or any other person. We now know what he must be and what he must do in order to qualify for the title "messiah." That is methodologically the right way to proceed: to work from a job description to assessing the credentials of any possible messiah candidate.

We should resist the bogus interpretive method of assuming that a specific person is messiah and then scouring ancient writings for hints that they foretold this particular individual. That's like making up our minds that a person is guilty of first-degree murder and then looking for elements in his background that might support this claim, for instance, displaying an angry disposition, consorting with the wrong crowd, owning a gun, and the like. That is faulty methodology. Not every person who owns a gun is angry, or who hangs out with the wrong crowd is a criminal. We can't assume what the point at issue is and then look backwards for corroboration. Rather, we need to start with a description of what constitutes first-degree murder and then consider evidence whether the person in question is or is not guilty of this crime.

The author of the Gospel of Matthew started this suspicious retrospective interpretive maneuver by saying "this . . . was done so as to fulfill . . .", the former being some event in the life of Jesus and the latter being some passage in the Old Testament. Matthew assumes that Jesus is messiah—without any description of what constitutes a messiah—and then retroactively scans passages in the Old Testament that might bolster this belief. He calls this "fulfillment."

Fulfillment theology represents flawed methodology. For one thing, it lifts the original passage in the Old Testament out of its larger textual and historical context and ignores what the writer of his time was trying to say to his audience. It simply twists an ancient text to suit a current agenda.

Matthew is no stranger to altering texts. Recall that the author of the Gospel of Matthew made a huge change to the trial narratives. The author of the Gospel of Mark had blamed the Roman authorities for ordering the death of Jesus. Matthew, however, with the Gospel of Mark right in front of him, shifted responsibility for Jesus's death from them to the Jewish leaders. Their culpability fitted his evangelical purposes more than placing responsibility upon the Romans, Roman citizens being his primary missionary target. That shift has had massive disastrous consequences throughout history. Media manipulation and fake news are not modern phenomena.

The messiah is not someone who has come forth out of Egypt as Matthew suggests (Matthew 2:15). That passage refers to Hosea Chapter 11, where God declares his love for Israel:

> I fell in love with Israel
> When he was still a child;
> And I have called [him] My son
> Ever since Egypt. (Hosea 11:1)

145

The NRSV translation puts it, "When Israel was a child, I loved him, and out of Egypt I called my son." It was Israel that came out of Egypt during the Exodus, and Israel whom God declares to be his son. Matthew's methodology, applying this passage to Jesus, obscures the meaning of the original.

Matthew is the only gospel that says that Mary and Joseph took Jesus into Egypt shortly after birth, because of danger to his life. The Gospel of Luke, however, has Mary and Joseph going into Jerusalem on the eighth day for Jesus's circumcision and the ritual purification of Mary after childbirth (Luke 2:21–24). So did the family take Jesus right into the heart of Herod's power, or did they migrate to Egypt for a while to escape his wrath? More likely, is this fulfillment passage part of Matthew's "created Jesus" so as to be able to apply the sentence in Hosea 11:1 to him, as "my son." Is this fake news on Matthew's part, creating an incident so he can apply a passage from the Old Testament that he thinks is somehow messianic?

Fulfillment interpretive methodology is reflective of an attempt to remove Israel's heritage and apply it to Christian circumstances. Sometimes called "replacement theology," it represents the attempt by some Christian leaders to say that the church has replaced the synagogue and that the Hebrew Bible is not meant for Jews, but for Christians interpreting it in the light of Jesus's sayings and actions.* This retrospective interpretive methodology represents at best, cultural misappropriation; at worst, cultural theft.

There is also no indication that messiah has a special or virgin birth. That view, found in the Gospels of Matthew and Luke, is based on a mistranslation as is now widely recognized at least in scholarly circles.† Those gospels used the Septuagint version of the Bible. That Greek version translated the Hebrew for "young woman" (*almah*), who may or may not be biologically virginal, as "virgin" (*parthenos*). The word *almah* focuses on youthfulness, not virginity.‡ The passage also refers to events hundreds of years before Jesus

---

*   Paul makes this startling claim, that Jews do not understand the Hebrew Bible, only Christians. See 2 Corinthians 3:12–18.

†   See, for instance, James D. Tabor, *The Jesus Dynasty*. New York: Simon & Schuster, 2006, Chapter 1; John Selby Spong, *Born of a Woman: A Bishop Rethinks the Virgin Birth and the Treatment of Women by a Male-Dominated Church*. New York: HarperSanFrancisco, 1992.

‡   The Hebrew word for virgin is "bethulah."

(Isaiah 7:14). It's a sign from God to Ahaz in the 8th century BCE, saying that by the time a young woman bears a child who has reached maturity, the threat from enemy kings will be over. It's saying that the political threat will be over in 10 or 12 years. As a sign to Ahaz about the politics of his era, a reference to some event 800 years or so later is just nonsensical.

Retrospective mining of biblical texts represents backwards methodology. It assumes the conclusion and then works backwards to find possible evidence. It can lead to absurd conclusions as the following considerations illustrate.

For example, if Peter is "the Rock," and Mary the Magdalene is "the Tower," that does not mean that all references to rocks and towers in the Old Testament refer to them.*

Similarly, when Zechariah 9:2 and Psalm 72:8 say of the ruler that he shall rule "from sea to sea," this is not a reference to either the United States as God's kingdom ("from sea to shining sea") or to Canada whose motto is "a mari usque ad mare" ("from sea to sea"). Furthermore, since the ruler is a king, this is not a prophecy that the ideal form of government is a monarchy rather than a republic.

Similarly, Isaiah's condemnation of those who kindle their own fires instead of following the light of the Torah (Isaiah 50:11) is not a warning aimed at Paul centuries later who did attack the Torah. Paul did "kindle his own fire," but this isn't a prophecy about him. It's not specific: it's referring to any Jew (including Paul) who prefers his own set of rules to those of the Torah.

Moreover, the passage in Deuteronomy about not adding or subtracting anything from the commandments of God (Deuteronomy 4:2) is also not a prophecy about Paul, who did away with all Torah obligations and so subtracted all the commandments of God. Nor is it a prophecy condemning the Christian addition of 27 books to the Bible.

These are all absurd conclusions based on faulty historical analysis. Scouring ancient writings without regard for their historical context for hints about the future represents backwards thinking.

More importantly perhaps is this preoccupation results in peripheral trivia (like a supposed origin in Egypt, having a special birth) and ignores the big picture—what the messiah must do in order to qualify as such. That's key. A

---

* Or to Gibraltar or Newfoundland which are also said to be "the Rock."

messiah must be a king. When he arrives, the world will change dramatically. When we see those events taking place, we will know we are in the vicinity of messiah. The massive social and political changes will be evident for all to experience and they will be heralded as "breaking news" in all media.

With this checklist of what a messiah must do, various messianic claimants can now be assessed. We now have a job description and are therefore in a position to evaluate would-be messiahs. It's the kind of thing we would expect the author of a gospel such as Mark's to have provided, some evidence to back up Peter's claim that Jesus is the Messiah. But Jesus kills any discussion of himself as messiah. As already mentioned, the Gospel of Mark says he sternly ordered the disciples not to speak of this.

A Kaleidoscope of Future Hopes

A complex cluster of ideas play into hopes for a brighter future—overcoming a life-threatening crisis, reestablishing an independent Jewish state, living in an era of universal peace, witnessing the return of Jews from the Diaspora, purifying the religion, enjoying eternal life in the world to come, experiencing a restored Paradise, and so on.

These represent jumbled themes. Likely for most people, most of the time, future hopes were a remote concern. People hearing Jesus, John the Baptist, the Teacher of Righteousness, Hillel, or Paul, for instance, would not have entertained clear-cut future scenarios. As the disciples' report indicates, no one thought of Jesus in messianic terms. While most if not all would long for a somewhat better world, the details of such a political turn of events would have been exceptionally hazy. Perhaps a bit more food or a lot less suffering would suffice.

Most people could not read the ancient scrolls, and even if they had heard the ancient Hebrew texts read in synagogues, they would have to have had it explained in Aramaic. Some of these explanations—called *targumim*—still exist. Any ideas they entertained about better times would likely have been gleaned from surrounding culture—"the word on the street"—that is, when they had time to think of such matters in the midst of struggling with life's daily preoccupations. Thinking about a vastly improved lot would likely be far down most people's bucket list and such hopes and dreams would have been dismissed as far-fetched.

So, a better world? The details of such a hope would have been an unstable kaleidoscope of mixed ideas and emotions . . . and considerable skepticism.

The presupposition in all these hopes and dreams is that someone powerful will come along with a solution. A messiah, a superhero, or a savior is above all, a rescuer, a catalyst, or a person who brings about—or helps bring about—a better world.

Looking ahead into the 1st century of the Common Era, messiah talk explodes, first with Jesus and his Kingdom of God message, and then with Paul who introduces the concept of a Christ figure. As we shall see, Paul changes the concept of messiah radically.

Much later the religious search for messiah migrates into the political and secular realms in the 20th century. Powerful political saviors emerge promising to shape society in a positive way. Popular superheroes, often in teams, come to the fore to rescue humanity.

IV

HOW DID THE CONCEPT
OF THE MESSIAH
EXPLODE ONTO
THE WORLD STAGE?

12

JESUS—THE KINGDOM OF GOD

———∞∞∞———

W e now have a job description for a messiah, a set of behaviors against which any possible candidate can be measured. So when the author of the Gospel of Mark has Peter blurting out to Jesus, "You are the Messiah," what exactly did he have in mind?

Maybe Peter's response frightened Jesus, so much so that he quickly changed the topic. According to Mark that's exactly what Jesus immediately did, shifting the talk away from messiah to Son of Man/the human. Given the enormity of the task, Jesus would have had every reason to be afraid. The messiah would oversee a dramatically transformed world and nobody's life would be untouched. Nations will be realigned, power structures demolished, a new world regime would emerge under the leadership of Israel, dispersed Jews would return, and a wonderful peace would ensue. If Peter meant some or all of this, then Jesus would have had a very good reason to be afraid.

Peter stands alone. There is no indication in Mark's gospel that any of the other disciples shared his perspective. Whatever Peter meant, it signified that he saw Jesus as a major political figure on the world stage, perhaps even a rival to the divine-human Roman emperor, maybe even surpassing the prowess of Greek and Roman gods such as Pan. He would have to be, if he were to carry out the duties of a messiah.

Some individuals before Jesus had actively opposed the government of the time with brute force. Judas Maccabaeus in the mid 2nd century BCE had led a resistance coalition against Antiochus Epiphanes and enjoyed military success, liberating Jerusalem in 164 BCE, cleansing the Temple, and instituting the annual festival of Hanukkah. Josephus mentions three Jewish armed insurrections just prior to the time of Jesus. These were led by Judas the Galilean, Athronges, and Simon of Peraea. Athronges in particular set himself up as "king" (Josephus, *Jewish Antiquities*, Book 17, Chapter 10, Sections 5–7). These were individuals who decided not to wait for God to act. They took up arms, attracted followers, and engaged in skirmishes. Nothing came of these movements. These rebellions were quickly put down by the Romans who were very sensitive to military challenges to their imperial might.

Positioning Jesus as a significant player in contemporary world politics was a daring move on Peter's part. People might then come to place him in the category of an insurrectionist, yet another military leader, perhaps another Simon of Peraea or Judas the Galilean. Likely some of Jesus's contemporaries who were Zealots may have hoped he would evolve into this role and spearhead an armed revolt against Rome. Perhaps even one of his own disciples—Simon the Zealot (Mark 3:18)—shared this view.

People today do not often think of Jesus in political terms. This is strange because whatever is meant by "messiah," it is intensely political. "Messiah" began as designating a King-Messiah, a ruler of Israel. Perhaps Peter thought of Jesus as the new David. Or perhaps more than a David. In the *Psalms of Solomon*, the King-Messiah came to denote a powerful political leader capable of presiding over an entire new world order. Did Peter think of Jesus in these grandiose terms? If so, then Peter is way out on a limb.

Recall, too, that the disciples' audience impact reports did not see Jesus in messianic terms. If he were like John the Baptist, he might be a radical teacher with a mission to baptize. If like Elijah, maybe a forerunner to a messiah. If like a prophet, then a teacher providing insight into current issues of the day. But King-Messiah? A new powerful political ruler? That was not one of the categories into which he was placed by the masses.

Jesus's Core Message

We know very little about Jesus prior to the late 20s. The Gospels give two dates for his birth, either before 4 BCE (Matthew) or at the time of the census of Quirinius around 6 (Luke). He was born in Bethlehem, just a few miles south of Jerusalem and was brought up in the small village of Nazareth in the Galilee, just a few miles southeast of the large Gentile city, Sepphoris.

His was an observant Jewish family. Jesus was circumcised on the eighth day in Jerusalem. The family made annual pilgrimages from Nazareth to Jerusalem for Passover—a good three-day trek each way. They would have adhered to the dietary laws, refrained from work on the Sabbath, and observed the annual round of Jewish festivals.

He had four brothers—James or Ya'akov/Jacob, José, Judas, Simon (Mark 6:3)—and two sisters who are not named. He was said to be a cousin of John the Baptist, who was from a priestly family. We do not know the economic status of Jesus's family. His father was a *tekton*, that's a Greek word meaning "carpenter," or, more likely, a "contractor" or "builder." Joseph may have worked in the nearby city of Sepphoris where there was a construction boom. We do not know his social status, but there is no good reason to suppose that his family was poor.

We know nothing of Jesus's upbringing, how he interacted with his siblings, his grandparents, aunts, uncles, and so forth. We have no information concerning his education, how he accessed scrolls containing the writings of the Hebrew Bible, or how he learned the ancient language of Hebrew in addition to the Aramaic which he spoke. We do not know if Nazareth was large enough to support a synagogue or if the congregation there was sufficiently wealthy to afford scrolls.

From the time he was eight days old to his early 30s, we know of only one incident: his visit to Jerusalem for Passover at the age of 12. As a result, there's a significant gap in his résumé of some 30 or more years, except for this one trip.

Perhaps he married. There are no writings that say he was not. Jewish rabbis were expected to marry, in order to comply with the very first commandment in the Bible, "be fertile and increase" (Genesis 1:28. NRSV has "be fruitful and multiply"). If he were married, then Mary the Magdalene would be the most likely candidate as his life partner. She provided funds for his mission. She was with him at his crucifixion. Perhaps most tellingly, she helped prepare his body for burial. That could indicate that she, like his mother, was a close relative—that's not a task a casual follower would be expected to perform.

Moreover, when arguing for celibacy—"To the unmarried and the widows I say that it is well for them to remain unmarried as I am" (1 Corinthians 7:8)—Paul cites his *own* example but not that of Jesus. He never says Jesus was unmarried. That's a curious omission since otherwise, it would have clinched his argument. So, Jesus may have been married. The Gnostic Christians certainly thought so, his marriage being viewed theologically as reconciling the primal fault within the universe, the bifurcation of the human into two disparate parts.

Jesus lands on the stage later in life, when he is in his early 30s. He moves from Nazareth to the larger town of Capernaum. There he forms a group around him, a teacher with students. He speaks to crowds around the northern rim of the Sea of Galilee, carefully avoiding the major city in the area, Tiberias.

We should not imagine Jesus as a loner, but as the leader of a fairly large entourage. His 12 students would have been married, each with perhaps large numbers of children, plus relatives. They might have had four or five children each, maybe more. So we have Jesus, plus 12 disciples, plus their 12 wives, plus at least 48 to 60 children. That equals 73 to 85 individuals. A sizeable group. And that doesn't include extended family members—parents, in-laws, aunts, uncles, brothers, sisters, and so on.

The movement seems to grow. Somewhat later in his mission, Jesus manages to send out 70 or 72 individuals in pairs to various towns and villages Jesus intended to visit. Their message? "The kingdom of God has come near to you" (Luke 10:9). The infrastructure to mobilize such a large number of advance teams testifies to excellent organizational skills and a sizeable entourage. Eusebius records the names of some of these delegates (*Ecclesiastical History*, Book I, Chapter 12).*

Jesus had connections to powerful wealthy women. As mentioned, Mary the Magdalene helped bankroll Jesus's enterprise. We do not know how she became wealthy. Possibly, she was involved in the fishing industry around the Sea of Galilee, salted fish being a valuable commodity and a major export.

In the New Testament writings, Mary is always "Mary *the* Magdalene," not "Mary Magdalene," and not "Mary from Magdala." The phrase "the Magdalene" is a title, meaning "the Tower." She is "Mary, the Tower Lady"—clearly an impressive person and a force to be reckoned with, one of Jesus's preeminent followers if not the most important. As the Gnostic *Gospel of Mary Magdalene* points out, the disciples turn to her for instruction, to teachings Jesus had conveyed to her in private that he had not shared with them. One of the students, Levi, points out jealously to Andrew and Peter that, "surely the savior knows her well. That is why he has loved her more than us."[†]

Jesus also enjoyed political connections with Joanna, the wife of the chief of staff to Herod Antipas. She, too, helped finance his organization, and was very close to the power structures of her day. Herod Antipas was the tetrarch or ruler of the political jurisdictions in which Jesus operated—the Galilee and Peraea. Joanna would have been well aware of Jesus's mission and movements. Was she perhaps a spy for Jesus in Herod's camp, warning him of any threat from the government? Another benefactor was Susanna, as well as other unnamed individuals about whom we know nothing (Luke 8:2, 3).

So Jesus had a powerful female "Board of Directors." How did he attract such well-heeled and well-placed supporters? According to a fanciful mid-2nd century writing, *The Infancy Gospel of James*, Mary, Jesus's mother,

---

* According to Eusebius, these individuals included Barnabas, Sosthenes, a Cephas (not the disciple called Peter also known as Cephas), Matthias, and Thaddeus. We know none of the details of this mission—where they went, how they were received, or Jesus's follow-up visits to the towns he intended to visit. All we are told is that "The seventy (or seventy-two) returned with joy." (Luke 10:17).

† Marvin Meyer, *The Gnostic Gospels of Jesus*, p. 41.

seems to have come from a wealthy family. So perhaps there was money and influence in Jesus's extended family.

So Jesus built a large base of support, a potential political threat to the powerful Jewish elites and Roman overlords. He was a force to be reckoned with.

The Kingdom of God

As already noted, Jesus's central message is this: Kingdom of God is coming soon; take the message seriously and prepare by repenting.

He explains what he meant by the "Kingdom of God" typically in parables, intriguing stories designed to prompt people to think creatively about what God's sovereign rule might mean. He describes how the kingdom would grow, who would be part of it, and what it would look like. These parables will be examined more closely later on.

Jesus contends that the kingdom would come soon . . . a matter of months perhaps, years maybe, but certainly not centuries later. He tells the crowds that they would be living when the kingdom manifests itself:

> Truly I tell you, there are some standing here who will not taste death until they see that the kingdom of God has come with power. (Mark 9:1)

With a maximum lifetime expectancy of 30 to 40 years, this means very soon. At best, within a decade or two at the most.

His prayer—the Lord's Prayer—expresses the number one priority:

> Your kingdom come. Your will be done, on earth as it is in heaven. (Matthew 6:10)

And the kingdom is an earthly one, not a celestial one.

Being alive to witness the advent of God's kingdom, praying for God's will to be done on earth—all these tantalizing details ignited the hope for a better world, perhaps even an ideal world. As we have seen, his audience would have brought many diverse hopes and aspirations to bear upon his words. They were living in desperate times and any straw that held out hope for something better would have been grasped. Jesus's message was one such straw. While likely unclear about details, Jesus's listeners would have understood him to say that God was about to intervene in a decisive way in world events. That message resonated and provided reassurance that, in spite of dreadful times, God was in charge of history. Jesus's message was similar to that of *Psalms of Solomon*—terrible times will usher in a new world order.

Whether they thought that Jesus himself would have a hand in bringing this about is not clear. Was he the new King-Messiah who would restore independence to a beleaguered nation? Was he merely announcing it? Or what? There were many possibilities as Jesus's audiences tried to make sense of what he was promising.

Like the group (perhaps the Essenes) who had formed a community of righteousness down by the shores of the Dead Sea, and like the Pharisees who devoted their lives to teaching people the Torah, Jesus is portrayed as a strict observer of Jewish Law. For Matthew, Jesus and his followers observe the dietary laws and he encouraged strict observance of Torah, even more so than the Pharisees did. More than that, according to Matthew, Jesus then extends the boundaries of the law from overt actions to inner thoughts, saying that the commandment not to commit adultery includes not just the actual act, but also thinking about it (Matthew 5:27–30). That's a much stronger obligation than what either the Pharisees or Essenes required. Jesus's interpretation of the Torah was strict. In addition to outward behavior, Jesus places emphasis on inner attitude as well. As we shall see, this emphasis on the inner self extends to his teachings in the Parables of the Kingdom.

We should not picture Jesus, then, as a rebel against Judaism. He was a thoughtful teacher actively engaged with leaders of his time who wrestled with biblical issues. His message would have appealed to many of the people to whom he spoke—they would want to believe that a better world was in store. More than that, they'd rejoice that they'd have a share in it. That was a very comforting prospect.

But they had to *do* something. It was not sufficient just to hear; they had to repent. Repentance, as we have noted, requires action, a change in conduct, turning around and orienting one's life around the commandments of God.

So the picture of Jesus that emerges from this substratum of the gospels is that he is a Torah-observant Jewish teacher, proclaiming that God is about to enter human history in a powerful and sudden manner. Life will be better . . . soon, very soon.

The Political Jesus

Few people realize just how political Jesus was.

As we have seen, the Jewish messianic expectation included a strong political component. Jesus was not just a healer, not just a preacher with a religious message. What he said stirred up powerful *political* hopes.

Jesus's Kingdom of God message gave his audiences reasons to expect a different world. *That* was the good news or gospel. The gospel was a message about a transformed world, this world. It would be a time when the righteous would be rewarded for their constancy in the face of abject social conditions.

If Jesus thought of himself as a messiah—and that's a big *if*—he would have entertained ideas about being enthroned in Jerusalem as God's King-Messiah. He would then preside over all the tremendous changes that were expected to happen at that point in human history. Receiving delegations from the various nations of the world, he would welcome the returning exiles, and restore true worship of the one God in the Temple. He'd be a King-Messiah under the sovereignty of God, the new David, head of an independent Jewish state.

Jesus may very well have envisaged a role for himself as king. If so, then his disciples would have been trained to be his cabinet as leaders in the new world order. There are hints that this was the role Jesus envisaged for his disciples. According to Matthew, each one of the 12 would be the head of one of the reconstituted 12 tribes (Matthew 19:28). If this passage is correct, then they were training to be leaders in the Kingdom, not missionaries; politicians, not clergy; princes of each of the reconstituted tribes, not itinerant preachers.

Thus what Jesus was promising was a new world government, not a new world religion.

In one of the great ironies of history, when the king-apparent was killed and the Kingdom did not materialize as expected, Jesus's students ended up removed from the center of political power. They were relegated to a religious fringe, on the edge of Judaism, far away from political influence and favor. So if Jesus thought of himself as King-Messiah, he would have died disappointed.

Moreover, as we shall see, the disciples were vastly overshadowed by Paul, a far more powerful individual who had never known Jesus. So influential was he that we know very little about Jesus's family after his death—his mother, brothers, sisters, perhaps his wife—or the travels of his 12 original disciples to whom he provided a three-year mentorship. These individuals were largely erased from history as focus in the New Testament shifted to Paul, his teachings, and his travels.

The Roman authorities understood Jesus's message to be political. Jesus himself was killed by the Romans in the early 30s for political insurgency. He was executed for political reasons, the Romans viewing him as a threat, as "King of the Jews" (Matthew 27:37). It had nothing to do with any religious claim, nothing to do with the beliefs or practices of Judaism. The Romans clearly understood his message in the way Jesus intended: he was proposing regime change.

After his death, Jesus's family and close associates were targets for Roman reprisal. While his brother James remained in Jerusalem, other family members felt they had to leave town. Legend associates Mary, Mother of Jesus, with Ephesus, and Mary the Magdalene with southern France. The disciples were in trouble as Jesus's shadow cabinet. Thomas, for instance, seems to have gone east into what is now present-day Syria, Iraq, and India. Peter winds up in Rome. But we know very little of the original 12 disciples.

Not all escaped being killed. Earlier, Jesus's cousin, John the Baptist, was beheaded by Herod Antipas. Jesus's brother, James, was thrown off Temple Mount in 62 and clubbed to death. Josephus mentions that the high priest delivered James to be stoned (*Jewish Antiquities* Book 20, Chapter 9, Section 1). The charge? James and some others were allegedly breaking religious law (Torah). No specifics were given, and the charge defies logic given his deep commitment to the Torah. James was a Nazirite; that is, one who has taken a vow of strict obedience to the dictates of the Torah. According to Eusebius quoting a 2nd century Christian, Hegesippus (*Ecclesiastical History*, Book 2, Chapter 23), his nickname was "James the Righteous" (*Ya'akov ha-Zadik*). Being a *Zadik* was a title of great honor, signifying dedicated commitment to the principles of the Torah. It was a trumped-up charge and the high priest was quickly dismissed from office, but not before James had been killed.

Eusebius says that James was thrown off a corner of Temple Mount and beaten to death with a club (*Ecclesiastical History*, Book 2, Chapter 23). Eusebius then quotes Hegesippus who gives a longer account. Again James is thrown from the edge of Temple Mount—"cast down the just man, with everyone saying, 'stone the just man.' And then he is beaten with a club." Eusebius doesn't indicate where James was thrown down. The southeast corner of Temple Mount is one likely possibility.

In 70, after capturing Jerusalem and destroying the Second Temple, the soon-to-be-emperor Vespasian ordered a hunt for all the family of David so that no one would be left among the Jews who was of royal stock (Eusebius, *Ecclesiastical History*, Book 3, Chapter 12).

In the mid-80s the emperor Domitian personally interviewed two children of Judas, one of Jesus's brothers. He wanted all the royal descendants of David killed. Finding them simple-minded, he released them, and they lived until the reign of Trajan in the early 2nd century (Eusebius, *Ecclesiastical History*, Book 3, Chapters 19, 20).

Around 106, the emperor Trajan crucified Simeon, another relative of Jesus, either a brother or a nephew, who had succeeded James as leader of Jesus's first followers in Jerusalem. Evidence from Hegesippus says he was 120 years old at the time (Eusebius, *Ecclesiastical History*, Book 3, Chapter 32).

As these accounts show, three major Roman emperors—Vespasian, Domitian, Trajan—went after Jews of the lineage of David related to Jesus. This shows dramatically how serious of a political threat that Jesus and his family represented, and that they were treated as such at the highest levels of the empire. Other would-be messiahs, for example, Judas the Galilean,

Athronges, and Simon of Peraea were all killed by the Romans. John the Baptist had been beheaded. Only with Jesus and his family did the Roman emperors, in the midst of running a vast complex empire, take the time to hunt down his descendants.

Jesus and the Messiah

Our inquiry began with a startling passage in the Gospel of Mark: Peter says he thinks Jesus is "the Messiah" (*Christos*). We asked, what did Peter mean by this title? Especially since the Gospel of Mark—composed some 40 or more years after the event in question—doesn't tell us. Nor does Peter, the other disciples, nor Jesus himself. That was the problem with which we began as we traced the evolution of the messianic expectation in biblical and related texts.

If Peter meant that Jesus was messiah in the sense of *mashiach* in the *Psalms of Solomon*, then he was mistaken. When measured against the checklist for being a messiah, Jesus did not fit the bill. He did not become King-Messiah in Jerusalem ruling over an independent people. He did not defeat the Romans. He did not put the nations of the world in their place. Jews from the Diaspora did not return. People did not become more righteous. Universal peace did not break out. The Jewish people did not experience better times. He did not fulfill the criteria for being messiah. So Jesus was not *mashiach*, even if Peter hoped he would be.

Moreover, the author of the Gospel of Mark would have known that Peter was mistaken if that is what he meant by "messiah."

The composer of the Gospel of Mark probably wanted us to read Peter's insight as a statement that Jesus was *Christos*, along the lines of Paul's concept of the Christ. That idea will be explored in the next chapter. The idea of Jesus as a cosmic Christ was a concept very much in vogue around the year 70 when the author of the Gospel of Mark was writing. But saying that Jesus was the messiah in the sense of a Christ-figure was not something that the historical Peter could have said to the historical Jesus. After all, Paul's concept of the Christ had not yet been developed when Peter was traveling to Caesarea Philippi with Jesus.

However dramatic, Peter's breakthrough insight never occurred. The whole scenario is part and parcel of Mark's "created Jesus." It was something he retrojected back into the time of Jesus.* The Gospel of Mark is not capturing history. He is creating myth and attributing to Jesus an identity that could not have arisen during his life.

So, however important his teachings may be, and however tragic his death, Jesus is not a messiah. He did not fulfill the tasks a *mashiach* must perform. The world still awaits the Jewish messiah.

Sometimes people ask, why did the Jewish people of his time not recognize Jesus as messiah? That's the wrong question. The question should be, Why would anyone at that time think of him in such terms? What evidence could they cite in favor of the claim that he was messiah?

Did Jesus even claim to be a messiah? Only at one place in the Gospel of Mark does Jesus say that he's messiah. It's at his trial, before the high priest. As we have noted, there are problems with the trial narratives. We do not know who might have been present from Jesus's entourage during the interrogation . . . they had all fled, in fear for their lives. As a result we do not know who's providing the information regarding the conduct of the trial, let alone how accurate their recollections were.†

If Jesus were the messiah, then the high priest would not have had to ask the question. The truth would have been self-evident. There would be massive geopolitical changes taking place: Romans packing up and leaving, Jews swarming in from the Diaspora, the Temple getting ready for a King-Messiah coronation ceremony, people returning to serious Torah observance and study, and so forth. So if Jesus were the *mashiach*, the world would have been in the midst of dramatic changes and the high priest would not have had to ask the question.

Jesus being dragged before religious authorities is likely part of Mark's "created Jesus." Putting Jesus in front of the high priest reduces Roman

---

* The gospels were written after Paul's theology had taken hold and the movement had become predominantly Gentile. In other words, the gospels were written after Paul's transformation of the message away from the Kingdom of God towards theological beliefs about Jesus as a divine-human atonement for sin.

† See Gary Greenberg, *The Judas Brief: Who Really Killed Jesus?* New York: Bloomsbury Academic, 2007.

involvement although that gospel, unlike later ones, does place blame on the political authorities for Jesus's execution. There is nothing in Jesus's teachings that would run afoul of biblical law, so much so that he'd merit capital punishment.

So, no, Jesus did not claim to be the messiah. That's something his later followers promoted, interpreting him not as *mashiach*, but as *Christos*. Interestingly, many who knew him best during his mission did not think of him as messiah. The crowds around the Sea of Galilee did not place him in the messiah category. The Gospel of Mark mentions that his townspeople in Nazareth "took offense" at him speaking in the synagogue (Mark 6:2, 3). So the people amongst whom he grew up did not think of him in messianic terms. And the Gospel of Matthew portrays Jesus cursing the inhabitants of Chorazin, Bethsaida, and Capernaum for not responding to his message and actions in the way he thought they should; that is, by repenting (Matthew 11:20–23). These were all towns in which Jesus had spoken extensively, and Capernaum was his home base. Clearly those who knew him best in the late 20s and early 30s did not think of him in messianic terms.

Did Jesus perhaps secretly think of himself as a possible *mashiach*? That we can never know, but it's not likely. Certainly he did not think of himself that way in the Gospel of Mark, his focus being on the Kingdom of God and how to prepare for it. He ordered his disciples not to engage in messiah talk. That just wasn't his focus.

When we do pay attention to *his* focus, however, we notice something quite startling: Jesus never mentions hoping for messiah, being a messiah, or even entertaining the smallest suggestion he could be one. There's no petition in the Lord's Prayer, for instance, asking God to send the messiah. The absence of messiah talk in the Gospel of Mark give us an important clue how he thought about messianic thinking. He was opposed to it . . . at least as conventionally understood. And, as we shall see, he proposed a radical alternative.

∽

Meanwhile, where's the Kingdom Jesus promised was coming soon? What should be made of his mission? Was it just a failure?

13

THE PROBLEM—
NO KINGDOM

That better world—the one Jesus promised was coming soon, within the lifetime of his audience—did not materialize. He died, disappointed. As Matthew writes:

> Jesus cried with a loud voice, "Eli, Eli, lema sabachthani?" that is, "My God, my God, why have you forsaken me?" (Matthew 27:46).

In other words, with only a few minutes of life left, Jesus cries out to God to make good on what he had promised, the Kingdom of God. But it did not happen.

So the Kingdom of God did not appear as Jesus thought it would.

The failure of the Kingdom of God to materialize on earth sparked a major crisis within the various groups that emerged from Jesus's teachings. "Why the delay?" thoughtful people asked. Why had Jesus not returned quickly to do what was required of a messiah, especially after what Christians understood to be his resurrection?

The question would have been most acute in the mid 60s, some 30 or more years after Jesus's death. At that time Jesus's family members, students, and initial followers were either dead or close to death. They had been promised the Kingdom within their lifetimes. That hope was rapidly fading. Within three decades of Jesus's death, from 66 to 70, Israel was convulsed by a devastating war with Rome with massive casualties in the Galilee and over a million in Jerusalem. No one was buying a "better times ahead" message . . . at least not for Jews.

Had Jesus's mission failed? Some followers likely did call it quits, judging him to be yet another in a series of failed messianic hopefuls—Judas the Galilean, Athronges, and Simon of Peraea, amongst others. And when the promised Kingdom of God did not appear on earth in a timely fashion, replacing Roman rule and oppression, probably many might have recalled how to discern true from false prophets: "If the prophet speaks in the name of the Lord and the oracle does not come true, that oracle was not spoken by the Lord (*YHVH*)" (Deuteronomy 18: 22). Some might have rejected him on these grounds, a false prophet whose message did not come true.

There were, however, other strategies for coping with seeming failure.

Strategy #1: Wait

One group was led by Jesus's brother, James (Ya'akov, Jacob). He remained in Jerusalem, along with some of Jesus's students. He was Jewish, as were the members of his group. Torah-observant, their approach was to adopt a low profile: wait for the Kingdom to appear, just as Jesus promised it would.

According to Christian belief, Jesus was resurrected. But resurrection did not change their attitude towards a coming Kingdom of God. According to a late 1st century writing, written some 60 or 70 years after the event in question, the disciples asked the figure they took to be the resurrected Jesus: "Lord, is this the time when you will restore the kingdom to Israel?" (Acts 1:6). They clearly still expected great events to take place and they did not tie in his resurrection to the promised Kingdom. They expected a transformed world. Jesus avoided the question saying that it was not for them to know the timetable.

Being resurrected and being a messiah are not the same. A resurrection has to do with what happens after death. A messiah transforms the social conditions of this life.

James and his entourage would not have stood out from fellow Jews. The Essenes would have shared his general messianic outlook, as undoubtedly did some Pharisees and many Zealots. Who James identified as the eventual messiah is the one distinguishing mark of this group. Very likely James looked forward to the day when his brother would be the new King-Messiah. Then the world would be altered, and he and the disciples would form the political leadership of this new world order. Like other Jews of his time, he would have kept kosher, rested on the Sabbath, enjoyed the festivals, visited the Temple, and practiced generosity in dealing with other people.

The Sabbath liturgy mentioned in *The Didache* (late 1st century) may reflect the communal meal of James's group.* Following Jewish tradition, the first blessing is over the wine, followed by the blessing over the bread. In this evening meal, there is no equation of bread with body or wine with blood. Paul's version (1 Corinthians 11:23–26) reverses the order of the blessings, not following Jewish tradition. Moreover he equates drinking wine with the consumption of blood, an act expressly forbidden in Torah (Leviticus 13:10–12). Both these factors are strong indications that Paul's decoding—wine with blood, bread with body—did not originate with Jesus.

James was killed in 62, before any of the gospels were written. So his scripture was the Hebrew Bible/Old Testament. Like Jesus, we know nothing of James's upbringing, education, linguistic skills, or occupation. He was followed as "bishop" in Jerusalem by ten Jewish leaders up until the time of the Bar Kokhba revolt against Rome, from 132–136. Their names have been preserved by Eusebius (*Ecclesiastical History*, Book 4, Chapter 5): after James, there were Simeon, Justus, Zaccheus, Tobias, Benjamin, John, Matthew, Philip, Seneca, Justus Levi, Ephres, Joseph, Judas. Eusebius notes, "At that time the whole church under them [in Jerusalem] consisted of faithful Hebrews . . ." In other words, all these leaders were Jewish.

---

* See *The Didache* in Bart D. Ehrman, *Lost Scriptures*, p. 215.

Nothing is known about these individuals who faced tremendous challenges: a changing Judaism after the destruction of the Temple in 70 on the one hand and a Gentile movement focused on the Christ led by the followers of Paul on the other.

Strategy #2: Reinterpret "Kingdom of God"

Perhaps, though, there were alternatives to thinking of the messianic era as an earthly Paradise restored. There are hints within the gospels that some followers of Jesus thought of the Kingdom as something interior, some deeply personal state. Perhaps the promised Kingdom could be accessed in the here and now, not at some future time. At one point, Jesus was said to have proclaimed: "the kingdom of God is among [or within] you" (Luke 17:21).

Building on this perspective, some wondered if the kingdom might be something spiritual. That, of course, would represent a departure from the Jewish idea of God's eventual sovereign rule on earth. When that terrestrial era had not arrived it was only natural to contemplate alternatives. Perhaps what Jesus meant by "the Kingdom of God" had to do with some personal transformation, a change of orientation so as to create an enhanced relationship with God and fellow human beings.

That thought provided the point of departure for Gnostic Christians. For these followers of Jesus, the Kingdom was discoverable and attainable through a process they termed *gnosis*. *Gnosis* represents an interior way of knowing and coming to consciousness of oneself as a spiritual being having an earthly experience, connected to God and other people. For them salvation had nothing to do with a sacrificial atonement for sin. Rather salvation concerned coming to know through *gnosis* (spiritual insight) who they really were, where they had come from, and where they were going.

Discovering through the process of *gnosis* their true origin, identity, and destiny—these quests constituted the focus of these Gnostic Christians:

> The savior said [to Thomas] . . . "Since it is said that you are
> my twin and true friend, examine yourself and understand who

you are, how you exist, and how you will come to be." (*The Book of Thomas*)*

Gnostic writings such as the *Gospel of Thomas*, *Gospel of Mary Magdalene*, and the *Gospel of Philip* contain no birth, trial, or resurrection accounts. They do not provide biographies. There are no attempts to provide a narrative or a chronological account of Jesus's movements from one place to another. For the most part they simply list sayings in a seemingly random order. There are also various "secret books" attributed to John and James, a *Dialogue of the Savior* as well as a *Treatise on the Resurrection*.

Many of these writings are attributed to Jesus's close associates and, while likely not written by them, perhaps these attributions are a hint that there was another early movement in early Christianity besides the two we know most about. Perhaps alongside James's Torah-observant community and Paul's Gentile group there was another non-Jewish movement, one that came into prominence in the 2nd century as Gnostic Christianity. Whatever its 1st century origins, this widespread and influential movement was gradually sidelined by another group which achieved dominance in the 4th century. Growing out of the teachings of Paul, this latter group became the faction of Christianity favored by emperors Constantine and Theodosius. That group—"Pauline Christianity"—predominated. For one thing, it fashioned the Nicene Creed in 325. In so doing it excluded Gnostic Christian beliefs. For another, recall that in 367, one of its major archbishops, Athanasius of Alexandria, enumerated the books that would from henceforth constitute the "New Testament." All other writings were excluded including all the writings of Gnostic Christianity. So the New Testament that we have today reflects a 4th century decision. Prior to that time, different Christian communities had different sets of scripture. In 380, Emperor Theodosius declared this Pauline form of early Christianity to be the official religion of the Roman Empire.

Whether in its Eastern Orthodox, Roman Catholic, Anglican, Protestant, or Evangelical form, the shape of the Christian Church today—its creed, Bible, infrastructure—dates from decisions taken in the 4th century.

---

* Marvin Meyer, *The Gnostic Gospels of Jesus*, p. 209.

Strategy #3: Change Concept of "Messiah"

Beside waiting for an earthly kingdom to manifest itself or reinterpreting the concept of the Kingdom of God as spiritual, a third strategy emerged: change the concept of what a messiah should be. That was Paul's genius and in so doing he forged a concept of messiah that a non-Jew could understand . . . and, importantly for Paul, one with whom a non-Jew could identify.

Who was Paul? How did he carry out this groundbreaking conceptual transformation, one that resulted in a highly successful world religion?

14
PAUL AND THE MESSIAH AS CHRIST

—∞∞—

Paul—Mystery Man

One of the most influential Jews who ever lived was Paul. This is ironic because of all the Jews who ever lived, Paul denied the validity of Torah and considered Jesus to be a divine-human. These two moves propelled Paul and his followers out of the Jewish orbit into a quite different realm.

The Torah—"Law," "Teaching," or "Instruction"—is not a minor detail. Just a reminder that it is, after all, the flipside of the Covenant between the people of Israel and God. Observing the Torah is the responsibility of each and every Jew as part of the covenantal agreement. As we have noted, the Torah is far more than a collection of laws: it represents an all-embracing lifestyle, a pattern for living, a rhythm to life as part of something much larger, a relationship with God, the creator of the universe and of humanity. Attitudes and actions are involved, the result of choices and values. It provides assurances that divine forgiveness awaits those who sincerely try to follow the path but who stray and repent.

The righteous guide their life along the path of the Torah. Psalm 1, for instance, contrasts two ways: the wicked *versus* the righteous:

> Happy is the man who has not followed the counsel of the wicked,
> . . .
> Rather, the teaching (*Torah*) of the Lord is his delight, and he studies that teaching day and night.
> . . .
> For the Lord cherishes the way of the righteous, but the way of the wicked is doomed. (Psalm 1:1, 2, 6)

Similarly the *Psalms of Solomon* say that the righteous are those whose lives are Torah-centered, even in the midst of extreme adversity:

> The Lord is faithful to those who truly love him,
> to those who endure his discipline,
> To those who live in the righteousness of his commandments,
> in the Law, which he has commanded for our life,
> The Lord's devout shall live by it forever;
> the Lord's paradise, the trees of life, are his devout ones.
> Their planting is firmly rooted forever. (*Psalms of Solomon* 14:1–4)

The righteous are described as "trees of life." Psalm 1 in the Bible compares the righteous to trees planted beside streams of water (Psalm 1:3). They flourish because of their roots. The Dead Sea Scroll Community saw itself as an "everlasting plantation" (*Community Rule*, VIII).* This "plantation" or colony had gone out into the wilderness of Judea, following the injunction of Isaiah (Isaiah 40:3)—"Prepare in the wilderness the way . . ." This passage they interpreted as follows:

> This [way] is the study of the Law which He commanded
> by the hand of Moses, that they may do according to all that

---

* All references to *Community Rule* are from Geza Vermes, *The Complete Dead Sea Scrolls in English.*

has been revealed from age to age, and as the Prophets have revealed by His Holy Spirit. (*Community Rule*, VIII)

The righteous, then, are those who let the teachings of Torah guide their life and who, as a result, function as strong role models for the movement. Community is very important for righteous living. Members of the Dead Sea Scroll group recognized that observance of the Torah requires more than individuals trying to follow this path on their own. It is not a do-it-yourself philosophy but rather it requires a collective of right-acting individuals. That observant community held out a remarkable future for those who walk in the path of righteousness:

it shall be healing, great peace in a long life, and fruitfulness, together with every everlasting blessing and eternal joy in life without end, a crown of glory and a garment of majesty in unending light. (*Community Rule*, IV)

Torah observance, righteousness, and eternal life are all intricately interconnected. Much is at stake.

So, while some Jews might ignore the teachings of Torah, and others might debate the meaning of specific injunctions, no Jew set aside the Torah and the Covenant with God. This includes Jesus, his family members, his disciples, Mary the Magdalene and the Jewish people around the Sea of Galilee and in Jerusalem to whom he spoke. They were all Jews and they all followed the Torah and the Covenant with God explicitly.

And no Jew would consider the Jewish human Jesus to be a divine-human.

Except Paul.

In the early to mid-50s, Paul rails against following the Jewish lifestyle of the Torah in his highly influential Letter to the Galatians. It's one of the most radical documents ever written, standing in utter contrast to the writings of the Hebrew Bible. Only six chapters long, it sweeps away the first five books of the Bible and all the prophets.

Paul's views depart company with the Torah focus of other Jewish leaders of his era. Notably it contrasts with such groups as James's community in

Jerusalem; John the Baptist's group that continued his teachings after his death; the Dead Sea Scroll Community with its Teacher of Righteousness; the teachings of the Jewish sages Hillel and Shammai and their disciples; as well as the teachings of Pharisees in towns and villages throughout Israel. All these leaders and groups were concerned with encouraging and maintaining a Jewish lifestyle within a hostile world. Paul's Galatians stands out as a remarkable writing . . . and it's an outlier. It purports to knock down the boundaries between Jews and non-Jews.

Paul's religion is oriented around Jesus conceived of as a Christ, a phrase he shortens to "Jesus Christ" or "Christ Jesus."

What does he mean by that, especially when the Greek word *Christos* translates the Hebrew word *mashiach*? Are the two concepts the same?

We know of Paul from several sources. First and foremost are his letters, 13 of which are included in the New Testament. Scholars today judge seven of these letters as genuinely from Paul: 1 Thessalonians, 1 and 2 Corinthians, Philippians, Galatians, Philemon, and Romans.[*]

Other letters included in the New Testament are attributed to Paul. Scholarly opinion is divided as to their authenticity. These include Ephesians, Colossians, 2 Thessalonians, 1 and 2 Timothy, and Titus.

There is also a heavily romanticized version of Paul in the late 1st century writing, the Book of Acts. This account, written decades after Paul's death, enhances his experience on the road to Damascus and traces his travels throughout the Mediterranean. The Book of Acts is one book we can factcheck. We can compare what Acts says about Paul with what Paul says about himself in his letters. Acts's Paul is not Paul's Paul.[†]

There is much we do not know of Paul. He was likely born in the first decade of the Common Era and died in the mid-60s. He was Jewish and also a Roman citizen. That sounds straightforward. But in what sense was he "Jewish"? He was likely ethnically, but not religiously, Jewish. We never see him preparing for the Sabbath, observing the dietary laws, going up to Jerusalem for Passover, or interpreting the Torah. He engaged in none of the

---

[*]   See Bart D. Ehrman, *The New Testament: A Historical Introduction to the early Christian writings*, p. 336.

[†]   See Barrie Wilson, *How Jesus Became Christian*, Chapter 12.

religious practices of Jesus and his students. Judaism seems to have been a religion he left behind in favor of something else. What was his new religion?

How did his Jewish family acquire Roman citizenship? What huge favor had they done for the Romans to grant them this exceptionally rare honor? Were they spies, snitches, or military heroes? Had they contributed vast sums of money to Roman coffers?

What, moreover, was the nature of Paul's upbringing in a Jewish family in the Diaspora, in Tarsus, a city that is today in southeastern Turkey? Likely they were a highly assimilated family in order to be accorded Roman citizenship. Who were his parents? What did his father do? Did he have siblings? An extended family? How long had the family been in Tarsus? What were the key formative influences on his life? What did he make of the Greco-Roman savior deities worshipped in Tarsus?

Did he attend synagogue? What kind of education did he have? In particular, how did he come to know the scriptures of Judaism? Could he read the writings of the Hebrew Bible—in other words, did he know Hebrew? Or, more likely, did he come to know the Hebrew Bible through its Greek translation, the Septuagint? The mythologized Paul presented in the Book of Acts contends that he studied under Rabbi Gamaliel in Jerusalem (Acts 22:3), but scholars dispute this.*

Paul's Religion

Different Focus

One of the key questions concerns Paul's relationship to Jesus and to James's group in Jerusalem. The problem is that Paul's message is not what Jesus taught.†

---

* See, for instance, Hyam Maccoby, *The Mythmaker: Paul and the Invention of Christianity.* San Francisco: Harper & Row, 1986, Chapter 6 *"Was Paul a Pharisee?"* and Chapter 7 *"Alleged Rabbinical Style in Paul's Epistles."*

† For the differences between Paul's message and that of Jesus, see Hyam Maccoby, *The Mythmaker: Paul and the Invention of Christianity*; Robert W. North, *"The Messiah's Unrealized Revolution*, Chapter 3 *"Paul's View of the Human Condition"* and Chapter 5 *"Paul's Goals;"* and Barrie Wilson, *Paul vs James*, New York: CreateSpace, 2018.

As we have seen, Jesus's core message was that the Kingdom of God was coming soon, within the lifetime of his audience. As we know—and as those living in the 40s, 50s, and 60s bitterly realized—this Kingdom of God had not come about as Jesus said it would. That in itself presented huge problems. What happens to people who die before this wonderful new world appeared? Were they doomed never to participate in it? Even more radically, did the delay perhaps signify failure? Had Jesus made a mistake? Were they deluding themselves hoping for something that would never come to pass?

In the midst of this angst, Paul's teachings were likely greeted as a breath of fresh air. His central message is this: if we can participate in Christ's suffering and death through faith, then we, too, can have the hope of being raised from the dead, just as he was.

Realizing that the Kingdom had not materialized as Jesus had promised, Paul shifts attention *away from* Jesus's teachings *to* Jesus's death and resurrection. In other words, Paul changes the focus—from the teachings *of* Jesus to teachings *about* Jesus. No longer is the gospel good news about a coming Kingdom; it becomes good news about the person of Jesus. That represents a major makeover of Jesus.

Gone is the idea of a King-Messiah ruling in Jerusalem along with the world-transforming scenario favored by Jewish writers. For Paul, Jesus's death was not just an untimely execution. Rather it represented a sacrificial atoning death, an act that rescued humanity from the power of death, paving the way for eternal life.

It was a powerful claim and it resonated with the Gentile audiences to whom he preached.

Different Origin

Paul claimed to have had a life-changing experience on the road to Damascus sometime in the late 30s. He mentioned this in his Letter to the Galatians composed in the mid-1st century. The Book of Acts repeated the account three times, 30 or 40 years after Paul wrote Galatians (Acts 9:1–22; 22:4–16; 26:9–18).

According to Acts, Paul had been chosen by the high priest in Jerusalem to arrest messianic Jews not in Jerusalem—his territory—but farther afield, outside his jurisdiction in Damascus. Who was Paul that he merited such a commission? How was he known to the high priest? What were his connections to this powerful religious and political figure in the Jewish establishment?

Moreover, Paul's mandate seems suspect—to bring men, women, and children back in chains to Jerusalem. Why, what was their offense? Holding messianic beliefs was not a crime. Furthermore, if the high priest wished to round up messianic Jews, there were many more right on his doorstep, right in Jerusalem, not only the first followers of Jesus, but also Essenes, some Pharisees, and Zealots. Why Damascus?

Paul went with a gang of bounty hunters to Damascus—he seems to have had companions. Where did these thugs go to after Paul had a change of heart? Did they just turn around and go home? Why did they not arrest Paul? When Paul returned to Jerusalem some time later on, why was he not arrested by the high priest and imprisoned for failure to carry out his assignment?

The road to Damascus incident raises many more questions than it solves. At any rate, after a hiatus of more than a decade, Paul set off on various journeys. He founded various congregations devoted to worshipping the Christ in the 40s, 50s, and early 60s in what is today's Turkey, Cyprus, and Greece. He died in Rome in the mid 60s where, according to ancient tradition, both he and Peter were killed.

Thus the origin of Paul's mission differs from that of Jesus's students. Paul did not have the advantage of Jesus's three-year mentoring process in the Galilee. A vision sufficed. In fact, if all it took was a dramatic experience to communicate what he wished to convey, why hadn't Jesus curtailed the three-year tutoring process in favor of a vision much earlier?

Different Teachings

Paul rarely references Jesus's teachings. There are no references to Jesus's parables of the Kingdom of God. No mention of the Lord's Prayer. No reference to any of the teachings found in the Sermon on the Mount—no emphasis on keeping Jewish Law even more strictly than the Pharisees. There is none of that. It is as if what Jesus said did not matter.

According to Mark and Matthew, Jesus had said there were two foundational commandments, love of God and love of humanity (Mark 12:28–34; Matthew 22:35–40). Paul simply says,

> For the whole law is summed up in a single commandment, "You shall love your neighbor as yourself." (Galatians 5:14).

Had he forgotten what Jesus was alleged to have said? Why no reference to Jesus here?[*]

Paul's teachings, as we shall see, went off in a different direction from those of Jesus, no longer focusing on the coming Kingdom of God and the need for repentance. The Preface to his Letter to the Galatians sets forth his thesis:

> Grace to you and peace from God our Father and the Lord Jesus Christ, who gave himself for our sins to set us free from the present evil age, according to the will of our God and Father . . . (Galatians 1:3, 4)

Paul's teaching centers on Jesus as a sacrificial atonement, the effect of which is to set us free from sin and its consequence (death), thereby making possible eternal life.

So the person of Christ takes center stage, not the Kingdom. Christ replaces the Kingdom message.

Different Religious Orientation

The issue Paul addresses in his Letter to the Galatians has to do with whether Gentile converts need to observe Jewish practices; that is, whether they have to follow the biblical laws as expressed in the Torah. Some individuals—we don't know who they were—had come into Galatia in what is now midcentral Turkey and had confused Paul's new converts. They

---

[*] Or possibly, writing later than Paul, why did the Gospels of Mark and Matthew get it wrong?

had maintained that Gentiles needed to be circumcised, for instance, an extremely onerous requirement for adult males in the 1st (or any) century.

The obvious answer is that no, they don't need to keep Torah—that's a specifically Jewish obligation. Non-Jews are required only to follow the seven Noahide Laws incumbent on all humanity: worshipping one God, not blaspheming, not murdering, not stealing, refraining from sexual immorality, establishing courts of justice, and not eating a limb torn from a living animal, thereby avoiding the consumption of blood. That's what James the brother of Jesus had ruled in the presence of Paul about Gentile obligations. This summit meeting had occurred just a few years before Paul wrote his Letter to the Galatians (Acts 15:19, 20). Had Paul forgotten this high-level discussion?

At any rate, a brief answer from Paul should have set things straight—Gentiles are only required to keep the Noahide Laws. That observation should have quickly cleared up any misunderstanding. It's not as if these Gentiles were converting to Judaism; they weren't. The letter should only have been, at worst, one chapter long.

That is not what Paul does, however. In his Letter to the Galatians, he launches into an angry tirade and his rage bristles through even after 2,000 years. He denounces the Torah, without any qualification. He's not saying that non-Jews (Gentiles) need not observe the commandments of the Torah—that is a position everyone would agree with. The obligations of Torah are only for Jews. He's making a much stronger claim: no one needs to now, not even Jews.

For Paul, the time of Torah has ended now that Christ Jesus has come. Paul advances a theology of history. He envisages three eras: pre-Torah (Abraham to Moses); Torah (Moses to Christ); and post-Torah (Christ onwards). Paul's Letter to the Galatians has played a major role in western thought: from this time forward, Christianity set aside Torah obligations.

Paul puts it this way:

> a person is justified not by the works of the law but through faith in Jesus Christ. (Galatians 2:16)

By "justified," Paul means a righteous human being qualified to stand before God. He advances several arguments concerning the need to set "the law"—that is, Jewish Law or Torah—aside. They are presented rather quickly, perhaps too quickly, as there are many loose ends in what he writes.* He appeals to the example of Abraham: "And he believed the Lord (*YHVH*); and the Lord reckoned it to him as righteousness" (Genesis 15:6 NRSV translation). This establishes the point, Paul says, that "those who believe are the descendants of Abraham" (Galatians 3:7).

This represents selective use of scripture. Paul neglects to mention that Abraham also had his household circumcised as "an everlasting covenant" (Genesis 17:1–14). Likely the people to whom Paul was writing would not have known this, not being Jewish and likely not having had the benefit of lectures on the Old Testament.

Another consideration ensues. The covenant between God and Abraham was made to him and his offspring. The true "offspring" of Abraham, Paul contends, *is* one person, namely Christ (Galatians 3:16). Note here that Paul takes the collective noun "offspring" as singular, referring to one individual, not to a nation or a large number of people. Paul's interpretation is very different from that of Second Isaiah who wrote:

> Look back to Abraham your father
> And to Sarah who brought you forth.
> For he was only one when I called him,
> But I blessed him and made him many. (Isaiah 51:2)

Clearly here the offspring of Abraham and Sarah are "many." Paul, however, forces a collective into a singular noun, claiming that the real offspring of Abraham is Christ. Christ is the real beneficiary to the contract. Presumably this extends to all those who are part of Christ. So the inheritance shifts from Jews to followers of Christ. Jewish claims about being heirs to God's Covenant or agreement with Abraham (Genesis 12:1–3) are set aside. They've been written out of the will.

Moving on quickly Paul contends that the era of the Law was temporary. It was given, he says, as a

---

* These arguments are examined in detail in Barrie Wilson, *How Jesus Became Christian*, Chapter 9, *"The Trouble with Paul."*

... disciplinarian until Christ came ... But now that faith has come we are no longer subject to a disciplinarian, for in Christ Jesus you are all children of God through faith. (Galatians 3:25, 26)

The Torah, then, was only operational for one stage in human history—like a tutor or nanny teaching children right from wrong. No longer is that necessary. Faith replaces the Torah for grown-ups.

The idea that the Torah is temporary contradicts many passages in the Old Testament. It would come as news to the song composer of Psalm 103, for instance. That remarkable piece of poetry celebrates a loving and merciful God who forgives, heals, and who understands human frailty. The psalmist proclaims, "He (*YHVH*) made known His ways to Moses, His deeds to the children of Israel" (Psalm 103:7). Have "his ways" changed? And, if so, on whose authority?

In Zechariah, when "the Lord (*YHVH*) shall be king over all the earth" (Zechariah 14:9), people from the nations of the world will go up to Jerusalem to worship God and to celebrate the festival of Succoth (Zechariah 14:16–19). The prophet Malachi declares that when God will separate the righteous from the wicked, people should remember "the Teaching (*Torah*) of My servant Moses" (Malachi 4:22).

Recall, too, that for the biblical Psalms as well as the *Psalms of Solomon*, the righteous are those who observe the Torah (for example, Psalm 1; Psalm 119; *Psalms of Solomon* 14). As the author of the *Psalms of Solomon* sees it, the King-Messiah, himself righteous (that is, Torah-observant) will rule over "a holy people whom he will lead in righteousness" (*Psalms of Solomon* 17:16, 29, 32).

Jewish and biblical tradition does not concur with Paul that the laws of Torah are temporary. This is something new, something that Paul made up. The implications are that God has now changed his mind and that everything said by way of an agreement or Covenant in the Hebrew Scriptures is now null and void. Paul tears up the agreement between God and the Jewish people *unilaterally*—there's no consent given by the two parties to the contract. That's hardly a strong legal position. It's tantamount to a third party coming along and destroying a person's will.

Again, likely those first recipients of Paul's letter would not have had the background to assess the merits of his argument. Nor, perhaps, would they have cared, being now the will's beneficiaries.

Quickly Paul goes on to say, there are now no ethnic or religious differences—"there is no longer Jew or Greek"* adding that "if you belong to Christ, then you are Abraham's offspring, heirs according to the promise" (Galatians 3:29). So, as Paul sees it, there is now a new humanity, no ethnic differences, and God's promise of a great nation to Abraham's has come to pass . . . not through the Jewish people but through those who "belong to Christ."

It should be clear from these remarks that they are general in nature and not qualified. Again, it is important to note that he is not saying that non-Jews have no need to observe the Torah. That everyone agrees on. Only Jews need to observe the Torah; the rest of humanity should observe the Noahide Laws. Paul's arguments are universal in scope. He's saying no one should now follow the path of Torah.

To reinforce his point, Paul refers to obedience to Torah as slavery (Galatians 5:1) and contends that anyone who wants to be justified by the law has "fallen away from grace" (Galatians 5:4), ignoring Torah teaching that forgiveness is always available to those who repent. In this connection see, for instance, the "Thirteen Attributes of God" in Exodus in which God is described as "forgiving iniquity, transgression, and sin" (Exodus 34:7), as well as Moses's subsequent prayer for forgiveness (Exodus 34:9). Repentance was also central to the proclamation of both John the Baptist and Jesus who were both Torah-observant.

He concludes that he wishes that those who perform circumcisions would let the knife slip and castrate themselves (Galatians 5:12). Tough talk. Paul is very angry.

Consider the implications of Paul's Letter to the Galatians.

Doing away with Jewish Law or the Torah sweeps away the Ten Commandments, the great festivals of Judaism (Rosh Hashanah, Passover, Succoth, Shavuot, Hanukkah), the Sabbath, the dietary laws, and ethics. It does away with the Books of the Torah and the teachings of the Prophets, along with various other writings that focus on the need to observe the

---

* He means "Gentile."

teachings of Torah fully and whole-heartedly as part of the Covenant with God. It gets rid of rich and valued traditions, foundational ethical injunctions, and principles of worship of the one God in one fell swoop. It attacks the beliefs and practices of such Jews as Jesus, his mother, his family members, the disciples, and their families, Mary the Magdalene, and the crowds that Jesus preached to.

Moreover, it is nothing less than an assault on Judaism. With no Torah, there is no Jewish Covenant with God, no Judaism, no point in being Jewish. It also reduces, if not eliminates, the relevance of the Old Testament to Paul's religion.

Galatians is indeed a radical document.

As soon as Paul does away with the Torah, he recognizes a problem. What now is his ethical frame of reference? Does anything "go" with this newfound faith freedom? Are ethics to be decided by social mores, personal whims, or the mood of the times? His answer is brief: "Live by the Spirit" the fruit of which would be "love, joy, peace, patience, kindness, generosity, faithfulness, gentleness and self-control" (Galatians 5:16, 22, 23). These are fine attitudes, but note that with the Torah gone, there is no overarching ethical framework: no Ten Commandments; no commandments against murder, theft, envying other people's possessions; no injunction to honor parents, worship one God, and observe the Sabbath; no *Shema*, the injunction that God is one; and so on.

It is interesting to contrast Paul's ethical position with the religious orientation of the Dead Sea Scroll Community. While encouraging strict Torah-observance as interpreted by their Teacher of Righteousness, this group identified two spirits operating within each person's personality. They are described as a spirit of truth or life, and one of injustice or darkness. A human being embodies these two spirits or forces. The challenge before each human being is how to conduct life so as to favor the inherent force of life over the force of death. People differ in terms of how they balance these two inclinations within their personalities. For members of the Dead Sea Scroll group, community plays a vital role in helping individuals stick to the right path guided by the spirit of truth.

This widespread community coexisted at the same time as Paul's creation of Christ congregations. They were found not only at Qumran down by the shores of the Dead Sea, but also in Jerusalem, and scattered in villages throughout Israel, perhaps even in Egypt where a similar or identical group called the Therapeutae existed. They described the path of true righteousness as follows. The righteous person will have the following orientation:

> A spirit of humility, patience, abundant charity, unending goodness, understanding and intelligence; [a spirit of] mighty wisdom which trusts in all the deeds of God and leans on His great loving-kindness; a spirit of discernment in every purpose, of zeal for just laws, of holy intent with steadfastness of heart, of great charity towards all the sons of truth, of admirable purity which detests all unclean idols, of humble conduct sprung from an understanding of all things, and of faithful concealment of the mysteries of truth.
> (*Community Rule*, IV)

That's a tall order! Righteous living includes the right attitude along with correct decisions, choices, and subsequent actions. It is all-inclusive. Both Paul and the members of the Dead Sea Scroll Community emphasized attitude in all undertakings. The difference is, however, unlike Paul, the Dead Sea Scroll Community did not discard the religious and ethical framework which underlies these attitudes.

So by the mid-50s when he penned his angry Letter to the Galatians, Paul has taken himself out of the orbit of Judaism and away from what other Jewish leaders and groups of his time were trying to achieve.

Paul's next step is even more radical. How should Jesus be understood, especially in light of the failure of the Kingdom to appear?

Different View of Jesus

At Caesarea Philippi, when Jesus asked the disciples for feedback on his identity, no one placed him in any category other than human. He was like John the Baptist, or a prophet, or a forerunner of messiah. All see Jesus as human. He was not thought of as a divine being on par with or greater than the Greek God Pan and the divine-human emperor. While Peter said Jesus was messiah, there is no indication that he thought of him in anything other than human terms. That's what we'd expect: a messiah in Jewish thought was to be human, just as King David was.

Paul, however, views Christ as a divine-human. In his Letter to the Philippians he writes:

> [Christ] who though he was in the form of God,
> did not regard equality with God
> as something to be exploited,
> but emptied himself,
> taking the form of a slave,
> being born in human likeness. (Philippians 2:5–8)

So Paul conceives of Christ as a preexistent being, "a form of God," who became human. Christ does not use his "equality with God" as leverage. That is, Christ does not exploit or showcase his unique powers. Rather, Paul says, Christ humbled himself.

Why Paul thought of Christ as a divinity in human form is not clear. It's not because Paul thought of Jesus as resurrected. Resurrection does not prove that the resurrected person is divine. Resurrection is solely the activity of God. So if Jesus were resurrected, it would be testimony to the power of God resurrecting a righteous person. That person is still human.

So, what's the evidence: why does Paul depict Christ this way?

In his Letter to the Philippians Paul writes:

> Therefore God also highly exalted him
> and gave him the name
> that is above every name,
> so that at the name of Jesus
> every knee should bend
> in heaven and on earth and under the earth,
> and every tongue should confess
> that Jesus Christ is Lord
> to the glory of God the father. (Philippians 5:9–11)

The thought here is complex. Christ, although equal to God, does not "self-exalt:" God exalted him. That's strange if we are to think of Christ as equal to God: God exalting God-in-human-form.

Moreover, why would God need to exalt God?

In this passage Paul substitutes Jesus for God. The Old Testament reserves "bending the knee" (that is, homage) solely to God. As Second Isaiah says,

> Turn to Me and gain success [be saved, NRSV translation]
> All the ends of the earth!
> For I am God, and there is none else.
> . . .
> To Me every knee shall bend,
> Every tongue swear loyalty
> They shall say, "Only through the Lord (*YHVH*)
> Can I find victory and might." (Isaiah 45:22–24)

As Paul interprets Christ, he is God. Moreover, according Paul, Christ had a hand both in the creation of the world and also in sustaining that which has been created: "one Lord, Jesus Christ, through whom are all things and through whom we exist" (1 Corinthians 8:6). So Christ represents a divine force who permeates all things.

Christ is God himself who chose to assume human form. But was Christ coexistent with God always, right from the beginning? Or was he a created being? Whether written by Paul or by a follower shortly after his death, the Letter to the Colossians provides the following portrait of Christ:

> He [Christ] is the image of the invisible God, the firstborn of
> all creation; for in him all things in heaven and on earth were
> created . . . all things have been created through him and for
> him. He himself is before all things, and in him all things hold
> together. (Colossians 1:15–17)

So Christ is the firstborn of God, equal to God, the one through whom God created and sustains all that is. He is the glue holding together all that exists. He is the reason why the universe does not fall out of existence. How being "firstborn of God" relates to "equal to God" is not made clear.

Why did Christ/God become human? Paul's Letter to the Colossians addresses this issue:

> For in him [Christ] all the fullness of God was pleased to dwell, and through him God was pleased to reconcile to himself all things, whether on earth or in heaven, by making peace through the blood of his cross. (Colossians 1:19, 20)

So Christ embodies "the fullness of God." Through the sacrifice of Christ as atonement for sin, people, for whom death is the consequence of sinfulness, are now returned to a right standing with God. It is a reconciliation. Death as a penalty for sin has been overcome and now people are able to stand before God the way they were in Paradise before the primal couple sinned.

Sometimes in Paul's writings it seems as if only those who "believe" in Christ share in eternal life. This would make eternal life psychological, a matter of belief or faith.

Other passages, however, express a universal position: "For as all die in Adam, so all will be made alive in Christ" (1 Corinthians 15:23). Paul would have interpreted the Adam mythology as an historical event, and this gives rise to a different line of interpretation, a universal one. Just as Adam's misdemeanor interpreted as a historical event infected all humanity, so, too, the victory of Christ over death interpreted as an historical event also applies to all people. Otherwise the parallelism doesn't work. If Jesus's resurrection—like Adam's fall—is interpreted historically, then the psychological interpretation of one (Jesus) but not the other (Adam) makes no sense.

We need not probe this contrast between these two who-will-be-saved interpretations here. Nor do we need to examine in detail what Paul understood by resurrection . . . that's a complex subject that Paul explores in 1 Corinthians 15.* Briefly, for Paul, resurrection represented

---

* For an excellent discussion on Paul's concept of resurrection as well as the traditional Jewish view, see James D. Tabor, *Paul and Jesus: How the Apostle Transformed Christianity*. New York: Simon & Schuster, 2012. See Chapter Two, *"Rethinking Resurrection of the Dead."*

a reembodiment of the person at some point after death. The reembodiment would not be the present body but a resurrected bodily form that encompasses the whole person in a manner appropriate to a postresurrection environment—something quite unimaginable to us in a preresurrection state. It's like a caterpillar imagining being a butterfly. This view contrasts with what might be termed a "Zombie" or physical interpretation of resurrection, as a resuscitation of *this* body. That's not at all Paul's view.

For our purposes here, it is sufficient to note how Paul describes the Christ. Piecing together the various descriptions above, we get the following: the Christ is a preexistent being, equal to God (but also firstborn), through whom God creates and sustains all that is, and who assumed human form, in which his divine fullness dwells. Through his suffering, sacrificial death, and resurrection, Christ created a new relationship with God for humanity, overcoming sin and death, thus enabling eternal life for his followers.

So Christ (*Christos*) is a savior, a creator of a new humanity now restored to the right relationship with God as God intended all along. Just as the effects of Adam's actions were universal in scope, so, too was Jesus's resurrection. It was a universal event the effects of which apply to all humanity, which has now been re-created and restored to wholeness before God.

15

UNFINISHED BUSINESS

———

So how does Christ relate to Messiah?

Christ *versus* Messiah

P aul moved a long way from Judaism. Doing away with Torah immediately removed him from a Jewish matrix. So, too, did declaring
a human being (Jesus) divine, equal to God, creator and savior.
These two moves make it clear that Paul developed a new religion focused
on an interpretation of the significance of Jesus's death, not his teachings.

Make no mistake: this is a new religion. It is not an outgrowth of an
existing one. It's not as if Jesus taught and then Paul came along to organize
and systematize his teachings. Paul's religion is radically different. It is a
Christ religion, not the religion Jesus taught or practiced.

Paul had no gospels in front of him. He taught and died before any of
the gospels had been written. If the New Testament were presented historically, Paul's letters would come first, and then the gospels. The current
ordering is highly misleading with the four gospels being placed before

Paul's letters.* The arrangement of writings in the New Testament creates the false impression that Paul knew all the sayings and doings of Jesus reflected in the gospels. Paul had no gospels.

Nor was Paul tutored by James, Peter, or any of Jesus's original disciples. Paul assured us he did not get his message from any human being. His Letter to the Galatians begins with this statement:

> For I want you to know . . . that the gospel that was proclaimed by me is not of human origin, for I did not receive it from a human source, nor was I taught it, but I received it through a revelation of Jesus Christ. (Galatians 1:11, 12)

So, in addition to not having been based on written records, Paul's teachings were not the product of consultations with Jesus's students or family members. He got it directly, he says, from Jesus himself, that is, from Jesus after he had died.

Paul created a religion familiar to his Roman audience, a dying-rising savior movement similar to other Hellenistic religions. He then hooked that concept onto the person of a Jewish teacher, while at the same time rejecting Judaism. This served the purpose of giving his new religious movement ancestry, a pedigree, something ancient—an important feature for his Roman converts.

Paul also changed the image of Jesus, from a human being to that of a divine-human. His Christ is a savior, a divinity in human form, who has been sacrificed as an atonement for sin, a being who has been resurrected and who enables salvation for everyone (or, possibly, just for those who psychologically identify with him). This is a far cry from a King-Messiah, decidedly mortal, ensconced in Jerusalem, presiding over a transformed world in which the Romans would no longer be in charge, worshipping the one God of Judaism, and enjoying an era of universal peace.

Paul's strategy worked: *Christos* translates *mashiach*, but Paul changed the definition of messiah, and, in the process, stripped Jesus of his Jewish

---

* Even Paul's letters are not presented in historical order, but arranged in descending order of length.

background and context. There is no linkage in Paul to previous Jewish writings on the messiah. There is no attempt to show how his Christ concept ties in with previous Jewish ideas. It comes out of the blue, as a different way of understanding Jesus. No longer is he to be located within the Jewish set of ideas concerning a messiah but within a non-Jewish framework of a cosmic savior.

The differences are startling:

- A messiah is human; the Christ is a divine-human.
- A messiah transforms this world; the Christ rescues people from this world.
- A messiah rules as king in Jerusalem; the Christ is a savior whose sacrificial death enables eternal life.
- A messiah is born and dies; the Christ is eternal, forever divine.
- A messiah is not an atonement for sin; the Christ is an atonement for sin.
- A messiah confronts worldly social and political evil; the Christ battles death itself.
- The followers of a messiah are Torah-observant; the followers of Christ are not.

The anti-Roman pro-Torah religion of Jesus, James, and the disciples was transformed by Paul into a pro-Roman anti-Torah movement. He catapulted Jesus from his Jewish environment into a landscape more amenable and accessible to Gentiles. They knew of divine rescuers and here is Jesus as yet another one.

Judaism asserts that death is real, and that God and God alone saves the righteous of all the nations of the world. God is the sole savior who will resurrect righteous persons—sometime, somehow, somewhere. For Paul, while God saves, Christ conceived of as God in human form becomes the means to salvation through an atoning death. For Judaism no such sacrificial death is necessary, salvation being viewed as resurrection of the righteous by the power of God. The righteous, it should be noted, are not perfect. Like King David, the righteous are flawed human beings, doing their best to follow Torah, and asking for forgiveness for failures.

Thinking of Jesus as a divine-human, God in human form, posed problems for later Christian thinkers. Jesus, for instance, did not self-resurrect. The language used of Jesus's resurrection is often expressed in the passive voice, that he "was raised" from the dead (see, for instance, Matthew 27:64; Matthew 28:7). In other words, Jesus was raised by God, not that he raised himself.

Moreover, if Jesus were partly divine and partly human, did all of Jesus die on the cross? Did some part of Jesus not die since God, by definition, cannot die?

Jesus's avatar, the Christ figure created by Paul, is not the same thing as messiah. Responding to the failure of the Kingdom of God to materialize as Jesus promised, Paul proposed understanding Jesus's death as a sacrificial atonement for the sins of the world. While Paul enjoyed enormous success preaching a Christ figure for a larger Roman audience, this is not the Jewish understanding of messiah.

Paul's contribution can be understood positively as liberating the concept of messiah from a Jewish nationalist perspective to a universal one. His religion stripped away all the Jewish elements in favor of a belief system he thought all humanity could share.

Paul's religion also had the merit of shifting focus away from the Kingdom that had not materialized to that of a resurrected Jesus. It salvaged a failed mission and offered his followers the hope of eternal life. If Paul had not come along, then the religion that flowed from Jesus would likely have been a form of messianic Judaism within the larger Jewish family, or else a Gnostic movement built on personal insight into human identity and destiny.

Alternatively, Paul's contribution can be regarded negatively, as a sleight-of-hand substitution. In this view, Paul changed the concept of the messiah dramatically. A Christ takes Jesus out of his historic and Jewish context and places him in the Greco-Roman environment of savior divine-humans.

However we assess Paul's contribution, his innovative concept of the Christ differs from the Jewish concept of messiah.

Unfinished Business

The *Psalms of Solomon* establish an important pre-Christian Jewish understanding of messiah. As we have seen, that figure is a powerful human Jewish king who rules over a Torah-observant community at a time of universal peace. The king is righteous, as are the people. Jews from the Diaspora return to Israel to build up the nation. Thus when messiah comes there will be major religious and political realignments affecting the whole world. It will be a worldwide phenomenon, a seismic shakeup of all political structures. It will be available for all to see and will affect profoundly all those alive at the time.

The ultimate End Time, however, is seen as the prerogative of God, and God alone. Paradise restored, the Garden of Eden recreated, eternal life for all the righteous, the resurrection of the righteous dead—all these end-of-history developments are attributed solely to the power of God to create the world he intended for humanity. God creates the End Time scenario, not messiah. In particular, resurrection is God's business, not a messiah's . . . and not humanity's.

Jesus was not messiah, at least not in the way in which the messiah (*mashiach*) or messiahship was understood by Jews in his era.

Jesus's followers recognized that he was not the messiah. They acknowledged that he would need to return to accomplish what a messiah is supposed to do. That represents an important clue how they understood the concept of messiah, as a catalyst for massive world changes. They expected these changes, but first, Jesus had to return to do what he should have done first time around. The idea that being a messiah represents a two-stage operation is not something built into the Jewish concept of messiah.

Moreover, the kingdom Jesus promised as coming soon, within the lifetime of his audiences, has not yet materialized—at least as ordinarily understood, that is, as world transformation.

The delay of the promised kingdom posed a problem for Christians for centuries. A church, creeds, a clerical hierarchy, a new set of writing—these were not what people imagined Jesus was promising. Rather they expected a kingdom, massive social and political changes, a better world, where God's will would be done "on earth as in heaven." That didn't happen. Rather than the fortunes of Israel improving, after Jesus's death, the social situation deteriorated. There were two Jewish wars against Rome (in 66–70 and 132–136) with massive casualties along with the destruction of Jerusalem and the Second Temple.

So, centuries later, the world still awaits messiah and the Kingdom Jesus promised.

That's a lot of unfinished business.

The Search Continues

As we have seen, the longing for a messiah is most acute in times of deep distress. In 1919 in the wake of World War I, for instance, W. B. Yeats penned his famous poem, "The Second Coming." In part, it goes as follows:

> Things fall apart; the center cannot hold
> Mere anarchy is loosed upon the world,
>
> . . .
>
> The best lack all conviction, while the worst
> Are full of passionate intensity.
> Surely some revelation is at hand;
> Surely the Second Coming is at hand.
>
> . . .
>
> but now I know
> That twenty centuries of stony sleep
> Were vexed to nightmare by a rocking cradle,
> And what rough beast, its hour come round at last,
> Slouches towards Bethlehem to be born?

Set in the midst of such dire devastation, the poet asks, where is the Second Coming of Jesus? If not now, when? If not in times of dreadful wars, crusades, inquisitions, genocides, holocausts, then what possible unimaginably horrible conditions would have to exist in order to provoke messiah to appear (or return)? That's a question that reverberates across the centuries. Where is the messiah, especially when we need him *now*?

Religious people continue to pray for a messiah. During the central prayer of the Jewish liturgy—the *Amidah* or *Shemoneh Esrei* (Eighteen Benedictions)—Jews pray daily for the coming of a messiah: "Cause the offspring of Your servant David to flourish and hasten the coming of messianic deliverance."

Christians reach out to God in the Lord's Prayer that his Kingdom will come and that his will be done on earth as in heaven. Moreover, many Evangelical Christian movements see the creation of the modern state of Israel as the beginning of the dawn of redemption and the likelihood of Jesus's Second Coming in the near future.[*]

Hindu theology also envisages a world in need of periodic repair. The rescuer is Lord Krishna who becomes reborn in order to change the downward path of destruction. Based on the Hindu belief in reincarnation, the Sanskrit Hindu epic the Bhagavad Gita records the famous saying of Lord Krishna to Arjuna, the third son of King Pandu:

> Whensoever there is decline of religion and morals,
> then I loose myself into rebirth,
> for the destruction of the evil doer
> and for the restoration of the right.[†]

Some groups within Islam, too, are messianic, anticipating the eventual arrival of the Twelfth Imam who will bring about a peaceful world free from strife and vengeance.

The religious search for messiah sometimes leads to "mini-messiahs," charismatic cult leaders, who inspire a group of followers, often with devastating results. The devotees of Jim Jones's Peoples Temple group, for instance, considered their leader to be a reincarnation of several ancient religious figures, including Buddha and Jesus. In 1978, the group committed mass suicide in Guyana.

---

[*] The Jewish prayer for the wellbeing of the state of Israel begins, "Our Father in Heaven, Rock and Redeemer of Israel, bless the State of Israel, the first manifestation of the approach of our redemption. . . ."

[†] Passage supplied by Suresh Chawla.

More recently, the Branch Davidian cult viewed David Koresh as the final prophet, the one who would appear at the end of time, heralding the second coming of Jesus. The group was killed in a shoot-out with the FBI in Waco, Texas, in 1993.

Others followed the Korean religious teacher, the Reverend Sun Myung Moon, as messiah and gravitated to his Unification Church prior to his death in 2012. In the 1980s, many individuals flocked to Antelope, Oregon, to join the cult of Guru Bhagwan Rajneesh, a messianic figure who promised members of his community a far better world.

To The Rescue

There are a lot of titles that seem to blend in with one another: messiah, savior, redeemer, superhero, rescuer. Often these words are used interchangeably. These individuals, in turn, are associated with a wide range of ideas: communal or personal salvation, redemption, eternal life, Paradise, temporary reprieve from some threat, and the destruction of enemy forces.

One way of untangling these closely-related concepts is as follows.

A Jewish messiah is one specific form of rescuer denoting what the *Psalms of Solomon* describe: a righteous Torah-observant ruler presiding over peaceful nations. The view presupposes belief in God and that he has a plan for humanity, one that moves towards creating the perfected world God intends people to enjoy. It would be a world free from oppression, poverty, and fear. This view envisages a better world, one where Jews can practice their religion in their own independent state, in a world that is at peace.

The Jewish messianic vision also looks forward to what might ultimately become the best of all possible worlds where the righteous of all generations and all the nations of the world will be free from death, rewarded with eternal life in a Paradise. That development, however, will be by the action of God, and God alone.

A Christian savior is what Paul describes, a cosmic being who battles death and destruction terrestrially and universally. In his case, it was God entering human history in the form of Christ in order to defeat the forces of evil, thus rendering people free from the bonds of sin with its consequence, death.

In contemporary popular culture, superheroes deal with temporary issues, confronting concerns that arise in society from time to time. They use their intelligence, advanced technology, and their special powers to rid the world of some specific evil.

But all that said, "messiah" and "savior" are often used interchangeably referring to anyone who can provide rescue in a troubled world.

The overarching generic concept is "rescuer," the search for any being who can rescue us from whatever foe we face. Rescuer is the larger term and embraces messiahs, saviors, and superheroes.

Rescue or messianic thinking is fundamentally a rejection of the world as it is in favor of the world as it ought to be, brought about through the instrumentality of a savior. People yearn for improved living conditions—a good, better, perhaps even the best of all possible worlds. People pin hopes and dreams—many totally unrealistic—onto rescuers of all sorts, messiahs, superheroes, and saviors. This mental landscape makes getting through the day tolerable, holding out the audacious hope that sometime soon, world conditions will improve.

The rescuer dream takes many forms—avenging wrongdoings, overcoming evil and injustice, creating an earthly paradise free from strife, rescuing us from terrible enemies who have made the world a hell. In short, a genuine rescuer must transform present reality into something far better.

The flip side to hoping for a rescuer is the identification of the villain. This is the foe, the persons or groups held responsible for all that stands in the way of success, the ones who are perceived to have created the mess. Sometimes the enemy is the occupying oppressor, as in the Persians, Greeks, or Romans ruling ancient Israel. At other times, the enemy is evil or evil personified as a Satan or as the antimessiah, the Antichrist. At still other times, the enemy are genocidal human agents—for example, Turkish Muslims *versus* Armenian Christians, Nazis *versus* Jews, Rwandan Hutu *versus* Tutsi, and so on.

Rescuers stand *for* something and are *against* something. All rescuers have enemies. The rescuer's job is to defeat the enemy, everything that stands in the way of better social and political conditions. We can't do it, and so we project someone coming "to the rescue" onto our mental landscape.

Rescuer thinking is magical thinking—"someone" is the enemy; "someone" will save us.

It's always "someone else."

New Places to Search

When people look to religious beliefs or movements for a messiah, there is a lot of unfinished business with no world savior on the horizon. As people grow tired of waiting for the messiah, new cultural expressions arise that build on the desire for a rescuer.

While messianic fervor still exists within various religions today, the search for a rescuer has seeped into the secular world, to political saviors and pop cult heroes and heroines.

There are many reasons for this cultural shift, which need not be discussed extensively here. Very briefly, the seeds for this shift occurred in the 1800s and early 1900s with the rise of the psychoanalytic interpretation of religion as well as philosophical investigations into the nature of religious belief. These served to portray religion as less of a divine revelation and more of a human projection onto a mental conceptual landscape. In other words, religious belief systems are the intellectual and emotional creations of humanity rather than a description of actual real entities outside the self.

In 1841 Ludwig Feuerbach's *The Essence of Christianity* put forward the view that God is a chimera; that is, an imaginary projection of our inner nature and hence, not real—not real in the sense of describing a being who exists apart from ourselves. In 1927, Sigmund Freud's *Future of an Illusion* added to the attack on religious belief as illusionary. In both, religious belief is not regarded as descriptive of an external powerful creator of all that is.

Literature turned to humanism for an ideal person. In 1883, in *Thus Spoke Zarathustra*, Friedrich Nietzsche investigated the idea of an *übermensch* (superman) as an ideal towards which humanity can strive. This work influenced George Bernard Shaw who wrote the play *Man and Superman* in 1903.

While psychology, philosophy, and literature were exploring the implications of humanism, biblical writings began to be subjected to critical historical analysis. With respect to the Christian Scriptures, serious differences among the gospels were detected and a plethora of diverse movements within early Christianity were noted. In addition scholars began "the quest for the historical Jesus"; that is, an attempt to discern what can now be reliably known about what Jesus said and did. In the early 1900s, Albert Schweitzer's book *The Quest for the Historical Jesus: A Critical Study of Its Progress from Reimarus to Wrede*[*] spearheaded the search. Since then there have been a variety of approaches trying to discern the real historical Jesus under layers of cosmological and miracle mythologies.

Along with historical analysis, scientific discoveries into biological and cultural evolution undermined a literalist or fundamentalist interpretation of religion.

These developments impacted the observance of Christianity and Judaism in particular, with the result that many turned away from traditional religion with its portraits of political messiahs and cosmic saviors.

Terrifying historical events also played a crucial role in the rejection of traditional religion. The 1940s were especially devastating: one-third of all Jews in the world were murdered as the result of the Holocaust; millions of people across the globe were killed during World War II; millions more were maimed, uprooted, or displaced. In these dreadful times, no messiah came to the rescue. Why was that? Why was there no rescue by the messiah then? Could there be a worse time?

There have been many other recent mass deaths—Armenians; the Bengal famine of 1943 that killed two to three million; Serbians; Bosnians; Rwandans; Muslims and Hindus slaughtered at the time of partition of the Indian subcontinent in 1947; Indigenous peoples of the Americas; and many others. These horrible atrocities and unimaginable sufferings have prompted some to attempt to understand history theologically. How are events like these to be understood theologically within either a Jewish or Christian framework of a good, all-powerful deity who cares about humanity? Why has so much evil been allowed to exist if there is a good all-powerful God?

---

[*] Published in German in 1906; translated into English 1910.

Why has the messiah not appeared in such dreadful times as these? This is a serious challenge that any monotheistic religion must face honestly, and the answer is by no means clear.

Perhaps religious expression is not the place to search for a savior . . . maybe there are other places to search for rescue from our plight.

The new search for a rescuer focuses on persuasive politicians who seem to embrace our deepest aspirations for better social conditions. Their charisma and popular appeal propel these leaders above the crowd, with the hypnotizing promise of better times ahead. Media commentators swarm to personalities rather than platforms and people become enamored of political superheroes on the basis of emotion rather than intellect. Perhaps, though, political saviors can provide a way out and transport us to better times.

In addition to populist leaders, starting in the midst of World War II, powerful fictitious superheroes emerged. They heroically confront evil on our behalf, giving hope and comfort that somehow, some day, the world will be better. Batman, Superman, Wonder Woman, Spider-Man, Captain Marvel, a host of Avengers, and many others grew from midcentury comic-book characters to modern-day rescuers filling our screens with endless battles against evil. The fantasy cosmologies of DC Extended Universe and Marvel Cinematic Universe grip popular imagination around the world, replacing religious conceptual universes. Their blockbuster films have resulted in mega box-office successes, testifying to the immense popular appeal of these salvation narratives.

The world wants rescuing and has moved away from religion to politics and pop culture.

16

MODERN POLITICAL SAVIORS

———✸———

S ince the early 1900s, a number of world leaders have emerged who
have embodied the aspirations of people searching for a way out of
conflict in order to create a better world. Some political messiahs lived
up to the expectations they generated and benefitted humanity; others just
brought death and despair. Still others made promises that failed to materialize. In desperate times, people have looked to these leaders for salvation.

Woodrow Wilson and Adolf Hitler were two political saviors. The
contrasts are stunning. One was hailed as "Savior of Humanity." The other
consciously fashioned himself as the new messiah, the savior of a humiliated
and suffering nation but who, in the end, was a would-be savior whose decisions caused the greatest amount of death the world has ever experienced.
Both had tremendous impact upon the world, one for good, the other for
tremendous evil.

Woodrow Wilson (1856–1924)—"Savior of Humanity"

From a neutral perch in Washington, DC, Woodrow Wilson thrust the
United States onto the center stage of European and world politics. His

lifetime accomplishments were many. His involvement with the warring parties played a pivotal role in ending the bloody conflict of World War I. Somewhat of a visionary, he persuaded other world leaders of his time to create an international organization, one that he thought would help ensure a secure and permanent peace between nations. He enjoyed enormous international stature and he placed the United States prominently on the world stage.

World War I came to an end in 1918, after four years of fighting. The Entente Powers were pitted against the Central Powers. The latter group had started the conflict and included Germany, Austria-Hungary, the Ottoman Empire, and Bulgaria. The Entente group comprised Britain, its colonies and dominions (such as Canada, Australia, New Zealand), France, and Russia. This coalition came to include Italy and Japan, as well as the United States, which entered the war in 1917, three years after the war started.

The loss of life was tremendous. It was one of the costliest conflicts of human life in history. There were at least 40 million casualties: 15–19 million killed in combat and 23 million wounded.* The United States suffered close to 54,500 combat deaths;† Britain lost 744,000; France lost almost 1.2 million; Canada lost about 57,000. The Central Powers suffered close to 5 million combat deaths.

That's only a small portion of those severely affected. Families mourned loved ones killed in action, so millions more suffered. Many more were wounded on land, or lost at sea as naval vessels were sunk. People in occupied territories were displaced and their lives uprooted. Some simply went missing. The economies of Europe were ravaged, a whole generation of young men killed, cities destroyed, trade patterns disrupted, and political energies sapped.

---

* See *"World War I Casualties,"* Wikipedia which provides a breakdown of military and civilian deaths, military wounded, and population of each country in 1914–1918.

† *The International Encyclopedia of the First World War* available on-line indicates that "the USA lost more personnel to disease (63,114) than to combat (53,402), largely due to the influenza epidemic of 1918." Total Americans killed during the war whether in combat or due to disease was 116,516.

The Basis for Peace

Faced with the horrors of war in Europe, Woodrow Wilson sent a diplomatic note to all combatants asking them to state the terms upon which it would be possible for them to make peace. He did this in December 1916, several months before the United States entered the conflict. This peace-making initiative was an intriguing development, the view of an outsider, the leader of a neutral nation with little domestic interest in a European and Middle Eastern conflict.

The Entente Powers replied to this initiative in detail. The Central Powers only expressed a willingness to meet their adversaries to discuss peace.

The president addressed the Senate on January 22, 1917.* That speech by Woodrow Wilson to the Senate secured a leadership position for the United States and marked a significant turning point in helping to focus the combatants on the nature of an eventual peace. In it the president held out the vision of a supranational entity that would "hold the world at peace." While still a vague notion, his suggestion was that the world needed "a new plan [for] the foundations of peace among the nations." It would include establishing an international body that could render aggression by one state against another obsolete. It was the search for a powerful alternative to war, a supranational body.

Woodrow Wilson described the sort of peace the warring nations of Europe should seek as a "peace without victory." If it were instead a peace imposed upon the vanquished by the victor, Woodrow Wilson, said:

> It would be accepted in humiliation, under duress, as an intolerable sacrifice, and would leave a sting, a resentment, a bitter memory upon which terms of peace would rest, not permanently but only as upon quicksand.

---

* Woodrow Wilson, "Peace without Victory" speech. www.digitalhistory.uh.edu. Digital History ID 3898.

This speech was prophetic. The Treaty of Versailles in 1919 which concluded the war sparked deep German resentment and created a huge backlash. Although Woodrow Wilson was one of the key architects of that treaty, it included clauses on war guilt and reparations that he opposed. He concluded his speech by suggesting that the Monroe Doctrine of 1823 become "the doctrine of the world":

> that no nation should seek to extend its polity over any other nation or people, but that every people should be left free to determine its own polity, its own way of development—unhindered, unthreatened, unafraid, the little along with the great and powerful.

This, he maintained, could be the framework for peace.

At the time, his words fell on deaf ears. The leaders of the Entente Powers—notably the prime ministers of Britain and France, David Lloyd George and Georges Clemenceau—considered his ideas idealistic. Perhaps his proposals were ahead of the times, but at least the concept of an alternative to war had been articulated.

Germany extended the scope of its war efforts in a bid to reduce American supplies to Britain. This included attacks on the ships of neutral nations such as the United States. German U-boats and mines sank merchant vessels and passenger liners with loss of American lives and goods.

An intercepted telegram from the German foreign secretary, Arthur Zimmerman, to the German ambassador to Mexico in January 1917 also played an important role in shifting American public sentiment towards involvement in the war effort on the side of the Entente Powers. This Zimmerman Telegram* indicated that if the United States entered the war, Germany would help Mexico recover territory it had lost in the 1840s, notably Texas, New Mexico, California, and Arizona.

Nothing came of that threat to the southern border, but on April 6, 1917, the United States entered the war.

---

* See "Zimmerman Note," www.digitalhistory.uh.edu. Digital History ID 3900.

On January 5, 1918, the British prime minister, David Lloyd George, addressed an important Trade Union Conference in London.* Britain was then at the peak of its imperial power, representing almost 25 percent of the world's population. The British prime minister spoke on behalf of that global entity including not just the United Kingdom but also its colonies and dominions including Canada, Australia, New Zealand, South Africa, Newfoundland, and the Irish Free State.†

In that speech, Lloyd George acknowledged the important role Woodrow Wilson had played urging the combatants to state war objectives. He rejected the Central Powers' quest for "conquest and annexation." He concluded by setting forth three principles upon which peace might be possible. The third principle went as follows:

> We must seek, by the creation of some international organization, to limit the burden of armaments and diminish the possibility of war.

Along the lines of Woodrow Wilson, the British prime minister put forward the view that the world needed "to establish, by some international organization, an alternative to war as a means of settling international disputes." He, too, was searching for a means of avoiding future wars between nations.

Lloyd George also suggested something that would come to play an important role in the Treaty of Versailles, the need for serious war reparations from Germany. Exacting retribution in the form of monetary compensation constituted an important objective for the British electorate in light of the high casualty rate. It was also something the French prime minister favored. Lloyd George, however, also contended

---

* See "Address of the British Prime Minister (Lloyd George) before the Trade Union Conference at London, January 5, 1918" in Office of the Historian, Papers Relating to the Foreign Relations of the United States, 1918, Supplement 1, The World War, Volume 1. https://history.state.gov/historicaldocuments/frus1918Supp01v01/d4.

† The British "Dominions" did not have complete legislative independence from Britain until 1931 (Statute of Westminster). The Dominion of Newfoundland joined Canada in 1949.

that the eventual settlement should be "one which does not in itself bear the seed of future war."

How these two objectives—reparations and leniency—could possibly balance each other out would consume much of later discussions.

The Fourteen Points

Three days after Lloyd George's speech, Woodrow Wilson delivered an address at a joint session of Congress on January 8, 1918.* He addressed the "Gentlemen [sic] of Congress" and it is in this speech that he set forth his objective to make the world "fit and safe to live in." This was his important set of principles, the Fourteen Points. It reiterated some of the points Lloyd George had made just a few days earlier. While the British prime minister had spoken on behalf of the entire British Empire, it was Woodrow Wilson's address that became the most famous. That speech branded the basis for peace in a way that no other world leader had done.

Woodrow Wilson contended that this plan—the Fourteen Points—was "the only possible program" for world peace. He envisaged a world in which members of peace-loving nations would live out their lives, enjoying their own institutions while being "assured of justice and fair dealing by the other peoples of the world as against force and selfish aggression."

Wilson's points included the need for open agreements between nations (not secret treaties); freedom of the seas (which Britain opposed, being the foremost naval power of the time); settlement of colonial claims; and arrangements for various nations (e.g., return of Alsace-Lorraine to France, an independent Belgium, an independent Poland). His final point was "a general association of nations" to help ensure "political independence and territorial integrity to great and small states alike."

---

* See "Address of the President of the United States Delivered at a Joint Session of the Two Homes of Congress, January 8, 1918" in Office of the Historian, Papers Relating to the Foreign Relations of the United States, 1918, Supplement 1, Volume 1.

The Fourteen Points were not off-the-cuff remarks but the fruit of an extensive study called "The Inquiry," conducted by about 150 advisors led by Edward M. House.

Wilson's historic Fourteen Points played an instrumental role in ending the war. In October 1918, the German chancellor, Maximilian, Prince of Baden, sent him a note, bypassing the prime ministers of Britain and France, against whom Germany was fighting. He requested an immediate armistice, that is, a cessation of hostilities, not a surrender.

Prince Maximilian also requested that peace negotiations be based on Wilson's Fourteen Points. This did not mean that the German leaders agreed with his Fourteen Points. As Prince Maximilian stated in his *Memoirs*, "[The Supreme Command of Germany] probably saw in Wilson's programme a mere collection of phrases, which a skilful diplomacy would be able to interpret at the conference table in a sense favourable to Germany."[*] In other words, they thought that the verbiage was sufficiently vague as to work to Germany's advantage during peace negotiations.

Woodrow Wilson's Fourteen Points did the trick, getting the warring parties to the peace table. On November 11, 1918, an armistice was declared.

In time, Germany withdrew its forces from the occupied nations. Many German citizens were perplexed why the war had ended since there had been no surrender and no defeat.

The world was ready for discussions of peace.

Paris Peace Conference

"Savior of Humanity"

Woodrow Wilson set sail for Europe in early January 1918. He was hailed in Milan, Italy, as "the Savior of Humanity" and as "The Moses from Across the Atlantic."[†]

---

[*] Quoted in *War Memoirs of David Lloyd George*. Boston: Little, Brown, and Company, 1937, p. 257.

[†] Thomas J. Knock, *To End All Wars: Woodrow Wilson and the Quest for a New World Order*. New York: Oxford University Press, 1992, pp. 4, 5.

The idea of Woodrow Wilson as savior is particularly apt. His leadership and ideas helped stop the war, thus sparing many lives. His hope for an international body to block all future wars gave hope to a weary European populace. In a sense, Wilson did for Europe what it could not do for itself: he acted as an effective mediator, a savior rescuing the warring nations from continued bloodshed.

His reception by the other world leaders was somewhat mixed. Lloyd George, the British prime minister, wryly observed:

> Whilst we were dealing every day with ghastly realities on land and sea, some of them visible to our own eyes and audible to our ears, he [Woodrow Wilson] was soaring in clouds of serene rhetoric.[*]

Lloyd George added:

> I really think that at first the idealistic President regarded himself as a missionary whose function it was to rescue the poor European heathen from their age-long worship of false and fiery gods.[†]

Wilson himself played into the perception of savior. In discussions with the other three leaders regarding the possible development of a League of Nations, he explained why Christianity had failed to achieve its highest ideals:

> "Why," he [Woodrow Wilson] said, "has Jesus Christ so far not succeeded in inducing the world to follow His teachings in these matters? It is because He taught the ideal without devising any practical means of attaining it. That is the reason why I am proposing a practical scheme to carry out His aims."[‡]

---

[*] David Lloyd George, *Memoirs of the Peace Conference*. New York: Howard Fertig, 1972, page 139. Originally published 1939.

[†] David Lloyd George, *Memoirs of the Peace Conference*, p. 141.

[‡] David Lloyd George, *Memoirs of the Peace Conference*, p. 142.

According to Lloyd George, Clemenceau just rolled his eyes at the president's attempt to outdo Jesus. But Wilson was serious: a peace treaty without any overarching mechanism for enforcing peace, was, in his judgment, futile.

From January to June 1919, Paris became the capital of a "world government." It was ruled by the influential Group of Four: Woodrow Wilson, David Lloyd George, Georges Clemenceau, and the Italian prime minister Vittorio Emanuele Orlando.

This Group of Four was assisted, of course, by many others—advisors from each of these four nations plus representatives from other parties to the conflict. Well in the background, the British Dominions sought independent recognition at the Conference—not merely lumped in with Great Britain—and this request was granted. That meant that for the first time countries like Canada, New Zealand, and Australia had a voice on the world stage separate from that of the British prime minister.

Over six months, the Paris Peace Conference was dominated by these four individuals who met informally on a daily basis. The decisions were theirs'. They set the terms of peace, making five treaties with the Central Powers. They divided up Europe as best they could and dealt with the disposition of the German colonies. Most of the latter were given to the French and British as "mandates."

One outcome was the Treaty of Versailles; another, the League of Nations.

Treaty of Versailles
(June 28, 1919)

The tension in the discussions centered on a number of contentious issues—self-determination for the German colonies, freedom of the seas—but the matter of German reparations was especially intense.

On the one hand there was Woodrow Wilson's concern that the burdens placed on Germany not be too onerous, not enough to occasion resentment. On the other hand, the French and British prime ministers, backed by popular sentiment in both countries, sought reparations for all the costs of war. Having suffered the most of any of the Entente Nations, the people of these two major powers wanted Germany hobbled.

Clemenceau's objective was to ensure the on-going security of the French nation and he looked forward to a weakened Germany both militarily and economically. While Britain had not suffered any land devastation, British public sentiment supported strong measures to ensure that Germany would be unable to repeat its aggression of 1914. Hence it wanted demilitarization of Germany as well as compensation for their losses. This was to be a war to end all wars and they saw constraining the German economy as the means for achieving this objective. That, some thought, might be more effective than any international association of nations.

While Woodrow Wilson firmly opposed harsh treatment of Germany, several clauses in the Treaty of Versailles reflected the desire to recoup losses:

> Article 231. The Allied and Associated Governments affirm and Germany accepts the responsibility of Germany and her allies for causing all the loss and damage to which the Allied and Associated Governments and their nationals have been subjected as a consequence of the war imposed upon them by the aggression of Germany and her allies.

"Responsibility"—German leaders came to view this clause as nothing less than a national humiliation, an admission of war guilt. In time, this resentment would blossom and would fuel rising post-World War I German nationalism.

The intent of Article 231 was to provide the legal basis for setting reparations from Germany to the Allied and Associated Governments. It took several years for a final figure to be arrived at and over the years only partial payment was ever made by Germany.

Placing the United States front and center on the world stage, setting a framework for peace, establishing the basis for an armistice, and helping to moderate the terms of victory—these were among Woodrow Wilson's greatest achievements internationally. Henceforth, America would be a nation to be reckoned with.

League of Nations
(1920)

The League of Nations was perhaps Woodrow Wilson's crowning achievement, and in 1919 he was awarded the Nobel Peace Prize for this initiative. The league represented an intergovernmental organization whose objective was to maintain world peace. That goal was to be pursued through such tactics as disarmament and substituting negotiations and discussions in place of actual warfare.

It was founded on January 10, 1920, and eventually found its headquarters in Geneva. The reality did not live up to its promise of ensuring world peace. The League of Nations had no standing army and member nations were reluctant to become involved in conflict. So the mechanism "to hold the peace" was not in place as Woodrow Wilson wanted. The United States ironically did not join, chiefly for domestic reasons. Other nations such as Germany, Japan, Italy, and Spain withdrew. The Soviet Union was expelled. So the League did not have widespread support amongst the major powers.

The experiment failed, although the League lasted 26 years and was replaced by the United Nations after World War II.

Despite personal flaws and early political missteps, Woodrow Wilson was a political superhero, a savior on the world stage, and instrumental in ending World War I. A visionary, he probed ways of avoiding international conflict. He represented the hopes and dreams of millions who wanted an end to interminable wars and the horrors of World War I to never be repeated.

In that sense he was, indeed, a "savior of humanity."

Adolf Hitler
(1889–1945)

The evil generated by this individual is universally acknowledged. His destructiveness was unparalleled in human history and involved people from around the world. During World War II, the Allied Powers (the United Kingdom, the United States, the Soviet Union, and France before the

German occupation) suffered enormous casualties. It resulted in massive devastation of Europe, and, with the military involvement of Japan, much of Asia. Russians and Poles suffered immense losses, as did Germany itself. Six million Jews from all over Europe were exterminated and the European infrastructure of Judaism destroyed. Gypsies, homosexuals, the physically and mentally disabled, Jehovah's Witnesses, and many other groups were targeted. The list of death and destruction goes on.

World War II (1939–1945) represented the deadliest conflict in human history. The total death toll and number of wounded or displaced incalculable. Estimates range from 70 to 85 million people killed, both military and civilian.*

Why did another world war occur so soon, just 21 years after the conclusion of the first?

Many reasons are given for this bitter conflict, some of them growing out of German frustrations with the terms of the Treaty of Versailles, especially the "war guilt" clause (Article 231) and the reparation requirements that were deemed especially onerous. We should not jump to the conclusion that the failure by the Group of Four to reach a long-lasting peace treaty "caused" another war. But social conditions in Germany in the 1920s interacted with resentment to the treaty to create the climate for the emergence of a more radical outlook. The treaty ushered in two decades of bitterness.

Some German leaders began to blame, not the Big Four who determined the terms of the Treaty of Versailles, but their own politicians who went along with it. Many ordinary Germans had not experienced the war directly, apart from having family members serving in the military and loss of life on the war fronts. But Germany had not been invaded, and so ordinary German citizens had not experienced the ravages and savagery of the war. They were surprised that they had been defeated when Germany's army was occupying portions of other countries, such as Belgium and France. Why had fighting stopped? Why was there an armistice when everything seemed to be going in Germany's favor?

---

* See table of human losses on a country-by-country basis in "World War II Casualties," Wikipedia.

A popular notion arose called "the stab in the back": Germans blaming other Germans for having betrayed the nation. As mentioned before, Prince Maximilian had requested an armistice with Woodrow Wilson's Fourteen Points acting as the basis for peace terms. The Kaiser abdicated and a civilian government was formed that acted as the peace partner in arriving at the Treaty of Versailles.

For some German nationalists, including many military leaders, the treaty should not have been signed. General Erich Ludendorff claimed that the German army had been the victim of a "secret, planned, demagogic campaign" that had doomed all its heroic efforts to failure in the end. Ludendorff added, "an English general said correctly: 'the German army was stabbed in the back.'"[*]

Hitler's Speech, Munich, April 17, 1923[†]

In this speech, Hitler addressed the implications of the Peace Treaty of Versailles. He set forth themes that reoccur in many of his speeches.

Humiliation and Betrayal

> With the armistice begins the humiliation of Germany . . . this Republic [the post-war German government replacing the Kaiser] was founded at the moment when Germany was humiliated . . . It was no Treaty of Peace which was signed, but a betrayal of Peace.

Resurrection and Redemption

> So long as this Treaty stands there can be no resurrection of the German people: no social reform of any kind is possible!

---

* Quoted in Richard J. Evans, *The Coming of the Third Reich*. New York: Penguin Press, 2004, p. 61.

† Norman H. Baynes (ed.), *The Speeches of Adolf Hitler*. New York: Howard Fertig, 1969, pp. 54–57.

While the Entente Powers were to blame for the imposition of harsh terms on the German people, Hitler placed primary responsibility upon those Germans who accepted the treaty and signed it. Neither he nor his movement played any part in it. So, in his judgment, he and his party were "blameless."

A number of factors played into the rise of the National Socialist (Nazi) Party: the Fourteen Points were not used as the basis for the Paris Peace talks; the war guilt clause that Germany bore responsibility for the conflict was perceived as humiliation; and the reparations demanded were deemed excessive and beyond the means of Germany to comply. The "stabbed in the back" mythology also played an important role. The military had not been defeated . . . at worst they had reached a stalemate, but politicians, it was alleged, traitors to the true Germany, had sued for peace. This legend of betrayal became entrenched in the party platform of the Nazi party.

Hitler used Christian imagery to appeal to the crowds. Germany was a righteous nation. Its suffering was caused by betrayal, just as the righteous Jesus had been betrayed by Judas. It would experience resurrection and redemption with Germany rising from death, just as Jesus had done. The parallels, constantly reiterated, were profound.

Hitler's First Speech as Chancellor, Berlin, February 10, 1933*

Eleven days after being sworn in as chancellor, Hitler addressed not parliament, but the German people and the world. This speech was given in the Berlin Sports Palace and was preceded by a "warm-up" by Joseph Goebbels. The Sports Palace was filled to more than its maximum capacity of 14,000. Huge crowds gathered around loudspeakers set up in 10 open spaces in Berlin. A film audience reached over 20 million. Goebbels set the stage and waxed eloquently about how this represented a unique event in the life of Germany, a true national meeting.

As Hitler entered the auditorium with a procession of flags and important party members, he was greeted with overwhelming approval. Once the

---

* https://www.youtube.com/watch?v=jnf1bAWn2jE.

audience had quieted down, Hitler began softly, setting forth his agenda. He spoke of how he had "called this movement to life," thereby positioning himself as a life-giving spirit. He then went on to "call it to action in the second, decisive phase in the fight for German resurrection."

Acting as high priest, Hitler pardoned the German people:

> In the year 1918 when the war ended I was, along with the many millions of other Germans, guiltless of the circumstances of this war, blameless for our leadership's conduct of this war, and likewise guiltless of the resulting political form of German life.

A new Germany had been born.

Nazi Nuremberg Rally, September 5, 1934

The massive Nuremberg rallies were annual events, typically held over five days. The 1934 rally—the Sixth Party Congress—was especially important. It was filmed and widely distributed in many countries as a documentary. Over 700,000 Nazi party supporters attended.

Leni Riefenstahl was the director of this documentary produced "by the order of the Führer." Titled *Triumph des Willens* (*Triumph of the Will*), it opened with Hitler in an airplane, cutting through the clouds, and swooping down on an eagerly awaiting city. The gradual descent of the aircraft along the streets of Nuremberg is shown as a cross-like shadow. Hitler's dramatic arrival represents the advent of the messiah, coming from the clouds of heaven, making his second coming.

The preface to the film is especially significant since it highlights three key dates. The preface reads:

> 5 September 1934.
> Twenty years after the outbreak of the World War.
> Sixteen years after the start of the German suffering.
> Nineteen months after the start of Germany's rebirth.

These three periods represent key dates in Hitler's interpretation of German history.

20 Years Ago—Betrayal

Hitler attributed the outbreak of World War I to false leaders, especially Jews. In his April 17, 1922, speech in Munich on the Peace Treaty of Versailles,* Hitler said:

> Who were the real rulers of Germany in 1914 to whom war guilt might be attributed: not the Kaiser, not the Pan-Germans, but Messrs. Ballin, Bleichroder, Mendelssohn, etc., a whole brood of Hebrews who formed the unofficial Government? And in 1914 the real ruler of the Reich was Herr Bethmann-Hollweg, "a descendant of a Jewish family in Frankfort"...

Thus began Hitler's obsession with "the Jews." His early speeches blamed "the Jews" along with "Bolsheviks" for almost everything wrong in German society. They were capitalists; they were communists. They were part of an international conspiracy. They weren't German. The charges were as endless as they were baseless. Anti-Semitism was a theme that pervades his speeches over the decades, right from the outset, and it resonated with many in his audiences already predisposed to believe the worst of Jews.

In a speech on April 20, 1923, Hitler asked, "What then are the specifically Jewish aims?" And he answered: "To spread their invisible State as a supreme tyranny over all other States in the whole world."[†]

On April 13, 1923, he attributed the entry of the United States into the war as a result of Jewish efforts, not the German sinking of American vessels, nor its efforts to provoke Mexico into a war with the United States to recapture lost territory:

---

*   Norman H. Baynes (ed.), *The Speeches of Adolf Hitler*, p. 54.

†   Norman H. Baynes (ed.), *The Speeches of Adolf Hitler*, p. 59.

What cause finally led America to enter the war against Germany? With the outbreak of the World War, which Judah [sic] had desired so passionately and [for] so long, all the large Jewish firms of the United States had begun supplying ammunitions. They supplied the European 'war-market' to an extent which perhaps even they themselves had never dreamed of—a gigantic harvest! . . . A gigantic organization for newspaper lying was built up, and once more it is a Jewish concern, the Hearst Press, which set the tone of the agitation against Germany.[*]

As well, at the end of World War I, Hitler blamed nonpatriotic German leaders for the war-guilt clause: "murderers of our Fatherland who all the years through have betrayed and sold Germany . . . [plunging] us into the depths of misfortunes."

So, as Hitler reconstructed the War, some assortment of Jews, Bolsheviks, Jewish Bolsheviks, and nonpatriotic German leaders were responsible for the debacle, before, during and after the conflict. They represented the enemy against which he railed.

16 Years Ago—Suffering

"Sixteen years after the start of German suffering," that is, from 1918 to 1934, a period of time that, in Hitler's view, was a humiliating time of abject misery and misfortune.

In his April 12, 1922 speech, Hitler had said:

at the end of the World War Germany was burdened with her own debt . . . and beyond that was faced with the debts of "the rest of the world"—the so-called reparations. The produce of

---

[*] Munich, Speech of April 13, 1923. See www.hitler.org/speeches. The reference to "Judah" is intended to blur the distinction between Jews and Judas, the betrayer of Jesus.

Germany's work thus belonged not to the nations, but to her foreign creditors: "it was carried endlessly in trains for territories beyond our frontiers." Every worker had to support another worker.*

As Hitler sized up the situation, Germany had become a "colony of the outside world."

Nineteen Months Ago—Resurrection

"Nineteen months after the start of Germany's rebirth," that is, from the accession of Hitler as Chancellor, January 30, 1933 to the Nuremberg rally of September 5, 1934.

In many speeches Hitler referred to Germany's "resurrection," a rebirth, a new era in the country's history.[†]

Thus Hitler advanced a threefold theology of German history: betrayal; national humiliation and suffering; resurrection. Germans have suffered as a consequence of their betrayal by their leaders. That suffering is about to end with Germany's resurrection. *Triumph of the Will* shows Hitler, the new messiah, coming with power to give new life to a dying nation. It also positioned the National Socialist Party as the means of salvation. This powerful film represented a remarkable visual transposition of Christian teachings about Jesus into Hitler's own time.

Hitler's language was frequently biblical. In a speech in Hamburg, August 17, 1934, he referred to Germany as "this kingdom of Heaven,"[‡] reminiscent of Jesus's hope for a Kingdom of God. In Munich on May 1, 1923, he used Paul's memorable phrase of "faith, hope and love" (1 Corinthians 13) to structure his remarks. In a remarkable passage, Hitler positioned himself as a Jesus figure fighting against religious and political powers:

---

* Norman H. Baynes (ed.), *The Speeches of Adolf Hitler*, pp. 4, 5.

† Norman H. Baynes (ed.), *The Speeches of Adolf Hitler*, see references to resurrection of Germany on pp. 56, 89, 100.

‡ Norman H. Baynes (ed.), *The Speeches of Adolf Hitler*, p. 97.

In boundless love as a Christian and as a man I read through the passage which tells us how the Lord at last rose in His might and seized the scourge to drive out of the Temple the brood of vipers and of adders. How terrific was His fight for the world against the Jewish poison. (Hitler speech, April 12, 1922)*

As the *Triumph of the Will* documentary demonstrates, Hitler used the new media effectively in harnessing his vision of a better world for Germany. Throughout his speeches he constantly returned to the same messianic themes—betrayal, suffering, resurrection—and the identification of the enemy as Jews, Communists, and false Germans. The theme resonated with a largely Christian Germany and he was welcomed and supported by major elements of society, reinforced by the elimination of political opponents and by military and paramilitary units.

Throughout the late 1930s, as Germany expanded its borders, and with the onset of World War II in 1939, the world descended into horror. This would-be savior simply brought death, devastation, and destruction, not only to his own people but to millions around the world.

The siren song of political leaders who promise better times ahead can yield quite different results.

---

* Norman H. Baynes (ed.), *The Speeches of Adolf Hitler*, p. 21.

17

SUPERHERO SAVIORS: SUPERMAN, BATMAN, WONDER WOMAN

———∞∞∞———

W hy is there evil in the world? How is the existence of evil compatible with belief in a loving, omnipotent God, the creator of all that is?

Thus the age-old conundrum arises. If God is all-powerful, then evil should not exist. An omnipotent God should simply be able to stamp out evil. Similarly, if God is infinitely good, perfect in all respects, the creator and sustainer of all that is, then evil should not even exist. Such a perfect being would simply not tolerate evil.

Evil, pain, suffering, war, brutality, torture, torment, violation of the self, brutal extermination of peoples—all these forces of death and destruction stand in the way of affirming belief in the existence of an almighty and infinitely good God.

The existence of evil represents the biggest challenge to the credibility of all monotheistic religions. Such religions have no convincing answer how evil and an infinitely good, omnipotent God can coexist.

A variety of approaches to the problem of evil have been proposed. Maybe there exists a power slightly subordinate to the one God, a Satan or a Lucifer, a real being conceived of as a powerful superhuman force acting within the universe, a rival to a less than all-powerful God and challenging his supremacy. That's one answer. A lesser cosmic being with whom God battles. But quickly questions arise: how did this evil being come to exist? Could an infinitely perfect, good God create an almost almighty evil being? Moreover, if God has a rival, is God, then, less than all-powerful?

Another one is a Christian response, that evil, sin, and death have already been overcome through the death and resurrection of Jesus. That suggestion, however, leaves us wondering: If this is the case, then why has evil continued to be present in the world for 2,000 years? Why has there been such an escalation of the forces of evil with so much suffering during the 20th century with its two world wars, Holocaust, genocides, and famines?

Moreover, what role does religion itself play in fostering evil, suffering, and pain? Why do monotheistic religions seem always front and center in world conflicts? Why do they appear to contribute to political and social warfare rather than being its cure?

Yet another answer is that we simply do not know why evil exists—perhaps it serves some purpose of which we are unaware. That response simply admits bafflement and fails to reconcile satisfactorily both of the existence of evil and a good all-powerful God.

Alternatively, we can blame humanity and exempt God. Perhaps there are destructive forces buried deep within us that occasionally win out over our good inclinations. It may have to do with choices we make, poor judgments that result in destructiveness rather than creativity. In this view, however, while God may not have directly created evil, he is at least accountable for creating the conditions under which evil arises and so is indirectly responsible.

Contemporary pop culture tackles these questions through superhero comics, films, and video games. Why is there evil? Can it be overcome? On whom can we rely in the battle against evil? Is there a savior? A messiah? A rescuer? Is there meaning to human existence?

Paw Patrol

Socialization into the world of powerful rescuers begins at a young age with such television shows as *Paw Patrol*. That popular kids' series first aired in 2013. Ryder, a 10-year-old boy, hears of or sees a problem, someone in distress. Clearly life poses serious challenges and wellbeing is threatened. That is instilled in us at a very early age. A problem has to be solved before we can move on with our day.

A fleet of savior puppies comes to the rescue; each dog has an individual identity and special skills. While Ryder can't solve the problem, although involved in all the missions, savior dogs such as Marshall, Rubble, Chase, and Skye can. Once alerted to the existence of a problem, the rescue dogs report to their base, the Lookout, where Ryder tells them of the problem. The appropriate rescue puppies slide down from the Lookout into their vehicles and complete the mission.

Through television, we teach children from a very young age that the world is full of problems too complex for them to solve on their own. Such socialization sets up a rescue mindset . . . we need superhero allies and saviors who help us solve the problems we face. Ryder needs the savior dogs in order to meet the challenges of everyday life.

Origins and Reboots

It is no accident that there has been a huge interest in fictional super-heroes as the power of organized religion wanes. Strong individuals whose super powers can crush evil beings of all sorts populate our pop culture literature, television, and films. Interestingly, these modern superheroes emerged during a time of great social trauma, World War II. Superman appeared in 1938; Batman in 1939; and Wonder Woman in 1941.

Many superheroes have suffered intense shock. Superman is thrust as an infant from his dying home planet, Krypton, and sent to the safety of earth where he is raised by human parents. Batman witnesses the death of his parents as a young child and dedicates his life to the eradication of crime in Gotham City. Wonder Woman hears of suffering in the world outside of her home of Themyscira and responds to the plea for help.

Secular superheroes fit the profile of a would-be saviors: born in a time of trauma, they use superior resources to combat evil and leave the world a better place as a result.

Superhero stories have been "rebooted" from time to time, to make the plotline relevant to changing circumstances. All use their powers to help make the world safer, but the problems change, the evil villains differ, and their powers evolve.

Rebooting of the plotline in superhero sagas is similar to the rebooting of ancient legends. The Robin Hood story has been rebooted many times, with variations ranging from Saxon peasants and Norman overlords to Rocket Robin Hood in space to a "men in tights" parody. The Arthurian legends have been rebooted numerous times over centuries. Disney has rebooted ancient fairy tales and 19th century Brothers Grimm stories to make them more palatable to modern audiences . . . less menacing and far less scary.

The gospels also represent a "reboot." The gospel authors took Jesus's early 1st century message and adapted it for different audiences and situations in the late 1st century. The gospels were written because the Kingdom of God did not materialize in Jesus's generation, as he said it would, and times had changed. The movement had become Gentile, not Jewish; pro-Roman, not anti-Roman. In this way the gospel writers extended Jesus's promise of the coming Kingdom of God for one additional generation.

The gospel writers also changed the focus. No longer was the "good news" about the coming Kingdom of God but about the person of Jesus as a Christ figure. Extending the promise of a coming Kingdom of God for later generations while altering the message from what Jesus taught to what was taught about him—that was an amazing reset.

The DC Extended Universe (DCEU) represents a remake of various superhero stories, tying them together in some respects so that the separate universes of Superman, Batman, Wonder Woman and others begin to coalesce and intersect. Instead of many parallel superhero universes, we now have one gigantic DCEU universe which they all inhabit.

The DC Extended Universe has released the following seven films in their rebooted series: *Man of Steel* (2013), *Batman v Superman: Dawn of*

Justice (2016), *Suicide Squad* (2016), *Wonder Woman* (2017), *Justice League* (2017), *Aquaman* (2018), and *Shazam!* (2019).

More releases are planned for 2020 including *Wonder Woman 1984*, along with *The Batman* and *The Suicide Squad* in 2021.

Similarly, the Marvel Cinematic Universe (MCU), has rebooted its superheroes. Since 2007 it has released 23 films in several groupings or "phases." These include: *Iron Man* (2008), *Thor* (2011), *The Avengers* (2012), *Guardians of the Galaxy* (2014), *Avengers: Age of Ultron* (2015), *Ant-Man* (2015), *Thor: Ragnarok* (2017), *Black Panther* (2018), *Captain Marvel* (2019), and *Avengers: Endgame* (2019).

MCU offers an alternative universe to our own, and to DCEU's. The cosmologies of superhero saviors are extraordinarily complex.

Man of Steel (2013)—
"Make a Better World Than Ours, Kal"

So says Superman's mother, Lara, to her infant son (Kal-El) as she faces imminent death and her own planet's destruction.

Directed by Zack Snyder and written by David S. Goyer, *Man of Steel* raises a number of important existential themes. What would a better future look like? Is there hope for beings on planets which have used up their natural resources? How would people react if they knew there were other beings in the universe? How do gifted people come to find their true identity?

Above all, however, the film raises the question: Can good conquer evil? If so, how?

As it turns out, evil exists not just on Earth but also on other planets as well. The cosmic dimension of evil is reminiscent of Paul's claim that the human battle against evil is not just against malevolent human beings, but against much more powerful spiritual forces that pervade the universe:

> For our struggle is not against enemies of blood and flesh, but
> against the rulers, against the authorities, against the cosmic

powers of this present darkness, against the spiritual forces of evil in the heavenly places. (Ephesians 6:12)*

For Paul, evil is a universal power that must be combatted by nothing less than divine force. The same is true in *Man of Steel*. The battle for the future of Earth is a continuation of a battle begun in the heavens on planet Krypton.

Krypton is a doomed planet. Shortly before its implosion Jor-El, the planet's leading scientist, and Zod, the planet's chief military leader, fight over the future of their species. Is it to be on some other planet? If so, where? How should the genetic code of the Kryptonian form of life best be preserved—in a being or encased in a Codex registry?

Both Jor-El and Zod are trying to ensure the continuity of their race. Just before Krypton explodes, Zod kills Jor-El. However, Jor-El and Lara's son, Kal-El, escapes.

That Kryptonian war is reminiscent of "a war in heaven" with the arch-angel Michael and his angels fighting against "the dragon" and his angels. That dragon, the devil or Satan, "was thrown down to the earth, and his angels were with him" (Revelation 12:9). Just as the dragon and his cohort are hurtled from the heavens to Earth, evil appears on our planet in the form of General Zod who has been thrown out of Krypton via a sojourn in the Phantom Zone.

These evil beings possess a "World Engine" capable of transforming Earth into a new Krypton, destroying all humans in the process. That is how Zod wishes to perpetuate the Kryptonian species. How should Earth confront this more powerful humanity-destroying force?

The Protagonists

Before depicting the Superman-Zod confrontation, *Man of Steel* delves into the back story: the origins of Superman and his rival, Zod. This represents

---

* As already mentioned, the Pauline authorship of Ephesians is disputed. But if not written by Paul then it was written by one of his close followers not long after Paul's death in the mid 60s.

a rebooting of the Superman saga for a new generation. It also prepares the way for the eventual formation of an association of superheroes which emerges in *Justice League* (2017).

So, what do we learn about Kal-El/Superman?

Superman's home planet, Krypton, is threatened with destruction as a result of overmining, resulting in planet destabilization. Superman's father, Jor-El, tried to persuade the leaders of Krypton to build spaceships, to transport the population to another planet. When they refuse to heed his warnings of planetary doom, he places his newborn son in an arklike vessel preprogrammed to travel to Earth. Jor-El and Lara's son is named Kal-El.*

Unlike the genetic programming practiced on Krypton for reproduction, Kal-El has been born naturally. Infused with the Codex containing Krypton's genetic material, the ark beams across space, landing on Earth near Smallville, Kansas, where he is raised by Jonathan and Martha Kent.

The biblical parallels are obvious. The vessel is like Moses's basket floated down the Nile River to a place of safety. Kal-El has a special birth (in his case, a natural one) just as Jesus was alleged to have had a special birth (a virginal conception and a virgin birth). He's brought up by two individuals—Martha and Jonathan—whose names are somewhat similar to Jesus's human parents, Mary and Joseph. Kal-El derives his superhuman powers from the sun; Jesus was depicted in early Christianity as Helios, the sun god,† and his resurrection is celebrated by Christians weekly on the Sunday.

Named Clark by his human parents, he grows up and, as an alien, tries to find his place in the world of humans. His special powers have to be curbed and as he matures he goes in search of his true identity, just as Jesus did in the temptations in the wilderness.

The Jewish creators of Superman—Jerry Siegel and Joe Shuster—were not likely to have heard of the 2nd century Christian gospel, the *Infancy Gospel of Thomas*. In that apocryphal writing, the young Jesus is depicted as exploring his remarkable powers, for example, making clay birds and

---

* "El" is one of the Hebrew names for God.

† This is a theme that is explored in Simcha Jacobovici and Barrie Wilson, *The Lost Gospel*, Chapter 10.

bringing them to life or killing a child who annoyed him.* Both Superman and the young Jesus have to learn to curb their amazing abilities.

While searching for his true identity, he comes across an abandoned Kryptonian scout ship sent centuries before to Earth. He activates an AI device which gives him a hologram of his real father who explains to him the circumstances of his transference to Earth. Jor-El encourages Kal to guide the people of Earth and give them hope. He explains the meaning of the Superman symbol: it means hope and a belief "in the potential of every person to be a force for good." Kal-El has found his identity and is given a mission.

Lois Lane from the *Daily Planet* tracks down Superman's mother and learns that Clark's human father had sacrificed himself in order to protect his real identity. She decides to honor that extraordinary commitment.†

Zod is the villain, but also, in his own way, a would-be savior of his people, but at the expense of another species. Taking over Earth's electrical systems and commandeering TV stations, he announces to the world in many languages, "You are not alone." He wants the return of Kal-El.

The Crisis

The arrival of Zod, his space ships, his message, sparks panic amongst leaders. Descending from the sky like a Christ-like figure, Kal-El decides to surrender, to avoid, he hopes, world destruction. Lois Lane accompanies him. Zod explains his purpose and demands the genetic template from the Codex registry.

Zod releases the World Engine which begins the destruction of Earth.

"Bridge between Two Peoples"

Kal's father, Jor-El, says to Superman that he can act as a bridge between two peoples. He reinforces his message with the plea:

---

* The *Infancy Gospel of Thomas* is pure fiction. No one considers it historical. For a translation of the *Infancy Gospel of Thomas*, see Bart D. Ehrman, *Lost Scriptures*, pp. 57–62.

† The relationship between Lois Lane and Clark Kent (Superman) is as ambiguous as that between Mary the Magdalene and Jesus.

You can save her [Lois];
You can save all of them.

And Kal does.

A megabattle ensues between Kal-El and Zod. It is not, however, a one-on-one battle. Fighting the forces of evil requires more than simply Superman's superior powers. He is assisted by a team—the American military, Lois Lane, and by the spirit of Jor-El.* This team effort paves the way for the eventual DCEU theme that evil is now so powerful that it requires more than one individual to succeed.

It also establishes that extraterrestrial evil has been conquered, at least from the direction of Krypton.

But will other sources of evil emerge?

Batman v Superman:
Dawn of Justice (2016)

If evil does not stem from cosmic sources—no Satan, no Devil, as in Christian theology—then what accounts for the presence of evil in the world? The answer from DCEU seems to be that evil arises from deep within the human personality. The film series espouses a Jewish view of wrongdoing, that destructive behavior stems from an evil impulse (*yetzer hara*) within the human makeup. According to Judaism, there is no cosmic being who rivals God or who tempts human beings and punishes wrongdoers in a Hell. So there is no cosmic dualism. Existence is fundamentally good, and humans have a choice to either do good or evil. The potential for either is inherent in humanity.

Batman v Superman is directed again by Zack Snyder and written by Chris Terrio and David S. Goyer. One of the villains is Lex Luthor, a flawed human who acts maliciously and malevolently. He brings Batman and Superman together and orchestrates a colossal battle.

---

* It is interesting that in spite of the fact that all humanity is threatened, no international body is involved, no UN, NATO, or NORAD, for instance.

The superheroes include Batman, Superman, Wonder Woman, and even the Flash. Their previously separate universes have been united. Together they will fight evil (and, in Batman and Superman's case, each other).

The film poses the question: Are these powerful superheroes purely good? In other words, is goodness pure? Can good agents sometimes cause evil, perhaps even inadvertently, while doing good? Can good exist without evil?

Batman, as human, experiences the inner conflict between good and evil impulses, giving way to his resentment of Superman's overwhelming powers. His evil impulse sways his judgment and he plots to kill Superman. In a sense, he is also a villain along with Lex Luthor, who designs a powerful entity that ultimately kills Superman. Superman, not a human but an alien who has adapted to Earth's environment, is exempt from this powerful tug of conflicting emotions, although he does have reservations about Batman's seemingly excessive need for revenge against wrongdoers.

All the protagonists have lost fathers. Superman lost both his biological father (who was killed on Krypton) and his real father (who sacrificed himself in a tornado to protect Clark's true identity). Batman witnessed his parents' death. Lex Luthor had an abusive father. Wonder Woman's father, Zeus, was killed by Ares. All have experienced deep personal loss and know the power of death. They all seek order and the removal of chaos encompassing Earth.

Power Politics

Lex Luthor is preoccupied with the implications of power and goodness. As he says to Superman,

> See, what we call God depends on our tribe, Clark, 'cause God is tribal. God takes sides. No man in the sky intervened when I was a boy to deliver me from Daddy's fist and abominations. I figured out way back if God is all-powerful, He cannot be all good. And if He is all-good, then he cannot be all-powerful. And neither can you be. They [the people of Earth] need to see the fraud you are.

What are the limitations to powerful beings? In a question to an American senator, Luthor asks an important question: "Do you know the oldest lie in America, Senator? It's that power can be innocent."

The film begins with the ending of *Man of Steel*. While Superman wreaks havoc on the streets of Metropolis conquering Zod and his cohorts, Batman is on the streets looking after some of the victims. In the wake of Superman's battle are thousands of dead innocent victims and terrible destruction. Perhaps this "collateral damage" can be waived aside as the better of two bad alternatives, limited carnage *versus* the destruction of the human race. But, still, there is massive death and destruction. And Superman is held responsible. It would appear that in trying to do good, much evil is created. Perhaps evil is, then, the by-product of good.

People on Earth do not know what to make of Superman. While acknowledging that he saved humanity, is he perhaps more of a rogue agent than a true savior? Batman harbors suspicions about Superman's behavior and resents Superman's seeming recklessness. Others ask, is Superman bound by American law? Can lawmakers in Congress harness his powers for beneficial purposes? How should power be used? Could members of Congress even compel a being like Superman to testify?

The film ends with a battle orchestrated by Lex Luthor who kidnaps Lois Lane as well as Clark's mother. He tells Superman to kill Batman in order to save his mother's life. While Superman tries to avoid conflict with Batman, the latter attacks him. Luthor creates a monster genetically engineered from Zod's DNA and his own blood. Diana Prince arrives on the scene and reveals her true identity as Wonder Woman. She kills Luthor's monstrosity but before dying, this creature kills Superman. Superman dies.

Batman eventually becomes remorseful for having failed Superman. He indicates that he is planning to form a team of "metahumans" to help protect Earth now that Superman has been killed. The earth covering Superman's coffin begins to rise, leaving us to wonder if a resurrection is about to take place. The film ends.

Superheroes are not divine. They are human (or Kryptonian) with special powers, but they are mortal, nonetheless. Even Superman. While powerful, they are not all-knowing and not always vigilant. For instance, Superman does not see the bomb inside the Senate chambers, and while he hears (and saves) Lois falling off a tall building, he does not hear his mother when she is abducted. Superheroes can be swayed by their emotions and can commit evil, as Batman was. They also cause immense collateral damage to innocent civilians while pursuing justice. Their power does not prevent them from wrongdoing. The superheroes of today's films are like the Greek gods—they can be born, they can die, they can do good, they can create havoc. They are super humans. And they are many.

The defeat of evil caused by humans now requires a team approach of powerful metahumans, all inhabiting the same conceptual universe. Thus we now have the "dawn of justice."

Wonder Woman (2017)—
"The Bridge to a Greater Understanding between All Men"

(Steve to Diana)
I can save today.
You could save the world.

Who was responsible for the evil known as World War I? That is the question *Wonder Woman* (2017) seeks to answer. The film is directed by Patty Jenkins from a screenplay by Allan Heinberg, and story by Heinberg, Zach Snyder, and Jason Fuchs.

In 1941 at the height of World War II, a German Lutheran New Testament scholar, Rudolf Bultmann, proposed a method of biblical interpretation he called "demythologizing." In particular, he suggested that the gospels in the New Testament need to be demythologized.*

By demythologizing, Bultmann meant that the gospels should be stripped of their ancient mythological framework—for example, a three-tiered universe (heaven, earth, hell), disease as demon-possession, and miracles. This should be done so that their true meaning can be discerned.

---

* See Rudolf Bultmann, *Kerygma and Myth: A Theological Debate*. London: S.P.C.K., 1953. This contains Bultmann's essay, "New Testament and Mythology," originally published in German in 1941.

For him, the mythological framework of the 1st century that the gospels naturally presuppose prevents modern people, who hold a different cosmology, from truly grasping the power of the gospel message. Demythologizing thus aims to free the message from its ancient cosmological framework so as to become intelligible to people today.*

Wonder Woman (2017) does the same thing: it demythologizes Greek mythology in order to reveal a human truth.

Diana is the offspring of the Amazon queen Hippolyta and the Greek god Zeus. Her half-brother by a different mother is Ares, the God of War. The Amazons have been sequestered on a special island, hidden away from the evil Ares and the influences of the outside war. They believe that one day, Ares will return to start conflict.

Wonder Woman, then, is a divine-human who has a special birth. She comes from a different realm and enters into the human world. She is a goddess who becomes human, taking on the identity of Diana Prince. She is divine goodness—love, care, concern—incarnate in human form. Wonder Woman, then, is reminiscent of Jesus as God incarnate, a special divine human.

The story takes place in 1918, close to the end of World War I. Captain Steve Trevor is a spy whose plane crashes near Themyscira, the mysterious island home of the Amazons. He has been pursued by the Germans who likewise break though the protective barrier surrounding Themyscira. Diana saves Steve's life and the Amazons kill the invading Germans. During that battle, her mentor, Antiope, sacrifices herself in order to save Diana.

Diana comes to learn of the terrible war ravaging the world. She chooses to leave the safety of her island and become immersed in the world's problems.

Diana's task is nothing less than to save the world. She sees the conflict, not as a war between the Central and Entente powers, but as the intrusion of Ares into world events. Her mission, as she understands it, is to destroy

---

* It is interesting that the demythologizing proposal surfaces within the field of biblical studies at the same time as modern superheroes arise. Both represent attempts to conquer the forces of evil with a powerful message. In the case of Bultmann, it is a gospel liberated from ancient conceptual baggage. In the case of superheroes, it's powerful beings who liberate people from evil and rampant crime.

Ares, her half-brother and a powerful god in his own right. She thinks Ares is responsible for the world war.

Diana is not omniscient. While engaging the forces of evil on the front, she discovers truths about herself that she had not previously realized. Like Oedipus, she does not at first know her true identity. She takes from the arsenal on Themyscira a sword she believes is the "god-killer" weapon. She discovers later on that she, not it, is the weapon Zeus had left behind before dying. Diana is the god-killer, the goddess who is more powerful than her brother, Ares. By killing Ares, who had killed Zeus, she becomes the most powerful of all the gods, defeating the force of evil.

She misidentifies Ares, whom she thinks has become incarnate in the German General Ludendorff.* Killing him, she is baffled that the war does not immediately cease. If the god Ares had been responsible for the evil that was World War I, cessation of hostilities is what would be expected with his death.

As it turns out, Ares is really Sir Patrick Morgan, a fictitious member of the British Imperial War Council. In their confrontation, Diana's god-killer sword is destroyed. Once again, Diana is baffled when Sir Patrick reveals Diana's true hidden identity: she is the god-killer. Positioning himself as "the God of Truth," he confesses that all he can do is to whisper . . .

> . . . ideas and inspiration for formulas, weapons, but I don't make them [humans] use them. They start these wars on their own. All I do is orchestrate an armistice I know they cannot keep in the hope that they will destroy themselves.

Ares (Sir Patrick) suggests that Diana join forces with him to end all the pain and suffering and to recreate Paradise as it was before humans. Diana refuses. Upon the death of Ares, Diana comes to realize that the gods in general, and Ares in particular, are not responsible for human warfare. The choice is human.

---

* The real German General Erich Ludendorff did not die in World War I. He opposed the armistice and after the War promoted the view that Germany had been "stabbed in the back" by cowardly German leaders—Communist, Bolsheviks, and Jews. He died in 1937.

Diana concludes:

> I used to want to save the world
> To end war and bring peace to mankind.
> But then I glimpsed the darkness
> That lives within their light
> And learned that inside every one of them,
> There will always be both.
> A choice each must make for themselves.

So *Wonder Woman* (2017) demythologizes the Ares myth. The gods are not responsible for evil nor for World War I. Humans are responsible for both, by the choices they make. Diana also realizes that she now has a mission, to fight and "give for the world I know can be."

With these three films in place, we now have the back story to Superman, Batman, and Wonder Woman.

The Source of Evil

As rebooted within the past decade, one of the key features of pop culture superhero films is its identification of the source of evil. Evil does not fall from the sky in the form of evil beings. Both *Man of Steel* and *Wonder Woman* (2017) destroyed this notion—at least in the DCEU series released to date.

Evil occurs not because of malevolent gods or aliens invading our planet but because of human wrongdoing. Evil arises when people chose to follow their evil inclination. Their values are warped and the choices they make lead to death and destruction rather than to life and creativity. Evil comes about as a result of human agency and actions. So we are to blame, not somebody else.

According to the superhero genre, we have many villains. These are humans who have chosen to do evil acts creating havoc and suffering in society. They must be confronted.

How, then, is human-generated evil to be confronted? Pop culture superhero films always portray a way out by some powerful mega- or metahuman. There is always a rescuer who arrives on the scene.

Interestingly, no longer is one superhero sufficient. The conquest of evil today now requires an army of superheroes—a "Justice League"—who join forces to help bring about a better world. Batman, Wonder Woman, Superman, the Flash, and many others team up to arrest and destroy evil in the world. The need for a league, a team, reflects our perception that the world we live in is a mess and that very powerful destructive forces beset our society.

V

WHERE'S TOMORROW'S MESSIAH TO BE FOUND?

18

"SOMEONE ELSE"

⚬⚬⚬

Centuries ago, the Hebrew prophet Micah expressed the desire for a better world. He envisaged the Temple of the Lord standing high above the mountains with people from around the world flocking to it for teaching and guidance:*

> For instruction (*Torah*) shall come forth from Zion,
> The word of the Lord (*YHVH*) from Jerusalem.
> Nation shall not take up
> Sword against nation;
> They shall never again know war;
> But every man shall sit
> Under his grapevine or fig tree
> With no one to disturb him.† (Micah 4:1–4)

---

*   This oracle is also found in Isaiah 2:2-4.

†   The NRSV translates the last line as ". . . and no one shall make them afraid."

Micah yearned for a world at peace with people enjoying life free from fear. He had no idea when this world would occur, simply projecting it into "the days to come." That idyllic stress-free future represents the hope of many, then and now.

How will such a world come to be?

In the quest for a better world, many people place their trust in saviors or messiahs—rescuers who promise a brighter future ahead. A rescue orientation gives rise to a conceptual framework, a way of understanding the world. It goes as follows:

> The world is a mess.
> Someone will come to fix it.

There are two elements in rescue thinking. First of all, there is a "someone" responsible for the mess—some identifiable entity, a force or a person, who has caused the problems. There is thus someone to blame: some problem-maker.

Secondly, there is the someone who is the chosen messiah or savior, someone selected to deal effectively with the situation: the problem-fixer. Religious and political realms in particular are scoured for that someone onto whom we can pin our deepest hopes and dreams. This person is to "rescue us from all our foes."*

Rescue thinking is essentially an optimistic outlook. Problems exist, but so do solutions. Challenging problems in life can be resolved successfully. There is a catch, however, and it's an important one: it requires someone else to effect change.

The hope for a rescuer isn't just an ancient preoccupation. We find rescue thinking rampant in contemporary society, in religious, political, and pop culture circles. In the video game universe, for instance, enemies abound and danger awaits. Obstacles crop up fast and furious. Each one has to be overcome by some "good guy" or avatar within the game.

This kind of thinking can spill over from the virtual world into real life where getting along can perceived as a succession of economic, health,

---

* A line from a popular Christian hymn, "Praise, my soul, the King of Heaven," based on Psalm 103.

social, and political challenges to be confronted and solved. Life then becomes a game like playing "whack-a-mole." As soon as one "mole" is dealt with, another one pops up. We can never get ahead of the moles.

News media reinforce this perception with commentators breathlessly trying to keep up with "breaking news," one crisis swiftly following another, so much so that most newsworthy incidents only last in our attention in-basket for a day or two, if that.

Rescue thinking is found today in Christianity, Islam, and some forms of Judaism which look patiently for a messiah—either a returning messiah or a first-time savior who will change the course of history, likely through cataclysmic means. Wars and rumors of wars in the Middle East are sometimes interpreted as harbingers of apocalyptic earth-transforming events. Some view these developments as heralding the imminent advent of messiah, recognizing that his arrival will involve the most terrifying warfare the world will ever see.

Apocalyptic rescue thinking borders on a self-fulfilling prophecy, encouraging risky political maneuvers so as to create the massive destructive conditions that would precede the appearance of messiah. The cataclysmic scenario depicted by Second Zechariah, for example, is never far from the minds of some devout messianic believers. That writing envisages nations descending on Israel to bring about the End Time. Some try to figure out the divine plan, identifying contemporary Iran (and its proxies Hezbollah and Hamas in Lebanon, Syria, and Gaza) and Russia as the current villains in this apocalyptic scenario.*

Rescue thinking is present, too, in contemporary American political circles. Reagan will fix things. If not him, then Bill Clinton. Obama will fix things. And if not him, then Trump. And if not him, then who? What strong popular leader will emerge to create a better society, a celebrity political superstar who will work collectively and collaboratively for the good of all? Who is the new political fixer who can bring about legislation to provide better education and healthcare, jobs that support middle-class aspirations with justice for all citizens regardless of ethnicity or gender? Where is such an effective political hero to be found?

---

* See, for instance, John Hagee, *Jerusalem Countdown, Revised and Updated: A Prelude to War*. Charisma Media, 2013.

Rescue thinking represents the search for an external agency, to fix things. It's rooted in a feeling of powerlessness and desperation. We cannot solve crime, horrors, injustices, tragedies, and atrocities on our own, so where's that more powerful being to whom we can attach ourselves? Where's that savior when he is most needed?

Where is that "somebody else" who will save us?

Rescue Thinking—Some Issues

Thinking we have to rely on someone else to fix problems represents a flawed perspective.

For one thing, rescue thinking reflects a paranoid mindset. This orientation sees the world as a dangerous place. Survival is understood as a challenge involving an endless series of evils to overcome. There's a problemmaker lurking out there, some enemy who must be defeated. The threat level to one's personal well-being is high.

The villain is someone else, some human being or perhaps some group perceived to threaten our personal aims and ambitions. For Hitler, it was "the Jews." For liberals it's "conservatives." For conservatives, it's "liberals." For others, it's Trump, or Obama, or immigrants, or nonwhites, or globalists, or a secret new world order society, or some behind-the-scenes organization like the Priory of Sion or Elders of Zion. A paranoid orientation plays into the politics of fear.

According to this mindset, evil beings or malevolent forces exist who are intent on destroying our plans and ruining our well-being. They threaten our basic security and comfort. Constant vigilance is demanded. Meissner observes that a rescue mindset needs . . .

> . . . an enemy in order to bolster its own inner resources and to maintain its own inner sense of value and purposiveness.*

---

* W. W. Meissner, *Thy Kingdom Come: Psychoanalytic Perspectives on the Messiah and the Millennium*. Kansas City, MO: Sheed and Ward, 1995, p. 258.

The enemy is the someone on whom we focus our anger. That someone stands in the way of personal happiness and fulfillment.

A rescue-oriented personality seeks out powerful allies, saviors in the struggle against the perceived evil. The quest to overcome the enemy motivates people to become attached to a cause, group, or ideology that will help in the quest to rid the world of the perceived evil. By becoming affiliated with a larger group, the individual through his identification with the rescuer becomes a force to be reckoned with, something more powerful than just that person alone.

Associated with social affiliation comes attachment to belief systems—religious or political or both—which reinforce the outlook that the world is a dangerous place. A community of shared belief surfaces that provides a framework for understanding the world, providing security and freedom from anxiety. The world becomes tolerable and existence takes on meaning and purpose . . . perhaps even a mission. As Meissner points out:

> The paranoid construction, in a sense, rationalizes the pattern of projections so that adherents to the belief system and members of the in-group are viewed as bearers of truth and goodness, while those who reject or oppose the belief system or belong to deviant out-groups are regarded as the agents of falsehood, error, even evil. This projective necessity requires the existence of an enemy who becomes the target and bearer of projections; the projections themselves do not stand alone but require a sustaining matrix within which they can find confirmation and rationalization.[*]

The matrix is the community, the social group which supports and sustains belief. In terms of religious messianic thinking, the community of belief provides a way in which the individual can confront a world which is perceived as fundamentally flawed and threatening. The thinking becomes, "If I can't mend the world, then perhaps a savior, a messiah or even God

---

[*] W. W. Meissner, *Thy Kingdom Come*, p. 258.

himself, will subdue the evil forces, creating a world more amenable to the way in which I think it should be."

Paul appealed to such a psychological dynamic. We can't conquer death, but by becoming attached to Christ who overcame death, perhaps we, too, like him can surmount this evil. Paul not only proposed this religious perspective, but went on to form communities of right-believing individuals. The congregations of the Christ reinforced this perspective in its members, focusing on recalling, celebrating, and participating vicariously in Jesus's death, sacrifice, and resurrection through ritual identification with his body and blood. The focus of this religious movement was Christ attachment—personal identification with the Christ figure. Right believing, correct personal attachment, became what counts, not right action. Orthodoxy supplanted orthopraxy.

Secondly, rescue thinking is inherently dualistic. Forces of good battle forces of evil and so confrontation replaces cooperation. Those who disagree with our deeply held religious or political positions are deemed suspect, if not downright evil. The *Psalms of Solomon* are inherently dualistic: the righteous *versus* sinners, each with separate eternal futures. A person is either one or the other. So, too, are the writings of the Dead Sea Scroll Community. They contrast their holy members against the unrighteous of the world in a battle to the finish and world supremacy. Similarly other religious perspectives segment the world into believers and nonbelievers, leaving little room in the middle for those who are uncertain or who vacillate between positions.

A dualistic perspective tends to vilify opponents. That mindset avoids the type of rational discourse that enjoys examining the merits of differing positions, looking at pros and cons of different ideas with a view to improving one's own position. People holding divergent views are just dismissed and their positions not only rejected but vilified. Since they are demonized, they are to be destroyed—locked up, sent back, or simply condemned.

Contemporary vile personal attacks in the comments section of newspaper articles and blogs bear out the depth of animosity towards the "other." Many comments are simply personal jabs or a rejection of other people's views simply because of their supposed affiliations—you only say that because you are a "retarded liberal" or "blind conservative" (and much worse) for instance. Such attacks often occur with such hot topics as border security, migrants, immigrants, Israel, Palestine, Muslims, climate change, or the United Nations. The views of political and social opponents are not debated, just attacked, often viciously. Civilized discourse is abandoned, and discussion is reduced to a series of likes and dislikes.

Thirdly, within a conceptual framework of antagonism, social, political, and religious conversations become tribal in nature. They become "my group," and my beliefs are correct *versus* those of all other groups who oppose my views. Strong ideologies take root, with no tolerance for dissenting perspectives. No longer is the 1960s optimism of Canadian social theorist Marshall McLuhan greeted with enthusiasm, that the world is becoming a global village.* Suspicion, anger, and distrust flourish as globalism itself comes under attack in favor of the security and comfort of our own tribe.

The tribe is not, of course, necessarily ethnically defined, although race, gender, and sexual identification play a role. It's a belief system characterized by those who share the perceptions and opinions we hold concerning the identity of the foe and the fixer.

Tribal orientation creates deep polarized chasms between opposing affiliations: Republican *versus* Democrat, liberal *versus* conservative, capitalist *versus* socialist/Communist, Sunni *versus* Shiite, progressive religious believers *versus* fundamentalists, and so on. It's "us"—whoever we are—*versus* whoever we perceive "them" to be. Discourse becomes dichotomized and there is no middle ground. With a wide gulf in personal opinions, dinners with family members who hold differing political beliefs or religious views can rapidly become confrontational. The tension can be palpable, and anger quickly surfaces as conflict and rancor prevail over the enjoyment of food and good times.

A tribal perspective is frequently encountered in comments on social media and news outlets. Opinions are rejected if they are "other" or accepted because they fit with our preconceived ideas. Complex issues are reduced to tweets and these are usually personal in nature and not substantive. People choose television networks based on the filtering ideologies of the news

---

* Marshall McLuhan, *Understanding Media*. New York: Signet Books, 1964.

providers. What used to be called reporting is slanted: it's opinion or information from a perspective. Thus what we consume from the external world by way of news/information reinforces our paranoia. A shared uncritical perspective gives us comfort that we are not alone in our take on life.

Moderate views that see some good in opposing perspectives are abandoned. As Yeats pointed out in his poem "The Second Coming" written at the end of the World War I, "the center cannot hold." In desperate times, there is no middle ground, and extremes rule. President Obama pointed to the fractures in current political discourse:

> The audacity of hope. That was the best of the American spirit,
> I thought—having the audacity to believe despite all evidence
> to the contrary that we could restore a sense of community to
> a nation torn by conflict. . . . *

Such conflict comes from extremist positions fueled by a dualistic understanding of the world in which we live: either you are for me and the right-thinking people who share my opinions, or else you're against me. There's no chance that if you hold a contrary position you could possibly be right. Those who disagree become the enemy, not just people who simply hold a different view. Their views are to be shouted down; the speakers banned from speaking. Rescue thinking is fundamentally divisive.

Fourthly, rescue thinking sets the groundwork for disappointment. Leaders generating huge expectations for a better day cannot always accomplish what they set out to do. Indeed, rescuers often fail to live up to their promise. Leaders generating huge expectations for a better day cannot always accomplish what they set out to do.

Jesus, for instance, promised imminent world transformation. When that failed to come about within two or three decades after his death, some disappointed followers abandoned his cause while others radically reinterpreted his message spiritually.

---

* Barack Obama, *The Audacity of Hope: Thoughts on Reclaiming the American Dream*. New York: Three Rivers Press, 2006, p. 356. Obama attributes the phrase "audacity of hope" to a sermon by the Rev. Jeremiah A. Wright, Jr.

Woodrow Wilson trumpeted the League of Nations as a way of ensuring peace. His ideas found root in Europe but not in the United States which refused to join the League of Nations. And less than a generation after the end of World War I, the allure of Germany's resurrection touted by Adolf Hitler led to that country's destruction, massive killing on a worldwide scale, and unimaginable worldwide suffering. Decades later, the audacity of hope movement by Obama generated huge excitement and high expectations, only to flounder by forces outside any one individual's power to combat.

Pinning all one's hopes on the one to carry the burden of the many is a certain path to disillusionment and crushed expectations.

Disenchantment with a savior creates a backlash. If Obama can't fix things, then perhaps a populist figure like Trump can. And if Trump can't live up to his promises, then who can? The search for a rescuer, a present-day messiah, continues.

Other-Directed Attachments

Finally, a fundamental problem with someone else thinking is that it is "other-directed." The focus is placed on an external agency outside the self. Problem-solving is something an "other" must do, someone stronger—someone who stands out—a charismatic leader in politics, a popular preacher or wise sage in religion or a flamboyant hero from pop culture.

Rescue thinking reflects a sense of personal powerlessness. To overcome weakness, that individual aligns himself with something more significant, perhaps a major religious movement, a cult, a political party, a conspiracy, or worldview that offers an inside scoop that lets us in on what is really going on in the world and who is actually in charge. Such an affiliation gives the person a powerful platform, something larger that gives meaning and purpose. Some religious leaders, politicians, and superheroes play into this dynamic, tantalizing people with solutions that provide reassurance, comfort, meaning, and purpose to an otherwise powerless existence.

Paul did this by asking his followers to identify with Christ, to participate in his suffering and sacrifice so as to escape the consequences of sin. His group became "Christ-ians," Christ identifiers. Individuals who so self-identify take on a larger persona. Leaders across all religions and politicians of all parties build a base of followers. All they ask for is strong personal attachment and steadfast commitment.

Such attachment, however, comes at a price. Rescue thinking or other-directed attachment encourages passivity, waiting for someone else to change the situation. A rescue orientation embodies a specific view of our identity as human beings. It promotes the view that we are bystanders or voyeurs to the drama that unfolds in the world around us, positioning us as ineffectual witnesses to the battles of our era. Maybe we could rise to the level of a cheerleader by attaching us to some rescuer mentally or emotionally but not much more. We're not the doers, however. We are not the rescuers.

So the attitude becomes: there's nothing we can do to fix the mess. So wait for a charismatic political leader; wait for a superhero rescuer; wait for a messiah.

Waiting was the strategy James and his Jewish Torah-observant group clung to in Jerusalem, waiting for Jesus to reappear as king of the promised Kingdom of God. For 30 years they lingered, from the early 30s to 62 when James was killed in Jerusalem. What did they do during this time? What did they teach? It's difficult to imagine what they did during this period of time to promote the cause of the Kingdom.* No wonder this group was bypassed in history by the far more proactive Paul† who crisscrossed the Mediterranean's northern rim with his revisionist message.

In *Batman*, the superhero is always on call whenever a crime wave occurs. The city, its police force, and its citizens are often paralyzed and simply wait for the hero to respond to the Batsignal.

---

* According to the Book of Acts (Acts 6:1–7), this group set up a food distribution program.

† Ironically Paul, too, was a rescuer, salvaging a failed mission by changing the message from the Kingdom of God to one about the significance of Jesus's death. The alternative to Paul's interpretation is admitting that Jesus's Kingdom had not come about as promised or else interpreting Jesus's promised Kingdom as something spiritual as did the Gnostic group of Christians. The first alternative sees Jesus's mission as a failure; the second, as miscommunication.

In *Man of Steel*, the United States military is mobilized, but it is powerless to deal with Zod and his crew. Only Superman can muster the powers to confront the forces of extraterrestrial evil.

In *Wonder Woman*, while most of the leaders are trying to achieve an armistice, one individual is bent on sabotaging these efforts through enhanced chemical warfare. Wonder Woman and her band come to the rescue to help stem the violence. Without her intervention, evil would not be stopped.

Everyone counts on the superhero to do what has to be done to defeat evil.

Overall, rescue thinking creates a passive population looking for "someone else" to solve problems. Socialization via messiahs, saviors, and superheroes can result in a paralysis of the self. That quest for someone else represents a false attachment. It is searching for meaning and fulfillment in the wrong place: in an external agency, outside the self.

Is there an alternative to someone else kind of thinking?

19

THE REAL MESSIAH

⸺⊶⸺

An alternative to other-directed rescue thinking can be found in the teachings of Jesus. According to him, we should not look to someone else to provide rescue—not to him, not to anyone. In his core teachings Jesus was not the least bit interested in the idea of a messiah. That just wasn't his focus. For one thing, as we have seen, Jesus did not fulfill any of the Jewish messianic criteria outlined in *Psalms of Solomon*. He also stopped messiah talk in its tracks when Peter uttered his famous phrase, "You are the Messiah." Keep quiet about that was his quick response. At his trial before the Roman and Jewish leaders he mounted no defense, providing no evidence why anyone might think of him in those terms. Moreover, the religious authorities saw no evidence that the requisite messianic world transformations were in progress. His first followers knew he wasn't a messiah because they put forward the view of the Second Coming, namely that Jesus would have to reappear to do what he should have done first time around, had he been the messiah. A two-stage messianic operation was not part of the expectation.

So, why think of Jesus in messianic terms?

If not a messiah in the sense of *mashiach*, then what did this Jewish, human, and perhaps married individual teach? And why has this aspect of his teaching become so obscured? Why has an inner-directed religion become transformed into one that is profoundly other-directed?

This transformation from an inner-directed to an other-directed religion joins a long list of key shifts as the religion of Jesus became Christianity:

- from the teachings *of* Jesus to those *about* him
- from a focus on the Kingdom of God to Jesus as the Christ
- from the desire for a new world order to a new world religion
- from Jewish to Gentile
- from Torah-observant to non-Torah-observant
- from anti-Roman to pro-Roman

The transformation of the religion of Jesus was immense in scope. It represents a massive makeover of the message of Jesus.

Detachment
Detachment from the Idea of Messiah

When we examine the fundamental teachings of Jesus—what he really taught, not the religion Paul developed about Jesus—we find that not only was he not a messiah, he did not even promote himself as one. He didn't want people to think of him that way at all. He didn't even encourage people to hope for a messiah. Not an iota of messiah talk. He was silent on the topic, for good reason. A messiah fixing things would simply be an "other-directed" quest, a search for "someone else" to set matters right. That, for Jesus, was searching in the wrong direction: it's outer not inner-directed, other-directed not self-directed.

This finding may be surprising to those wedded to Jesus as a *Christos* as Paul taught. But look below the Pauline layer imposed on the gospels. Strip away all the Christ talk and see what Jesus himself actually taught, the good news of the Kingdom.

The absence of messiah talk in the Gospel of Mark gives us an important clue to how Jesus thought about messianic thinking. Being messiah wasn't part of his agenda and he made that very clear when he assumed a disguise as the Son of Man/the Human. Taking a cue from Jesus's silence on the topic, we should detach ourselves from thinking of him as a potential rescuer, that is, as a King-Messiah anointed to lead an independent Israel enjoying world peace.

So forget messiah talk. Detach from that false attachment. There's nothing in Jesus's core teachings about being a messiah. Let's now turn to what is included in the teachings of the Jesus of history.

Detachment from Things

Jesus opposed focus on externals. He taught turning away from alluring but harmful attachments, for example, the attachment to material goods. For instance, immediately after outlining the Lord's Prayer in the Sermon on the Mount, Jesus said:

> Do not store up for yourselves treasures on earth, where moth and rust consume and where thieves break in and steal . . . For where your treasure is, there your heart will be also. (Matthew 6:19–21)

Here Jesus urges detachment from material objects and from making the acquisition of things our purpose in life.

A consumer society binges on hoarding, desiring material possessions as markers of status, and personal self-esteem. Consumerism is other-directed. With attachment to the pursuit of things, stuff becomes part of who we are, a central part of our identity. Things become an extension of ourselves and our personal worth. Amassing expensive cars, clothing, furniture, collectables, and other goods can become an obsession. Accumulation can exceed the ability of our homes or apartments to house the stuff. Public storage facilities—a growth industry—rise to fulfill the need to store the stuff we have accumulated over and above what is in our closets, basements, and sheds.

A materially oriented person thus finds it very difficult to declutter, downsize, or to give up acquisitive habits. For a person devoted to things, decluttering, and overcoming consumerism is not the removal of neutral no longer wanted objects. Rather it takes the form of carving out bits and pieces of one's self. It's like cutting off a limb.

Jesus encouraged his followers to turn away from such other-directed behavior as material acquisition and to focus instead on nurturing one's self and enhancing one's true identity. Seeing the accumulation of things as the purpose in life represents a false but powerful attachment. Material goods cannot replace the void in other sectors of life, relationships, experiences, and a sense of self-worth.

This does not mean that material goods are irrelevant—shelter, clothing, food, transportation, and, in modern terms, phones and tablets—all have their place. But, for Jesus, we should not become wedded to them or regard them as an extension of our being. They are there to be used, as necessities. They are not part of us.

Jesus's core teachings are to be found in sources such as the Lord's Prayer, the Sermon on the Mount (Matthew 5:1–7:27), and the Parables of the Kingdom. These passages tell us what the Jewish, human teacher roaming around the Galilee in the late 20s and early 30s likely said—as opposed to the fiction Paul created later on to save a failed mission.* They set forth two key elements of his teachings: *detachment* from false values and *engagement* in activities that enhance creation.

Detachment from False Values

Setting Life's Priorities: The Lord's Prayer
This prayer establishes what is—and what is not—centrally important as far as the Jesus of history was concerned.

---

* That doesn't mean that these sayings have not been altered by the gospel writers addressing late 1st century concerns. All of Jesus's sayings have been filtered through that later perspective.

There are several versions of the Lord's Prayer, one in Matthew (Matthew 6:9–13) and a slightly shorter one in Luke (Luke 11:2–4).* The prayer is addressed to God as, "Our father, in heaven." The person praying is positioning himself as a child of coming before an infinitely compassionate and loving father. It begins by acknowledging the sacredness of God: "Hallowed be your name." We are entering sacred space. We are doing something out of the ordinary.

The Lord's Prayer is cast as an "us" prayer, not a "me" prayer. It's "our" father. It's not asking for what "I" want but what "we" need.

The Lord's Prayer then makes four petitions. First and foremost is the request that God's Kingdom become manifest. That establishes priority: the Kingdom before everything else. The Kingdom in the prayer is tied into world transformation: "thy will be done on earth as in heaven." The Kingdom is terrestrial, but other than that, the Kingdom is not described. It is a blank screen on to which we can project our hopes and ideas. Jesus's Parables of the Kingdom will fill in some details, as we shall see. But even there, the full reality of the Kingdom is not described, the emphasis being upon what we should do to help bring it about.

The second petition is that our basic needs be met—"Give us this day our daily bread." This includes material as well as spiritual requirements: we are to attend to both. The phrase "give us" does not imply that we just sit back, and wait for these necessities to be handed to us. It means something more like, "Help us in ensuring that our daily needs are met." So material goods are important but not as the focus of our existence.

Thirdly, the prayer asks for forgiveness from God. This is conditional on us having pardoned those who have transgressed against us. Forgiveness resets relationships amongst people, our network of family and friends. That means overcoming slurs, slights, harmful deeds, grievances—all the injustices and perceived wrongs that impede our getting along with other people. It means doing what is in our power to reestablish relationships, to forgive, even when there is no reciprocity or pushback by the other party.

---

* Another version is found in a late 1st century Christian writing, *The Didache*, which is not included in the Christian Scriptures/New Testament. *The Didache* (section 8). See Bart D. Ehrman, *Lost Scriptures*, p. 215.

If we can't forgive, then we have no basis for standing before God asking for forgiveness.

Like the Psalms of King David, the Lord's Prayer presumes that people can stand before God, even though sinful. It premises divine forgiveness on us having forgiven others, that is, to do what is within our power to create a harmonious and peaceful world. By forgiving others we are to do what they cannot do for themselves, that is, to be forgiven by us.

In modern terms, forgiveness is a reboot: it resets relationships, with other people and with God. So again the message is one of detachment—getting rid of all the barriers and resentments that stand in the way of relationships, with others and with God. There is much in our power to effect change.

Finally, "Lead us not into temptation but deliver us from evil."* The petition is that we not succumb to temptation, not to surrender to the evil impulse, and to recall the primary focus, the Kingdom. It's essentially a petition for help in avoiding sin.

Pope Francis recently proposed changing the wording. Instead of saying the familiar "lead us not into temptation," he suggests saying instead, "do not let us fall into temptation." That avoids positioning God as the agent of temptation. Furthermore it makes clear that this petition is asking for control of self: we have the means not to fall.

Several things are paramount in this prayer. For one thing, it does not seek to influence or to change God by itemizing a long list of things God should do. We ask for God's help in securing our daily necessities and avoiding the temptation to do evil, but there's no long list of sociopolitical actions God should be concerned about, simply because they are on our agenda. There is no long list pointing out the obvious to God, that the world we have made falls short in many respects and may indeed lead to disaster. God is not sitting back waiting for us to mention climate change, racism, poverty, crime, illness, and the like.

Nor does the prayer encourage us to think that God is going to tackle these issues.

---

* There are variants here—for example, some versions have "do not bring us to a time of trial." Other versions have "but deliver us from the evil one."

The objective of prayer is to change ourselves. We must become transformed.

In so doing it sets forth priorities. As children of God, we are to focus on the Kingdom, forgive others and resist the temptation to commit evil. The prayer is about *us* changing and about us *doing*. *We* must change; *we* must *do*. It's about self-transformation.

The Lord's Prayer does not include any mention of Jesus. Its focus is on God's Kingdom:* "thy Kingdom come." This passage aligns with the opening of the Gospel of Mark—the "good news" is good news about that Kingdom. That's the number one priority: forgiving and coping with temptations come ahead of personal needs.

The prayer's focus is not only on world transformation. The Lord's Prayer empowers the self through personal transformation. It is decidedly not someone else thinking and certainly not about a messiah coming to change the world. *That's the clue*: the complete absence of messianic thinking in Jesus's signature prayer. World transformation requires personal transformation. The kingdom requires us to be focused on changing ourselves; to recast priorities, reboot relationships, and avoid the inclination to commit evil.

Individual transformation through personal empowerment is the emphasis in Jesus's keynote prayer. It is not a prayer that says to God, send in messiah to fix this world. That is, it is not other-directed. Its focus is directed towards the self: change us.

This message is reinforced in Jesus's Parables of the Kingdom.

Detachment from Other-Directedness and Passivity

Preparing the Way of the Lord: The Parables of the Kingdom

The Gospel of Mark (Mark 1:3) begins by quoting Second Isaiah (Isaiah 40:3), "prepare the way of the Lord." This command suggests that we have to do something. But what? How should we "prepare the way of the Lord?"

---

* Even in versions of the Lord's Prayer that include as an ending, "For thine is the kingdom and the power and the glory, for ever and ever," the referent here is to God—it is God's kingdom, no one else's.

As we shall see, it has everything to do with personal self-transformation, not taking it easy and not wishing for a messiah to appear on the world stage. Other-directed thinking lets us relax, sit back and let someone else do the job. We relinquish responsibility and lapse into observers. Someone else thinking is a couch-potato stance.

Parables are short, sometimes puzzling stories meant to engage the audience. They are intended to provoke discussion and invite response. Parables represent mirrors in which we see ourselves. What we do with that image is up to us.

Jesus does not typically divulge the meaning of the parables. He lets people debate and discuss them. Some parables are decoded as allegories, but scholars suspect that these are elucidations by the gospel writers, not those of Jesus.*

The parables focus on values and actions. Jesus did not write out a list of prescriptive do's and don'ts. Rather, his parables tease and challenge people, allowing them to discern through dialogue and discussion what the Kingdom requires.

The Parable of the Sower

The Parable of the Sower (Mark 4:1–20) presents a situation where seeds fall on four different soil conditions: on places where they can easily be consumed by birds, or on rocky ground, overshadowed by thorns, or on "good soil."

Presumably audience conversation would then focus on a number of elements in the story—identifying what constitutes "seeds" and the "good soil," for instance. Or discussing what constitutes the fertile conditions for

---

* The Gospel of Matthew in particular interprets the parables allegorically. See, for instance, his take on the Parable of the Sower (Matthew 13:18–23) or the Parable of the Weeds in the Wheat (Matthew 13:24–30 with its interpretation given in Matthew 13:37–43). Allegorical interpretation of parables defeats discussion and debate, thereby rendering the point of telling parables pointless. If parables are so mysterious as to require allegorical decoding, then it would be better just to say the message than to tease people into thinking creatively as to its possible meaning. This is why scholars think that the allegorical interpretation of the parables is attributable to the author of the Gospel of Matthew, not Jesus.

the Kingdom message to prosper. In what environment does the Kingdom take root?

As this parable shows, the Kingdom message is interactive, between message and hearer. The hearer or responder has to think about the message, ponder various possibilities and consider various interpretations. Parables are designed to open up discussion, not close off debate.

Presumably these parables would have been told on many different occasions during Jesus's mission in the Galilee, likely in many different versions. Not all parables are included in each of the four gospels. Some are also found in the *Gospel of Thomas.** None of Jesus's parables are to be found in Paul's letters.

Parables of the Treasure and the Pearl of Great Value

The parables emphasize some critical themes about the Kingdom. For one thing, the Kingdom is vitally important, precious, something to be sought after and treasured. Sometimes the Kingdom is described as "a treasure hidden in a field" (Matthew 13:44) or as a "pearl of great value" (Matthew 13:45). As with the Lord's Prayer, the centrality of the Kingdom is the message.

Parable of the Talents

The Kingdom involves active participation. It requires thoughtful reflection, judgment, choices, and action. The Parable of the Talents makes this clear (Matthew 25:14–30).

The story proceeds as follows. A person goes away on a trip, entrusting his wealth to his servants. One gets five talents; another one, two talents; and finally one receives just one talent. A "talent" is delightfully ambiguous in English. Here it means a coin of considerable worth. It can also refer, of course, to the special skill set each person has. And the point of the parable is that "talent" means both.

---

* A chart of Jesus's parables and their biblical references can be found online. See, for instance, "Parables of Jesus" on Wikipedia.

The person who receives five talents uses this wealth to make five additional talents. Similarly the one with two talents makes two more. The one with one talent, however, hides the money in the ground and does nothing with it. The two who use their wealth to create more are praised and welcomed "into the joy of [their] master." The one who hides the money is condemned. He does nothing with what he has been given. As a result, he is to be thrown into "the outer darkness."

So, what does this parable mean? One line of interpretation pertains to the individual abilities and resources each person possesses. These personal skill sets are to be used. The Kingdom is not for those who sit passively, waiting for it to materialize. Instead, the Kingdom requires thoughtful action.

Presumably, then, those hearing this parable around the Sea of Galilee would start discussing what was required of them. How to maximize God-given gifts? How to use our potential, skills, and resources to benefit the Kingdom? In other words, the hearers understand that they have to do something. It's an inner-directed message directed towards the self.

Perhaps individuals in Jesus's audience would reach into biblical history and discuss leaders who took initiative to overcome crises. Perhaps they recalled individuals such as Joseph, Esther, or Judith who used their abilities, leadership, and courage to rescue their people.

The Kingdom Jesus talked about requires doing. In a sense, this parable condemns both the stance of Paul, who taught salvation by faith (not action), as well as James who simply waited (inaction) for the Kingdom to appear. The teaching here is much more in keeping with Micah 6:8, "He has told you, O man, what is good, and what the Lord (*YHVH*) requires of you: only to do justice and to love goodness, and to walk modestly with your God." These are all action verbs: do, love, walk.

Jesus's action-oriented religion is highlighted in other passages. For instance, one day, a lawyer encounters Jesus and asks him what he had to do to inherit eternal life. The question is posed as one of action—what he must *do*. Jesus asks the lawyer how he understands Torah. The lawyer replies as follows:

> You shall love the Lord your God with all your heart, and with
> all your soul, and with all your strength, and with all your mind;
> and your neighbor as yourself. (Luke 10:25–27)

Jesus commends the answer. The lawyer has referenced two foundational commandments: love of God and love of others (Deuteronomy 6:5; Leviticus 19:18). These laws include attitude, decisions, and actions. They are expressions of the whole person, the values we embody, and the actions that reflect who we are. That's consistent with the Jewish tradition in which both Jesus and the lawyer stood. Eternal life is built upon trust in God and treating people the way we wish to be treated ourselves. In other words, eternal life requires action and trust . . . not belief in a cosmic savior. This passage highlights the major difference between the religion of Jesus and that of Paul.

Parable of the Great Judgment

Jesus's action-oriented perspective is also reflected in the Parable of the Great Judgment (Matthew 25:31–46). The story envisages the day when "the Son of Man" will appear gathering people from all the nations of the world. He will separate people as a shepherd separates the sheep (the righteous) from the goats (the unrighteous). The righteous receive eternal life.

Who are the righteous? It turns out in the parable that they are those who respond to the needs of others. Welcoming strangers, feeding the hungry, giving water to the thirsty, and clothing the poor are the examples given. The righteous are not those who sit back and wait for someone else to help people.

Parable of the Good Samaritan

The lawyer who had asked Jesus about eternal life continues the discussion by inquiring, "Who is my neighbor?" Jesus then tells a story.

A person traveling on the road from Jerusalem to Jericho is mugged. He's robbed, beaten, and left for dead. Two other individuals pass him by on the road, one a priest and the other, an assistant priest (a Levite). They don't stop to help. However, another individual, a Samaritan, somewhat of an outsider,* stops. He attends to his wounds and takes him to a place of

---

* Samaritans were Jews who followed a somewhat different set of laws.

shelter, giving that institution funds to cover the injured man's treatment. So, who was the neighbor to the person who was hurt?

The lawyer responds that the neighbor is the one who showed mercy. He is the person who is moved with compassion, who sees an urgent need and who responds thoughtfully and thoroughly to the stranger's plight.

The Kingdom is comprised of individuals like this, who are aware of the plight of other human beings and who take the initiative and the time to help. The rescuer here is us. We're supposed to fashion ourselves after the Good Samaritan and proactively aid people in trouble. Again the message is not one of waiting for someone else to come along to help an injured person. Righteous behavior is not something to be delegated to another.

Engagement

Self-Transformation

That's the key: world transformation depends on personal transformation. Jesus's teaching is antimessianic in the sense that it is not other-directed. The parables do not direct Jesus's followers to wait, their hopes pinned upon someone else who is supposed to make the world better. The Kingdom will come whenever, but in the meantime, there is work to be done. Detachment from passivity means engagement, using one's insights, taking advantage of opportunities, and performing deeds that help to bring about the Kingdom. This means becoming co-creators with God of the Kingdom.

In the parables, Jesus shifts away from the idea of an external fixer towards the individual and that person's role in creating a better world. The parables make clear that people must use their own unique abilities to choose wisely, to make decisions and act in such a way as to help improve the human condition. Jesus's thinking is directed towards the self and what each person can and should do. The Kingdom is something that requires activity on our part.

The message of the parables is similar to the message in the Lord's Prayer. We are to make the Kingdom our focus. We are to be forgiving, sensitive to the needs of others. We are to act mercifully, take the time to help out others, use the unique abilities and talents we each have to benefit others, and perform good deeds. It is a message about doing, not believing, and not just yearning for someone else to do what we should be doing. We must do the heavy lifting . . . not Jesus or a leader or a superhero. There can be no abdication of personal responsibility.

World transformation begins with self-transformation. That's where the messianic quest should be: how to reform the self so that an improved world comes about.

So we've been looking for messiah in all the wrong places. We should not be looking outside ourselves for someone else to solve problems. Religion, politics, and pop culture all put forward an external fixer, the someone else who will come along to repair the world. Those are the wrong places to search. They are other-directed and promote passivity, but our complex problems require all of our inputs and participation to solve.

In the parables, Jesus is not encouraging us to look elsewhere for a messiah to resolve issues. That's why he is silent when Peter says he is one. Jesus isn't a messiah. He knows he isn't. And he doesn't endorse the search for messiah. The idea that people should hunt hither and yon for one is off message. Rather Jesus teaches that we are all responsible for helping to improve the situation in which we find ourselves. The task involves repairing the world . . . on the basis of a repaired self.

It is ironic that Jesus's core teaching of self-transformation becomes layered over by the quite different teachings of a subsequent individual, Paul, and his new religion. Paul shifts the focus away from the teachings *of* Jesus to teachings *about* him. In so doing he changes the emphasis from an inner direction to an outer, from personal transformation to reliance upon an other, a someone else, an external Christ-figure.

No wonder Paul never quotes the Lord's Prayer or the Parables of the Kingdom. For him, these items are off message.

The messiah is not "out there." The messiah is right in front of us when we look in the mirror.

We are all, each one of us, individually, **messiah**.

SELECTED REFERENCES

———∞∞∞———

PRIMARY SOURCES

Bible

"JPS"—*JPS Hebrew-English Tanakh*. Philadelphia: The Jewish Publication Society, 1999.

"NRSV"—New Revised Standard Version. See *The New Oxford Annotated Bible with the Apocrypha*, College Edition. Edited by Bruce M. Metzger and Roland E. Murphy. New York: Oxford University Press, 1991.

Douglas, J. D. (ed.). *The New Greek-English Interlinear New Testament*. Wheaton, IL: Tyndale House Publishers, 1993.

Old Testament Pseudepigrapha

Charlesworth, James H. (ed.). *The Old Testament Pseudepigrapha, Volumes 1 and 2*. New York: Doubleday, 1983.

Dead Sea Scroll Community Writings

Vermes, Geza. *The Complete Dead Sea Scrolls in English*. New York: Penguin, 1997.

Gnostic Christian Writings and Christian Pseudepigrapha

Meyer, Marvin. *The Gnostic Gospels of Jesus*. New York: HarperOne, 2005.

Ehrman, Bart D. *Lost Scriptures: Books that Did Not Make It into the New Testament*. New York: Oxford University Press, 2003.

SELECTED REFERENCES

Josephus

The New Complete Works of Josephus, Revised and Expanded Edition. William Whiston (trans.), Paul L. Maier (commentary). Grand Rapids, MI: Kregel Publications, 1999.

Eusebius

Eusebius' Ecclesiastical History. C.F. Cruse (trans.), Peabody, MA: Hendrickson Publishers, 2001.

SELECTED SECONDARY SOURCES

Books by the Author

Wilson, Barrie. *How Jesus Became Christian.* New York: St. Martin's Press; Toronto: Random House, 2008.

Jacobovici, Simcha, and Barrie Wilson. *The Lost Gospel.* New York: Pegasus; Toronto: HarperCollins, 2014.

Selected Biblical Studies

Bandstra, Barry. *Reading the Old Testament.* Third Edition. Belmont, CA: Wadsworth Thomson Learning, 2004.

Ehrman, Bart D. *The New Testament: A Historical Introduction to the Early Christian Writings,* 6th edition. New York: Oxford University Press, 2015.

———. *Lost Christianities: The Battles for Scripture and the Faiths We Never Knew.* New York: Oxford University Press, 2003.

Greenberg, Gary. *The Judas Brief: Who Really Killed Jesus?* New York: Bloomsbury Academic, 2007.

Tabor, James D. *The Jesus Dynasty: The Hidden History of Jesus, His Royal Family, and the Birth of Christianity.* New York: Simon and Schuster, 2006.

———. *Paul and Jesus: How the Apostle Transformed Christianity.* New York: Simon and Schuster, 2012.

Messiah

Brandon, S. G. F. *Jesus and the Zealots: A Study of the Political Factor in Primitive Christianity.* New York: Charles Scribner's Sons, 1967.

Charlesworth, James H. (ed.). *The Messiah: Developments in Earliest Judaism and Christianity.* Minneapolis: Fortress, 1992.

———. "From Jewish Messianology to Christian Christology: Some Caveats and Perspectives" in Neusner, Green, Frerichs, pp. 225–264.

Chester, Andrew. *Messiah and Exaltation: Jewish Messianic and Visionary Traditions and New Testament Christology.* Tubingen, Germany: Mohr Siebeck, 2007.

Collins, John J. *The Scepter and the Star: Messianism in Light of the Dead Sea Scrolls.* Grand Rapids, MI: Eerdmans, 2010.

Green, William Scott. "Introduction: Messiah in Judaism: Rethinking the Question." In Neusner, Green, Frerichs (eds.), pp. 1–13.

Klausner, Joseph. *The Messianic Idea in Israel: From its Beginning to the Completion of the Mishnah.* W. F. Stinespring (trans.). New York: Macmillan, 1955.

Meissner, W. W. *Thy Kingdom Come: Psychoanalytic Perspectives on the Messiah and the Millennium.* Kansas City, MO: Sheed and Ward, 1995.

Mowinckel, Sigmund. *He that Cometh: The Messiah Concept in the Old Testament and Later Judaism.* G. W. Anderson (trans.). Nashville: Abingdon Press, 1956.

Neusner, Jacob. *Messiah in Context: Israel's History and Destiny in Formative Judaism.* Philadelphia: Fortress, 1984.

———, William Scott Green, Ernest S. Frerichs (eds.). *Judaisms and their Messiahs at the Turn of the Christian Era.* New York: Cambridge University Press, 1987.

North, Robert W. *The Messiah's Unrealized Revolution Discovered in the Gospel of Thomas.* New York: CreateSpace, 2017.

Novenson, Matthew V. *The Grammar of Messianism.* New York: Oxford University Press, 2017.

Scholem, Gershom. *The Messianic Idea in Judaism.* New York: Schocken, 1971.

Schonfield, Hugh J. *Jesus: Man—Mystic—Messiah.* London: Open Gate, 2004.

Smith, Morton. "What is Implied by the Variety of Messianic Figures?" *Journal of Biblical Literature* 78 (1959).

Vermes, Geza. *Jesus the Jew: A Historian's Reading of the Gospels.* New York: Macmillan, 1973.

Psalms of Solomon

Atkinson, Kenneth. *An Intertextual Study of the Psalms of Solomon: Pseudepigrapha.* Lewiston, NY: Mellen Press, 2000.

———. *I Cried to the Lord: A Study of the Psalms of Solomon's Historical Background and Setting.* Leiden, Netherlands: Brill, 2004.

Bons, Eberhard, and Patrick Pouchelle (eds.). *The Psalms of Solomon: Language, History, Theology.* Atlanta: SBL Press, 2015.

Harris, J. Rendel. *The Odes and Psalms of Solomon: The Syriac Text.* Cambridge: Cambridge University Press, 1912.

Ryle, H. E., and M. R. James. *Psalms of the Pharisees, Commonly Called the Psalms of Solomon.* Cambridge: Cambridge University Press, 1891.

Trafton, Joseph L. *The Syriac Version of the Psalms of Solomon: A Critical Evaluation.* Atlanta: Scholars Press, 1985.

———. *The Psalms of Solomon: Syriac and Greek Texts. Supplementary Volume to the Syriac Version of the Psalms of Solomon*, 1985.

Wright, Robert B. "*Psalms of Solomon.*" Translation and Introduction. In James H. Charlesworth (ed.), *The Old Testament Pseudepigrapha*, volume 2. New York: Doubleday, 1985, pp. 639–670.

———. *The Psalms of Solomon: A Critical Edition of the Greek Text.* New York: T & T Clark International, 2007.

Superheroes

Daniels, Les, and Chip Kidd. *Superman: The Complete History: The Life and Times of the Man of Steel.* San Francisco: Chronicle Books, 1998.

Oropeza, B. J. (ed.). *The Gospel According to Superheroes: Religion and Popular Culture.* New York: Peter Lang, 2005.

———. "Superhero Myth and the Restoration of Paradise" in B. J. Oropeza (ed.), *The Gospel According to Superheroes*, pp. 1–32.

Schenck, Ken. "Superman: A Popular Cultural Messiah," in B. J. Oropeza (ed.), *The Gospel According to Superheroes*, pp. 33–48.

King David

Kirsch, Jonathan. *King David: The Real Life of the Man Who Ruled Israel.* New York: Ballantine Books, 2000.

Van Seters, John. *The Biblical Saga of King David.* Winona Lake, IN: Eisenbrauns, 2009.

Wolpe, David. *David: the Divided Heart.* New Haven: Yale University Press, 2014.

John the Baptist

Nir, Rivka, *The First Christian Believer: In Search of John the Baptist.* Sheffield, UK: Sheffield Phoenix Press, 2019.

ACKNOWLEDGMENTS

—∞∞∞—

F or millennia, people of faith in Judaism, Christianity, and Islam have embraced the idea of a messiah. But what's a messiah? Without a job description, how can we recognize one should one appear? That was the starting point for this book and so the Messiah Project was launched—are there criteria for identifying who's a messiah?

I am highly indebted to Nancy Mandell for urging me on several occasions to write up my investigations as a book. *Searching For the Messiah* is the result.

Several individuals from different backgrounds read portions of the manuscript in its draft form. I am highly indebted to them and took their comments to heart. Whatever errors or omissions remain are solely my responsibility. Readers of these early drafts included David Goldberg, Jonathan von Kodar, Marian Magrane, and Elaine Barkin. I also discussed Hitler's positioning as savior with James A. S. Thompson of the School of Continuing Studies, University of Toronto, and I'm grateful to him for pointing me towards the film *Triumph of the Will* and other speeches.

My children and their spouses provided encouragement along the way and constantly checked on how the writing was progressing. So thanks to

Jamie, Danielle, David, Sarah, Michael, Morgan, Dorothy and Jack for their sustained interest in the project.

I have dedicated the book to my grandchildren: the future belongs to them and I wish them all well, and hope they use their insights, abilities, and energies to make the world a better place.

I am personally pleased that my literary agents, Joelle Delbourgo and Jacqueline Flynn, recognized the book's potential, as did the publisher, Jessica Case at Pegasus. I hope readers enjoy the work and will use it as a platform for discussion.

My partner in life, Linda, read the entire manuscript, and that occasioned several rewrites and a number of discussions. As always, I'm highly indebted to her for her support, insightful criticism, and encouragement as this project unfolded.

Toronto, Canada
January 2020

INDEX

A

Abraham, 109, 180, 181, 183
accuracy of Gospel accounts. *See* interpretation of Biblical texts
action to change the world, 259–262
Acts, Book of, 44–45, 175–177
Adam, 60, 188, 189
Alexandra, Queen Salome, 131
Amidah, 63, 196
Amos, Book of, 10, 11
Anglican Christianity, 170
anointed leader, 69–73, 80, 82–83, 139
Antiochus Epiphanes, 56–57, 95, 113–114, 120, 154
anti-Semitism, 88, 90–94, 217–218
Ant-Man, 225
Aquaman, 225
Aramaic, 34, 38, 39, 56, 130, 149, 155
Aristobulus I, King, 131
Aristobulus II, 131, 133
Arjuna, 196
Ark of the Covenant, 74, 75
Athanasius, Archbishop of Alexandria, 42n‡, 170
Athronges, 154
Avengers, The, 225
Avengers: Age of Ultron, 225
Avengers: Endgame, 225

B

Babylonian exile
    end of Davidic lineage, 82, 104
    Isaiah's vision of end of, 99–102, 106, 108–112
    in Lamentations, 103–105
    punishment for sin, 100, 106, 109
Bar Kokhba revolt, 168
Bathsheba, 71, 75–76
Batman, 201, 223–224, 229–232, 236, 248
Batman, The, 225
Batman v. Superman: Dawn of Justice, 224–225, 229–230
Bethlehem, 73, 155, 195
Bethsaida, 3, 4, 165
Bhagwan Rajneesh, Guru, 197

Black Panther, 225
Branch Davidian cult, 197
Britain (UK), 203, 205–212
Bultmann, Rudolf, 232–233

C

Caesar, Roman Emperor, 6–7, 10
Caesarea Philippi
    Jesus's question to disciples at, 7–13
    journey to, 3–6
    Mark's version, 44–45
    Matthew's version, 36–41, 45–48
    Thomas' version, 42–43, 48–49
Capernaum, 4, 5, 156, 165
Captain Marvel, 225
Central Powers, 203–204, 206, 233
Chorazin, 165
"chosen ones"
    David as, 74, 80, 136
    Israel as God's chosen people, 101, 106, 125–126
    Paul as, 177
Christ/Christos. *See also* Paul: theology of
    cosmic Christ, 163, 197
    defining features of, 189, 192
    as divine, 186–187
    Jesus named as, 13, 22, 33–34, 149, 163, 175
    Kal-El (Superman) as, 228
    versus *mashiach*/messiah, 175, 190–193
    personal identification with, 244, 247–248
    replaces Kingdom message, 179–180, 224, 251
    as true descendant of Abraham, 181–182
Christian scriptures. *See* New Testament
Christianity. *See* church, founding of; Gnostic Christians
Chronicles, Book of, 71
church, founding of, 40–41, 44–45, 48–50, 190–193
Churchill, Winston, 30
Clemenceau, Georges, 205, 210, 211
Clinton, Bill, 241
Colossians, Letter to, 187–188
community as God's agent in world, 98–99, 112
Constantine (emperor), 170

INDEX

consumerism, 252–253
Council of Jamnia, 131
Council of Nicea, 49
Covenant
  with Abraham, 181
  with David, 71–72, 80–82, 136–137
  with Israel as "light of the nations," 101, 112
  and King-Messiah, 139, 143
  and Torah observance, 37, 81, 125–126,
    135–136, 172, 174
  unilaterally voided by Paul, 182, 184
"created" versus "historical" Jesus
  of gospel writers, 30–32, 35
  in Luke, 31, 146, 169
  in Mark, 164
  in Matthew, 19, 30, 36–41, 48, 116
  in Paul's writings, 33–34
Cyprian of Carthage, 125
Cyrus, King of Persia, 70, 99, 103, 105

D
Damascus, 175, 177–178
Daniel, Book of, 56–57, 114, 125
David, King
  affair with Bathsheba, 75–76
  character flaws of, 75–77, 192
  Covenant with God, 71–72, 80–82, 136–137
  defeat of Goliath, 73
  dynasty of, 80–82, 104, 114–115, 136–137
  Jesus as descendant of, 19–20
  as King-Messiah and son of God, 73–74,
    77–80, 122
  political achievements of, 74–75
  as prototypical messiah, 71–74
DC Extended Universe, xi, 201, 224–225, 229
Dead Sea Scrolls Community
  Community Rule of, 121–122, 185
  dualistic thinking of, 244
  and eternal life, 125
  origin of, 120
  Torah-observant; righteous, 8, 120, 173–174,
    184–185
  War Scroll of, 18
deaths - mass, 167, 195, 200, 203, 213, 220, 231
"demythologizing," 232–234
Deuteronomy, Book of, 82n*, 124, 147
Dialogue of the Savior, 170
Diana Prince. *See* Wonder Woman
disciples of Jesus, 3–5, 141, 160–161
Domitian (emperor), 162
donkey, king riding on, 115, 116
dualistic thinking, 244–245

E
Eastern Orthodox Christianity, 170

Egypt, 5, 86–88, 102, 109, 115, 145–147
Eisenhower, Dwight D., 29
Elijah, 9–11, 18, 70
Elisha, 69–70
End Time, 10, 118, 119–123, 144, 194, 241
enemy
  central to rescue thinking, 197–199, 242–246
  defeated by Judith, 96
  Haman as, 93
  Jews identified as enemy by Hitler, 218
Enoch, 119–122, 123, 125, 126, 144
Entente Powers, 203–204, 211, 215, 233
Essence of Christianity, The, 199
Essenes, 8, 18, 32, 159, 168, 178
  See also Dead Sea Scrolls Community
Esther, Queen; Book of, 88–94
eternal life
  by Christ's sacrificial death, 192
  not a focus of HB/OT, 98, 125
  and righteousness, 134, 136, 144, 174,
    259–260
  through belief in Christ, 177, 179, 189, 193
Eusebius, 162, 168
Evangelical Christianity, 170, 196
evil
  in *1 Enoch*, 121
  anti-Semitism as, 93–94
  combatted by Jewish messiahs, 18
  elimination of. *See* End Time
  Haman as force of, 88, 92–93
  in Hindu theology, 196
  and Hitler, 202, 212–213
  imperial oppression as, 114, 192
  in Judaic thought, 229
  in The Lord's Prayer, 255–256
  overcome by God, 87, 94
  in rescue thinking, 242–244
  Satan/Lucifer, 222, 226, 229
  in superhero films, xi, 201, 223–226, 229–232,
    234–236, 249
  theological questions about, 200, 221–222,
    225–226
  See also enemy; sin
Exodus, Book of, 88, 183
Ezra, Book of, 105, 111–112

F
Feast/Festival of Booths. *See* Succoth
Feuerbach, Ludwig, 199
films (movies) - superheroes, 224–236
forgiveness, 183, 254–255
France, 203, 205, 207–208, 210, 212, 213
Freud, Sigmund, 199
Fuchs, Jason, 232
fulfillment theology, 145–146

future: imagined by Jewish community BCE. *See also* End Time; new world order; Paradise, restoration of, 122–123, 126, 148–149
Future of an Illusion, 199

G

Galatians, Letter to, 174, 177, 179, 183–184, 185
Galilee, region of
  devastation of, 30, 116, 167
  Jesus's life and ministry in, 4–7, 11–16, 28, 32, 155–157, 258
Gamaliel, Rabbi, 176
Garden of Eden, 59, 114, 123, 144, 194
gender, concepts of, 60–62, 156
Genesis, Book of, 59–61
George, David Lloyd, 205, 206–207, 209–210
German nationalism, 211, 214, 215
Germany, 203, 205–206, 208, 210–220
gnosis, 42, 169
Gnostic Christians
  gnosis as spiritual practice, 42, 169–170, 248n†
  history of, 170
  marriage/of Jesus, 62, 156
  writings excluded from New Testament, 42, 49, 157, 170
God, role of
  as acting in human history, 97, 102, 135–137, 160, 194
  as ultimate savior, 98, 102, 116–118, 123, 144, 197
Goebbels, Joseph, 215
Goliath, 73
Good Samaritan, 260–261
gospels
  as biased and partisan, 24–25, 30–31, 35, 41, 43
  compared to modern media, 24, 28, 29–31
  "created" versus "historical" Jesus, 30–32, 35
  influence of Paul's theology on, 33
  not included in New Testament, 25
  sources of information for, 27–29
  time gaps in writing of, 25–26, 29–30, 34
  unknown authors of, 26–27, 29
  written for different audiences, 30–35, 41
Gotham City, 224
Goyer, David S., 225, 229
Greek empire, 113
Greek gods. *See* Pan
Group of Four, 210
Guardians of the Galaxy, 225

H

Haman, as anti-Semite, 88–94
Hanukkah, Festival of, 58, 154, 183
Hebrew Bible/Old Testament, 32, 124–125, 130–131
Hebron, 74

Hegesippus, 162
Heinberg, Allan, 232
Hellenistic religions, 191
Herod Antipas, 20, 47, 157
Herod the Great, 26, 130
Hillel (Jewish sage), 141, 149, 175
Hinduism, 196
historical Jesus, quest for, 31–34, 163, 200
historical scholarship, xii, 24, 27, 29, 50, 130, 147, 200
Hitler, Adolf, 212–220
  German history, version of, 217–219
  Jews identified as enemy, 217–218, 220
  Munich speech, 214
  savior/messiah imagery, 215–216, 219–220, 242, 247
  speech as Chancellor, 215–216
Holocaust, 111, 200, 213
Holofernes, 95–96
Hosea, Book of, 145
House, Edward M., 208
human beings: creation and "fall of," 59–61
Hyrcanus II, 131, 133

I

interpretation of Biblical texts, 24–26, 144–147, 200, 232–233, 235
Iron Man, 225
Isaiah (Chapters 40-55), 99–111
  Cyrus as rescuer of Israelites, 103–105
  Israel as model nation, 109, 110, 112
  Israelites as God's servant, 105–106, 108, 110
  justice, 101, 106–107, 109–110, 112
  liberation from Babylonian exile, 11–12, 99–103
  "light of the world," 106–107, 109
  and modern-day Israel, 111
  punishment for sin, 100, 104, 106, 108–109
  "servant songs," 105–110
Ish-bosheth, 74
Islam, 196
Israel: in Hebrew Bible/Old Testament
  as God's redeemed servant-nation, 101–107, 112
  independent Jewish state, 139–140, 148
  liberation and restoration of, 99–103, 115–119
  mission as "light of nations," 106–107, 109–111, 123
  persecution and oppression, 113–114. *See also* Roman empire
  sins of, 106, 108–109, 111
Israel: modern state of, 111, 196, 241

J

Jacob, 85–86, 101, 102, 103
James (Jesus's brother and disciple), 141, 161–162, 167–168, 170

James, Infancy Gospel of, 157–158
James, Letter of, 40
Jannaeus, King Alexander, 131
Jehu, 69
Jenkins, Patty, 232
Jerome, 86
Jerusalem
  destruction/occupation of, 32, 48, 103–105,
    117, 131–133, 137
  Jesus's entry on donkey, 28, 116
  during King David's rule, 74, 77
  over one million Jews killed in, 30, 116
  saved by Judith, 95–96
  as widow, 103, 106
Jesse, 73
Jesus
  birth and life of, 19–20, 26, 28, 146–147,
    155–156
  "created" Jesus. *See* "created" versus "histori-
    cal" Jesus
  death of, 26, 46–48, 52, 110, 161
  family and lineage of, 5, 19–20, 51–52, 155
  "historical Jesus," 31–34, 163, 200
  kosher or nonkosher, 37–38, 44–45, 155, 159
  and Mary the Magdalene, 4, 61, 141, 156–157,
    228n†
  Second Coming of, 195–196, 250
  supported by wealthy women, 157–158
  and Torah laws, 37–38, 44–45, 159, 174
Jesus as messiah/savior
  divine revelation as, 39
  does not meet criteria for, 163–165
  does not self-identify as, 13, 36, 164–165,
    250–252
  in Gospel of Mark, 51–52, 163–165
  identified as Christ/Messiah by Paul, 33, 163,
    185–189, 190–193
  identified as *mashiach*/messiah by Peter, 13–16,
    39, 153–154, 163
  and "messianic secret," 17
  not seen as such in his time, 16, 149, 154, 165,
    194
  silence about, 13, 16–23, 36, 148, 165
Jesus's identity
  as Elijah, 9–11, 154
  as John the Baptist, 7–9, 12, 38, 53, 62, 154
  as a political figure, 160–163
  as a prophet, 11–12, 154
  as Son of God, 39
  as Son of Man, 38–39, 53–65
  as teacher, 43, 156
  "who do people say that I am?," 7–13, 38–39
Jesus's teachings
  absence of messianic focus, 250–252, 256
  compared with Paul's teachings, 192–193, 260

  detachment from material things, 252–253
  in the Lord's Prayer, 253–256
  in the parables, 257–262
  personal transformation and action, 256–262
  on repentance, 159–160
  requirements of Torah, 15, 159
  See also Kingdom of God
Jewish Diaspora, 115–117, 123, 142, 148, 194
Joanna, 5, 157
Job, 135
John, Gospel of, 29, 47
John the Baptist
  beheading of, 20, 161, 163
  Jesus seen as, 7–9, 12, 38, 53, 62, 154
  ministry of, 8–9, 15, 175, 183
Jones, Jim (Peoples Temple Group), 196
Joseph: life of, and as savior, 85–88
Josephus (historian), 8, 9, 46, 72, 133, 141, 154
Judaism transformed to Christianity, 190–193, 251
Judas Maccabaeus, 154
Judas the Galilean, 52, 154
Judith, Book of, 95–96
justice: as Israel's mission, 101, 106–107, 109–110,
  112
Justice League, 225, 236

K
Kal-El. *See* Superman
Kennedy, John F., 26
King David. *See* David, King
"King of the Jews," 20
Kingdom of God
  as call to action, 16, 258–262
  failure to materialize, 30, 33, 40–41, 52,
    166–171, 177, 194
  as inner, spiritual change, 159–160, 169, 171
  as Jesus's central theme, 11–12, 14–15, 34, 156,
    158, 177
  in Jesus's parables, 253, 256–261
  in The Lord's Prayer, 254–256
  as new world order, 5, 12, 16, 158–160
  as political in nature, 160–163
  supplanted by Christ-centered teachings, 22,
    179
King-Messiah
  absent from Paul's theology, 177, 191
  as anointed human leader, 69–71, 79–80,
    82–83, 182
  David as, 72–74, 77–82
  described in Psalms of Solomon, 123, 137–144,
    194
  Jesus as possible, 159, 163–165, 252
  as political leader, 154–155
  Solomon as, 76
Koresh, David, 197

kosher/nonkosher practices
  of Gentiles/non-Jews, 45, 115–116
  of Jesus, 37–38, 44–45, 155, 159
  of Jewish people, 15, 57, 96, 113, 124
Krishna, Lord, 196
Krypton, 223, 226–227, 229, 230

L

Lamentations, Book of, 70, 100, 103–106, 112
League of Nations, xi, 209–212, 247
Lois Lane, ix, 228–229, 231–232, 232
"Lord of the Spirits" (*Enoch*), 119, 121, 122
Lord's Prayer, 22, 158, 165, 196, 253–256
Ludendorff, Erich (General), 214
Luke, Gospel of
  accounts of Jesus's birth, 19, 26
  blames Jews for Jesus's death, 47
  "created Jesus" of, 31, 146, 169
  Jesus as Son of Man, 63
  sources of, 28–29

M

Maccabees, Book of, 57, 62, 114, 125, 134
Maimonides (Jewish philosopher), 125
Malachi, 9–10, 11–12, 15, 182
Man and Superman, 199
Man of Steel, 224, 225–229, 231, 235, 249
Mark, Gospel of
  authorship/sources of, 26–28, 32, 44–45
  death of Jesus by Romans, 46, 145
  Jesus as Son of Man, 53–56, 58, 65
  Jesus questions disciples on his identity, 7–13
  Mark's "created Jesus," 164
  Peter identifies Jesus as Messiah, 13–16, 153–154
  silence about Jesus as Messiah, 16–17, 20,
    22–23, 36, 148, 165
Marvel Cinematic Universe, xi, 201, 225
Mary, mother of Jesus, 19–20, 124, 146, 157–158, 161
Mary Magdalene, Gospel of, 25, 42, 157, 170
Mary the Magdalene, 4, 26, 61, 141, 156, 157, 161
mashiach (messiah)
  Aramaic word used by Peter, 13
  as "Christos" in Greek, 175, 191
  meaning "anointed," 69–70, 73, 78, 103–104
  as meaning King-Messiah, 163–165, 194, 251
materialism, detachment from, 252–253
Matthew, Gospel of
  account of event at Caesarea Philippi, 24, 38–41
  blames Jews for Jesus's death, 46–48, 145
  church, built on Peter as rock, 39–41, 44, 45
  "created" versus "historical" Jesus, 19, 30,
    36–41, 116
  Jesus as Son of God, 39
  Jesus as Son of Man, 38, 41
  Jesus's birth and childhood, 26, 146

kept Jesus kosher, 37, 44
  sources of, 28–29
  use of fulfillment theology, 145–146
Maximilian, Prince of Baden, 208, 214
Meissner, William W., 243
messiah
  as cosmic Christ in Christian thought. *See*
    Christ/Christos; Paul: theology of
  Cyrus as, 103, 105
  desired during times of distress, 195–201
  false messiahs, xi, 52
  introduction to, x–xi
  messianic belief, 196–199, 243–244
  not a key focus of HB/OT, 124, 250–252, 256
  popularized in 1st century CE, 149
  as threat to Jewish and Roman power, 18
  See also Jesus as messiah/savior; King-Messiah;
    mashiach; savior
"messianic secret," 17
methodology. *See* historical scholarship; interpretation of Biblical texts
Micah, Book of, 239, 259
Michal (wife of King David), 74, 75
mishpat. See justice: as Israel's mission
monotheism, 9, 10, 221
Monroe Doctrine, 205
Mordecai, 88–94
Moses, 30, 38, 69, 183
Mount Hermon, 6
Mount of Olives, 117, 120

N

Nathan, 76–77
nationalism (German), 211
Nazareth, 7, 155, 165
Nazi (National Socialist) Party, 215–220
Nehemiah, Book of, 105, 111–112
New Testament, compilation of, 25, 31, 41–42,
  49–50, 170, 190–191
new world order
  as Kingdom of God, 5, 12, 16, 158-160
  of King-Messiah, 143, 153–154, 159
  Second Isaiah's vision of, 112–115
  as socio-political transformation, 194
Nicene Creed, 21–22, 42n‡, 49, 170
Nietzche, Friedrich, 199
Nixon, Richard, 30
Noah, 119
Noahide Laws, 126, 143, 180
Nuremburg Rally, 216, 219

O

Obama, Barack, 241, 246, 247
Old Testament. *See* Hebrew Bible/Old Testament
Orlando, Vittorio Emanuele, 210

P

Pan (Greek god), 6, 7, 10, 13, 43, 44, 154

Pandu, Lord, 196

parables of Jesus, 257–262

Paradise, restoration of, 123, 126, 144, 148, 194, 234

Paris Peace Conference, 208–210, 215

Passover, 28, 118, 124, 155, 175, 183

Paul

    author of NT writings, 26, 175

    creator of new religion, 190–191

    identity and life of, 175–178

    influence of, 161, 172

    road to Damascus revelation, 175, 177–178

Paul: theology of

    assault on Judaism, 184, 191–192

    Christ, concept of, 33, 181, 186–189, 190–193.
       See also Christ/Christos

    "created" versus "historical" Jesus, 33–34

    diverges from Jesus's teachings, 164n*,
       176–177, 178–179

    diverges from Judaism, 190–193

    divine power versus cosmic evil, 197–198,
       225–226, 244

    faith supercedes law/Torah, 180–182

    focus on person of Christ Jesus, 175, 177,
       179–181, 244, 247–248

    Jesus's death as atonement for sin, 177, 179, 192,
       193

    messiah, changed meaning of, 171, 191–193

    rejects kosher laws, 45

    rejects Torah, 37, 110, 172, 174–175, 179–184

    resurrection, 188–189

    strips Jesus of Jewishness, 191–192

    as universalist, 175, 179–180, 183, 188–189, 193

Pauline Christianity, emergence of, 170

Paw Patrol, 223

peace

    in *1 Enoch*, 121–123

    envisioned by Woodrow Wilson, 204–212

    installed by King-Messiah, 122, 143–144, 148,
       194, 197

    international body to oversee, 204–205, 212

    in Micah, 239–240

    Paris Peace Conference, 208–-210

    "peace without victory," 204–205

    in Second Zechariah, 115–118, 123

persecution of Jews (ancient times), 114

Persian empire, 88–91, 99, 112, 113

Peshitta Bible, 131

Peter

    "created Peter" versus "historical Peter," 31, 163

    identifies Jesus as Messiah, 13–14, 16–17, 22,
       39, 148, 153–154

    other accounts of Peter's insight, 38–39, 43, 45, 54

    as rock, foundation of church, 39–40

Peter, Gospel of, 25, 47–48

Pharaoh, 86

Pharisees, 32, 37, 159, 168, 175, 178

Philip, Gospel of, 170

Philippians, Letter to, 186

Philistines, 115–117

Philo (Jewish philosopher), 46

polytheism, 9, 10

Pompey, 104, 131–135, 137

Pontius Pilate, 21, 46–48

Protestant Christianity, 170

Psalm 2, 78–79

Psalm 23, 75, 125, 126

Psalm 47, 78

Psalm 103, 182

Psalm 137, 100

Psalms of Solomon

    and dualistic thought, 244

    history of, 130–131

    job description for messiah/King-Messiah,
       141–144, 182, 194, 197, 250

    Psalms 1–18, 132–140

    righteousness, 142, 173, 182

Pseudepigrapha, 130

psychoanalysis of religion, 199

Purim, 93

Q

Quest for the Historical Jesus, The, 200

Qumran, 8, 120, 184

    See also Dead Sea Scrolls Community

R

Rabbi Gamaliel, 176

Reagan, Ronald, 29

rebooting of myths/narratives, 224–227, 235

rebooting of relationships, 255, 256

reparations (Germany), 206, 210–211, 213, 215

repentance, 15, 159–160, 183

replacement theology (fulfillment theology),
    145–146

rescue figures as saviors

    Christian savior as cosmic Christ, 197. *See also*
       Christ/Christos

    Jewish messiah, 197. *See also* King-Messiah;
       messiah; superhero saviors in the Bible

    as overarching concept, 198–199

    populist political leaders, 201–202. *See also*
       Hitler, Adolf; Wilson, Woodrow

    superheroes in secular culture, 198. *See also*
       superhero saviors in popular culture

rescue thinking, 239–249

    and apocalypse, 241

    dualistic nature of, 244–245, 246

    enemy or evil to overcome, 240–245

failure to deliver, 246–247
in modern times, ix–xi, 240–241, 247–249
and new world order, 239–240
in Paul's theology, 244, 247–248
and political heroes, 241
and powerlessness, 242, 247–249
reliance on external agent, 247–249
tribal nature of, 245–246
resurrection
being resurrected not same as being messiah, 168
for faithful adherence to Torah, 57, 62–63, 192
of German people, 214–216
of Jesus, 167
not a primary focus of HB/OT, 125–126
not equated with divinity, 186
in Paul's theology, 188–189
as work of God, 194
Revelation, Book of, 226
Riefenstahl, Leni, 216
righteousness
characteristics of, 184–185, 260
co-exists with human flaws, 192–193
community, importance of, 177, 184
of King-Messiah, 143, 182
practice of Torah or Noahide laws, 124–126, 173–174, 182
rewards of, eternal life, 121–122, 134–136, 142
"the Righteous One," 119, 120, 121
Roman Catholicism, 125, 170
Roman empire
anti-Jewish violence of, 113, 130, 132–133, 167
context for gospel writers, 31–32
Jewish revolts against, 52, 57, 114, 154
killing of Jesus and his family/followers, 161–163
Pauline Christianity as official religion of, 170
power of, 6–7
Rosh Hashanah, 183

S
Sabbath, 124, 168, 183
Sadducees, 32
Salome Alexandria, Queen, 131
salvation, Christian - as exclusionary, 125
salvation of communities - in HB/OT, 98
Samuel, Books of, 69, 71–73, 77
Sarah, 109
Saul, King, 69, 72–73
savior. See rescue figures as saviors
Schweitzer, Albert, 200
Sea of Galilee, 4, 7, 12, 13, 32, 156
"Second Coming, The," (Yeats), 195
Second Isaiah. See Isaiah (Chapters 40–55)
Second Zechariah. See Zechariah, Book of
self-transformation, 261–262

Sepphoris, 7, 155
Septuagint, 146, 176
Sermon on the Mount, 30, 37, 252, 253
"servant songs" (Isaiah), 105–110
Shammai, 175
Shavuot, 118, 124, 183
Shaw, George Bernard, 199
Shazam! 225
Shuster, Joe, 227
Siegel, Jerry, 227
silence about Jesus as Messiah
in Gospel of Mark, 16–20, 22, 165, 252
by Jesus, 36, 148, 250–251
in Nicene Creed, 21–22
Simeon (Jesus's relative), 162
Simon of Peraea, 52, 154
Simon the Zealot, 154
sin
Jesus's death as atonement for, 188, 193
of people of Israel, 106, 108–109, 119–121, 134–135
Sirach, 71, 75, 87, 125
Snyder, Zack, 225, 229, 232
Socrates, 31
Solomon, 69, 70, 74, 76, 122, 130
Son of God, 39
Son of Man
in Hebrew Bible/Old Testament, 55–58
Jesus named as, 38–39, 53–55
as Jesus's refusal of other identities, 62–65
as perfected humanity, 58–62
Succoth, Festival of, 118, 124, 182, 183
Suicide Squad, The, 225
Sun Myung Moon, Rev., 197
superhero saviors in popular culture
Avengers, 201
Batman, 201, 223–225, 229–232, 236
DC Extended Universe, 201, 224–225, 229, 235
eras of social trauma, 85, 223–224
the Flash, 230
good versus evil, 201, 225–226, 228–232, 235–236
as human, not divine, 231
introduction to, ix, xi–xii
Justice League, 225, 227, 236
Lex Luthor, 229–231
loss of fathers in, 230
Man of Steel, 224, 225–229, 231, 235, 249
Marvel Cinematic Universe, xi, 201, 225
Paw Patrol, 223
power politics, 230–231
Robin Hood, 224
Spiderman, 201
Superman, ix, 201, 223, 224, 225–232, 236
team of superheroes, 236
Wonder Woman, 201, 223–225, 230–236

superhero saviors in the Bible
  introduction to, 84–85
  Joseph the Israelite, 85–88
  Judith, 94–96
  as ordinary people, 96–97
  Queen Esther, 88–94
Superman, ix, 201, 223, 224, 225–232, 236
Susanna, 5, 157

T
Tarsus, 176
Temple
  built by King Solomon, 74
  cleansing of, 154
  desecration of, 103, 131–133
  destruction of, 32, 41, 57, 113, 169
  envisioned restoration of, 102, 105, 118
Ten Commandments, 8–9, 10–11, 183–184
Terrio, Chris, 229
Tertullian, 48
Thatcher, Margaret, 30
Themyscira, 224
theocracy, Israel as, 78, 140
Theodosius (emperor), 170
Thomas, Gospel of
  different account of Jesus's words, 24, 42–43,
    48–49, 63
  Jesus as wholeness/"the human," 58–59, 61
  Jesus's parables in, 258
Thomas, Infancy Gospel of, 227
Thor and *Thor: Ragnarok*, 225
Thus Spoke Zarathustra, 199
Tiberius (Roman emperor), 48, 156
Torah laws/teachings
  adherence to by Jesus and all Jews, 12, 15,
    124–126, 159, 172, 174
  core tenets of, 8–9, 11, 81–82, 124, 172
  devoted adherence to, 134–136, 143, 172–174,
    182
  dietary (kosher) laws of, 44–45, 115–116
  Jesus extends requirements of, 159
  "light their own fires": Torah non-adherence,
    107, 109, 110, 147
  messiah as Torah-observant, 142–143
  opposed by Paul, 37, 110, 172, 174, 179–184
  permanence of, 182
  persecution for, by Romans, 114
  See also Dead Sea Scrolls Community; righ-
    teousness; sin; Ten Commandments
Tosefta Sanhedrin, 125
Trajan (emperor), 162
Treatise on the Resurrection, 170
Treaty of Versailles, 205–206, 210–211, 213–214,
  217
trinity, theology of, 22

Triumph des Willens, 216, 220
Truman, Harry S., 29
Trump, Donald, 241, 247
Twelfth Imam, 196

U
unfinished business, 194–195, 199
Unification Church, 197
United Nations, 212
United States, 203–205, 211, 212, 217
universal laws of humanity. *See* Noahide Laws
universal peace, 143–144, 148
Uriah, death of, 76–77

V
Versailles. *See* Treaty of Versailles
Vespasian (emperor), 162
villains. *See* enemy
virgin birth, 19–20, 146–147, 227
Virgin Mary. *See* Mary, mother of Jesus

W
Waco, Texas, 197
war, alternatives to, 204–205
war reparations (Germany), 206, 210–211, 213,
  215, 218
War Scroll, 18
"Who do people say that I am?," 7–13
Wilson, Woodrow, 202–212
  Fourteen Points, 207–208, 214, 215
  and League of Nations, 247
  Nobel Peace Prize, winner of, 212
  "peace without victory" speech, 204–205
  role in ending WWI, 204–205, 207–208, 211
  as "Savior of Humanity," xi, 202, 208–209,
    212
women who supported Jesus's ministry, 157–158
Wonder Woman, 201, 223–225, 230–236
Wonder Woman (film), 225, 232–235, 249
world government, 210
World War I, 203–211, 217, 232
World War II, 200, 201, 212–220, 223
Wrede, William, 17

Y
Yeats, W. B., 195, 246

Z
Zadok (priest), 69, 70
Zapruder, Abraham, 28
Zealots, 18–19, 32, 154, 168, 178
Zechariah, Book of, 115–119, 123, 182, 241
Zedekiah, 70, 82, 104
Zimmerman, Arthur, 205